AMSTERDAM ACID

By
Major Rogers

Illustrated By
Katie Barisic

MLRPRESS

ISBN: 9-78-06921-017-5-9

For Tamm. And the Good Doctor—both of them…To Muse.

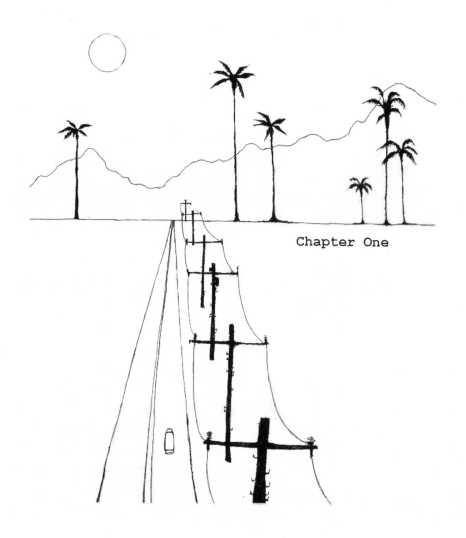

Chapter One

"Ride captain ride upon your mystery ship,
Be amazed at the friends you have here on your trip,
Ride captain ride upon your mystery ship,
On your way to a world that others might have missed."
Blues Image.

We were somewhere close to the heart of Bakersfield, California when I took my first drag on the glass weed pipe. It was Thomas, Alonzo and I heading south on the California 99 towards the Los Angeles airport to catch a trans-Atlantic flight. Our destination was a party, first in London and then on to Amsterdam for the 2006 Cannabis Cup. No reason not to start the festivities early while we were on our own soil. I remember handing the pipe to Thomas and saying something like, "You better hit this; you're driving like a maniac." He had been trailing a black Lexus in his white Mercedes sedan for the past twenty minutes, making good time and clocking an average eighty-seven mph, a tough speed for a passenger baked on grass; things outside the windows tended to lose focus.

"Keep that shit away from me," Thomas replied. "I don't want anything slowing me down." Just then the pop of a Corona bottle announced its presence.

"Good idea; take a swig of this," Alonzo said from the back seat, as he handed the driver a bottle of beer. "Thanks," Thomas said as he drank the pale yellow liquid as if dehydration had him in its grip.

"Here, hand me that," Alonzo said, looking at me as he reached for the pipe; but Thomas instantly handed him the empty bottle over his shoulder, assuming he was talking to him.

"Hand me a beer first," I said. *"Penche gringo,"* Alonzo replied as he pulled another beer from the bag, popped it and handed it up front. "Here," he said. "Now give me that fuckin' pipe." But it was too late; I had already started to drink. A small amount trickled from the corner of my mouth through my days-old whiskers and ran the length of my jaw and down my neck.

"Chingow cabron, you keep that up and they're not going to let us

on the plane because you'll smell like a wino," Alonzo said. I turned towards him mid-burp and replied, "Your brown ass can pass for an Arab—an Iranian at best; all eyes will be on you as we taxi on the runway.

They'll be happy to have some drunken cowboy on board to handle any ideas you have of bringing the ship down," obviously playing into America's newest age of xenophobic fears towards Arabs or Persians or any other person from a majority of the world's population.

Thomas suddenly took his foot off the gas pedal, and we slightly bumped forward with the decrease in speed. "Aww shit! He's got me," Thomas said, mostly to himself.

"What?" I said just in time to see a California Highway Patrolman passing us on his motorcycle, looking into the car where I still clinched the warm pipe, as my hand rested on my lap. I gave a large smile, showing lots of teeth, hoping it would keep his eyes on me and not my hand. He gave a lurch of speed as he passed and positioned himself between our car and the car in front of us, and his warning lights sparked to life. The cop turned around and motioned with his hand for us to pull over as he began to follow the front car to the side of the road; he was performing a dual citation.

I assume it was the drugs that gave me my next thought of genius; but I assure you, as the plan unfolded in my head it seemed harmless, even a little funny. "Dude," I instructed Thomas, "pull over to the outside lane like he instructed." Thomas followed the order with no questions. Once over, we drove about 100 yards more, keeping a bit slower pace than the cop and the lead car that were slowly making their way to the side of the road 100 feet ahead. "Now!" I said, "exit here!" And that was it; we were off the freeway at the next exit cleanly. At the end of the off-ramp, we hit a red light. "What do we do now?" Thomas asked with wide eyes and racing pulse, which for some reason made me laugh for a second; but that quickly changed. It was at that moment I realized that I had just instructed my friend to run from the police. At first I thought it was funny because the cop told us to pull over, and all we did was take his suggestion one step further and pull off the freeway altogether. But still, the reality was we were running from the State Police.

"Fuck it. Head northwest and we can catch Interstate 5; it's only fifteen minutes out of the way," I said. "We'll travel country roads and intersect the 5 as it nears the 99." We were silent for a few miles before I spoke again, "Chances are he may have radioed a few miles ahead to be on the lookout for our car. They won't suspect this move."

"He won't call anyone," Al said with a strange confidence. "It was probably his first attempt to pull over two cars at once, and he would be too embarrassed to tell anyone."

However, I had something else on my mind. Fifteen miles ahead was a CHP weigh station we would inevitably pass once we were onto the 5, as it was the only passage to LAX without a three- hour detour, which at that point was not an option. The weigh station would be a smart place for the cop to call, as most traffic traveling south would pass the station. And we had just damaged a cop's ego. Getting pulled over now would surely require taking some sort of police beating in retribution.

Thomas' car was a large sedan with the back windows blacked out. It was the kind of ride you would find some sort of third-world warlord or second-world diplomat driving around in. Not the newest model, but bright, clean and something easily eye-catching. A roadside cop would have no problem picking it out as it passed.

I could imagine what was in store for us. "STOP FUCKING MOVING!" they would order once they had us roadside. However, it is hard to stop moving while they zap you with a Taser and the body convulses. "I SAID, 'STOP FUCKING MOVING,' ASSHOLE," as another volt would force the body to jig, which gives more probable cause to beat us with clubs and season us with mace as they continue to order us to "STOP MOVING!"

The whole scene seemed very possible, as that was the outcome I had seen many times on TV. And why not? How can I blame the cops? We are the bad guys, the ones who seem to be wiping our asses with the law. But thank almighty baby Jesus, we live in an age where we could all blame the drugs; and society would go easy on us at sentencing, as long as we found Christ—and rehab before trial. After twenty minutes of country road driving we came to the 5. Moments later the weigh station appeared in the distance, and the car stayed quiet as we awaited our road karma for our behavior. "Pull along that semi and ride his tail in the blind spot," I told Thomas as he maneuvered the car in place with sober precision. He increased his speed to stay with the big rig as we passed the station; we were now traveling in the blindside of the truck. Thomas then took a large swig of beer, I assume for courage—or calming.

But no one was waiting. The two parked and empty CHP cars sat vacant outside the office with nobody running to them as we passed. "G'day, mate," I said to Alonzo. "That's not what they say in England, you know," Thomas informed me, though I already knew it was an Australian greeting.

"Fuckin'-a then, g'day, mate!" Alonzo replied.

"That's Australian, not English," Thomas directed us, but I acted like I didn't hear him. Moments later Alonzo cracked some beers and passed them around as we ascended into the Smoky Grapevine Mountain Range, which was rich with the pink and purple sunshine that was captured within the late afternoon's misty hills. We drove for an hour with little talk and more ponderous thoughts of what we had already experienced on our trip. An hour later we descended into the metropolis of Los Angeles and the sprawling flight deck of the LAX.

We drove into a private long-term parking lot just blocks away from our gate. They offered free valet parking, but we passed because we wanted to park ourselves and use the shelter of the car while we smoked out before our flight. Soon after we finished business, we walked to the shuttle that dropped us at curbside for departure. The early evening sky appeared deeper blue than usual, a beautiful sight that L.A. skies rarely let you in on, a beautiful place to fly into—a positive omen.

The jet was a titan of a craft, a Howard Hughes wet dream. I had hoped to get the seats at the front of the economy-seating section during check-in. These seats gave a few extra inches of space. However, I was told they had already been assigned to those in need. Once we boarded we saw they were given away to cripples and mothers with children. This made no sense to me being I wanted them for the extra leg room. Why does a kid or those who have trouble feeling their limbs need leg room? And here I was about to fly into another day with my knees greeting the seat in front of me. Soon after we found our seats, Alonzo, who had booked his flight separately, disappeared to the back of the craft to sit alone.

And just like that, we were off—flying into a new day, unto an old world.

"Fuck this, I'm taking some Vicodin; I can't handle it," I told Thomas moments into the flight as I dug for the pills I had been hoarding for months for this exact moment.

"You brought enough to share?" Thomas asked with angst.

"Mayyybe," I said as I poured eight pills into my hand.

"Good, then you can take one of these," he said as he exchanged a small pale-blue pill for four of mine.

"What's this?" I asked.

"It's good night, that's what it is," he told me, which sounded good, as I had not really slept the night before our trip. Pills have never done much for me, outside their medical intent, aside for an uncontrollable relaxation. But I will always try a new one, just to make sure I don't miss the party on any of them. We ordered our booze to chase the pills. Then we clicked our plastic cups in a toast, followed by our getting situated in our seats as our craft raced eastward, forward in time.

Our MP3 players were in place; the song "Ten Years Gone" by Led Zeppelin poured into my ears. Moments later I felt my seat seemed to turn into sun-warmed goose down; my stress evaporated. To raise my arm became too much work and not worth the effort. I looked to Thomas; he was in his special place too, eyes shut and thoughts somewhere miles from where we were. I blinked once, then twice and I too was gone.

I don't know if it were a murky dream or just the mind floating a thought while intoxicated; but I began to have visions in my head about the day we planned this trip almost six months prior.

"Is that dog shit in your dining room?" I asked Thomas as I stood at the entry of his home, moments after waking him with a pound on his front door at 2:30 p.m. He stood in the doorway, all six-feet-three of him looking as if he had combed his hair with the pillow.

"Where?" he replied, rubbing his eyes as I pointed out the fudge cigar that was planted in the mostly empty room that flanked the living room and kitchen. "It can't be; we don't have a dog," he said as he grabbed a paper towel and walked in to pick it up as if it were house custom. I figured it was better I didn't ask from the look of the house, which didn't look any more unusual than one where normal, savage beasts had loomed several hours earlier... beasts who foolishly gambled and drank from warm rum bottles as they grunted and snorted from a line of moon dust until the entire evening melted around them, only to be born into another day.

"What the fuck? Is that an ice tray?"

"Yeah," Thomas affirmed. "Why?"

"Why?" I asked. "Do you think it normal that a pile of dog shit and an ice tray are just lying on the floor in here?" He just walked by me shrugging his shoulders as if my question didn't make sense. "I told you, we don't have a dog," he said as he chucked the napkin and its contents out the front door. "You wanna smoke a bowl?"

"Sure," I said, giving up reason. As we walked to the kitchen, I saw Thomas' roommate Scottie on the living-room floor. He was with a gal on an inflatable mattress Scottie had pulled from the garage. He was locked out of his own room by some quick-acting party guest hours before. The two on the floor were locked in some sort of lustful embrace that seemed to make them oblivious to the world around them.

"Here," Thomas said as he handed me a freshly-packed glass pipe.

"Thanks," I said, taking it, adding flame and inhaling the dragon. I passed it back to him to repeat the action. Thomas had to be at work pouring spirits in a half-hour. An open, almost- empty bottle of spiced rum was on the counter, so I figured if you're going to start the day right, you may as well indulge in the fact. So I poured a glass and went to retrieve some ice.

"Are you shittin' me? You don't have any ice?"

"Well, at least you know where the ice tray is," Thomas said. "How the fuck am I supposed to drink this poison?"

"Drink it warm; it's how it is supposed to be drunk anyway," Thomas said. So I figured *what the hell* and took him at his word. I drew a swig straight from the bottle, my winced eyes relaxing when it turned out to be much smoother than I had anticipated.

"You wanna go to Amsterdam?" I asked Thomas as he passed the pipe back to me.

"Sure," he responded while exhaling, as if the question I asked was as simple as asking if he wanted to split a pizza. But his response didn't surprise me and that, for the most part, is why I asked. I wanted to go; I needed to go. I needed to get away from American life for a while. With the war in Iraq still raging several years after Bush raised his "Mission Accomplished" sign on the decks of an American aircraft carrier, America and its tribe seems to be the most hated place on Earth. They say they hate us and that we do everything wrong. We say they are all just jealous, all the while both sides failing to see they are each as right as they are wrong, just like fighting children. So I wanted to investigate world politics first-hand—without the bias of cable news. I anticipated returning with a new disdain *and* appreciation for my own country. A little fun within the process was also in order.

Travel is not foreign to me. I have been as far west as the Hawaiian Islands and as far east as Turkey. I have explored Alaskan glaciers by dog sled and have been given the royal treatment at a Dominican Republic resort, paid for by a bookie after I had a rare but lucrative football-betting season.

Thomas travels by saving his money and flying down to obscure places in South America, such as the time he toured the continent by bus before insulting some Columbians in poker by taking their money. Apparently after the card game, a few at the table had harsh words for him in a language Thomas didn't understand. So as he exited the room, he placed his hand under his chin and waved— "giving 'em the high sign" as Thomas described it—though as the story goes, he left the country quickly after on a jet to Maui.

By now it was apparent Scottie was getting a hand job by the vixen on his living-room bed. She tried to hide the fact with the covers, but if you stared long enough, you could tell what was going on. Of course, that all stopped when she looked up and saw me staring, making me feel like a pervert and then subsequently getting into an argument with myself as to who the real goddamn pervert was anyway? So I looked away and back at Thomas who was eyeballing the scene with an expression that led me to believe this type of behavior was the norm of the manor.

"I'm gonna get ready for work; why don't you get online and look at ticket pricing?" Thomas instructed. "Actually, why don't we stay a day or two in England and run around? I have a friend there who will let us use his flat, and then we can take a ferry or get a flight into Amsterdam," Thomas planned as he went. "I hear they have casinos on the ferries, and puddle jumpers run all the time for 100 bucks." I was already positioned at the computer. I knew Virgin Atlantic flew out of Los Angeles non-stop to London, and I proceeded to book our passage.

"Wow, flights are only $460.00 round-trip."

"Sweet, book it," Thomas said as he slid his arm into his white shirt. "Come down to the bar later and tell me about what we end

up getting." His next move was to grab the front door and head through it.

"Cool," I said as he closed the door behind him. I then turned to watch the portable porn show, but the participants were now napping, dreaming about carnal things while their bodies recharged for a later round, I'm sure. I looked back to the computer monitor and clicked on the "book your flight" key, only to find the total sum for both tickets was $1350.00 each! I was thoroughly confused. I thought for sure a currency exchange got mixed up and I was being quoted a different price. So I found Virgin's phone number and proceeded to investigate the sum.

As it turned out, after some pissed-off folks flew planes into a couple of buildings one September morning years back, a whole new list of fees was established "to keep it from happening again." But I guess that is the price of travel in the new reality of extreme world politics. Besides, you can't ride a bus or a train across the Atlantic or fly them into a building. So Virgin Atlantic it was.

"Ladies and gentlemen," a soft English accent broke my sleep. "We will now be seu-ving breakfast." I sat motionless in my seat for a moment, waiting, wondering where I was. It was an odd feeling, like when you wake from a heavy mid-day sleep and are momentarily disillusioned into believing it was morning; or when you wake staring at the wall of a hotel that you don't remember falling asleep in. But it all came back to me: where we were, where we were headed. I straightened up in my seat and turned to look at Thomas. But he was nowhere to be found.

"Breakfast, sir," another warm British voice spoke as the food cart was pushed next to me. "Yes, and leave one for my friend; he'll be right back," I requested. In reality though, I wasn't looking out for Thomas. The effects of the long nap, which had taken us through the night, had left me very hungry. I had hoped to eat my breakfast as well as Thomas's before he returned from wherever he had gone. Telling him when I woke, there was only one breakfast left, which I ate, assuming he had gone and sat next to better company.

I finished my egg and croissant sandwich quickly with little pleasure because of the speed at which I consumed them. Once I got the two largest menu items down, I could condense the other items from Thomas's tray and ditch the tray and plastic ware. I could eat my second sandwich a bit slower. But just as I reached for his tray, he appeared like some old junkyard dog that had developed a sixth sense when it came to the danger of losing his food.

"What are you doing?" Thomas asked as I reached over to scoop his food from his plate. "I'm, uh, putting my eggs on your plate; I don't want them," I responded as if it were the truth.

"Alonzo is sick, some sort of allergic reaction," Thomas told me. But I wasn't sure if he were serious or playing a pointless prank. I just stared at him wondering if our trip, or at least Alonzo's trip, had ended before it began. "His face is swollen like a tomato."

"Did you give him any pills?" I asked.

"Nope, he didn't want any; he was happy with booze."

So I got up to investigate. Sure enough, they had Alonzo stretched out on the floor. His face was puffy, and he had on an oxygen mask with tubing, which made the whole scene seem more serious than it really was.

Thomas said, "He looks better than he did five minutes ago," as the air stewards had already given Alonzo a Benadryl and its effects were upon him.

"Jesus, what happened to you? Get caught trying to light your shoes on fire?" I asked. He went on to blame the eggs and then the fruit given to us as the reason for his anaphylactic shock. Then Alonzo sat up and was able to return to his seat. He rested while the flight attendant checked on him every couple of minutes. Twenty minutes more and we landed, though no one was allowed off the plane until the medics, who were at the gate, were able to board and inspect Alonzo. Ultimately, after we held the plane departure up, we were cleared to disembark after the medics were satisfied with his stabilized condition.

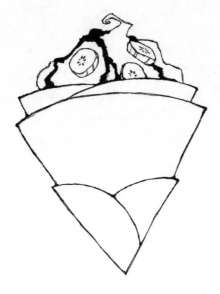

Chapter Two

We boarded a train and headed for our room in Russell Square, a thirty-minute ride. Once at the hotel I received my first lesson in British economics. Our room, which was in a large popular tourist hotel called The International ran us 150 pounds a night. In England money value is easy to understand if you are a Yank. Take the value of an American dollar, cut it in half and then expect to pay double or triple for items of lower quality than you are used to in America, where we are apparently spoiled.

The hotel lobby showed promise with a buffet restaurant, a small bar and a large official-looking bell desk. The check-in area was a long bar-type front with wood walls and clocks showing the different time zones of the world. It was dinnertime in Los Angeles, but lunch, where we stood... a day ahead. Several lines formed, all leading to the desk, all with a dozen or so weary travelers in them. Alonzo bought three pints, giving one to me where I sat and one to Thomas, who was now in the thick of the lines. We had three pints each waiting for check-in. Thomas emptied his last just as he stepped up to get our room keys.

Though the hotel lobby was nice, the room was a different story. It came with three small beds and amenities that belonged in a worn-out hostel or possibly an upper-class jail. The bathroom had a cramped shower, a stained toilet and something resembling a bidet that we could never get to operate properly, though it later served as a valuable asset as Thomas was able to vomit in it while never leaving the toilet seat.

As we set out to explore, I got into a day pack I had thrown into my suitcase. I had grabbed the bag quickly during packing back home. I was looking for my MP3 charger which I had misplaced or not packed at all. What I found was a little more dangerous, as I realized I should have been in jail at that moment. The day pack not only contained a joint's worth of old weed, but also a half dozen M-70 firecrackers in a pouch—about a half-a-stick of dynamite worth of explosives.

I just stared at the contents, which were left in the bag from the previous 4th of July celebration. I wasn't sure if I were relieved to not get arrested for carrying explosives into a country that was still shaky from the blast of a terrorist's bomb months before or if I were actually excited that I was going to hear the bell toll of Big Ben after smoking a joint. But my emotions were quickly figured out after the first drag of the thing, as we shared a communal smoke and out the door we went.

It is hard not to sit on a bench while waiting for your train in the Underground and imagine what a bomb blast would be like—the screams, the dust, the long echo, the silence, the large tubular structure collapsing itself as two fingers squash an ant. Don't dwell on it too long, or *the fear* will trickle down and the terrorist will win.

We arrived at the clock tower that hosts Big Ben, Houses of Parliament where justice and law has both been created and perverted, the London Eye, the circle in the sky, and the Thames River, which shimmered with shiny black, pink and purple strobes of sky reflections. At that moment, it did seem we were in The Queen's England. We were living the postcard.

Thomas spotted a street vendor making crêpes. We got in line and all three of us ordered Nutella as our spread; Alonzo added banana slices to his. Then, like a communal pack of dingoes who had plenty to eat before them, we sat somewhat quietly with our meal and consumed. There was no speaking, just chewing, and the eyes roaming the area still taking it all in.

From our point in the middle of it all, we returned to the Underground and emerged into Piccadilly Circus. The place was something close to the activity of Las Vegas, perhaps minus much of the sin or at least flagrant sin. Piccadilly buzzed with activity, neon lights and hints of the Far West's fashions and trends. It was chilly out, but it didn't stop the locals from filling the streets or sitting in public squares enjoying ice cream as if it were summer. We blended in as much as possible and drank as frequently as it was available, but always on the move. Another Underground ride and a surfacing in the SOHO District. The place must have been the original inspiration for the culture of San Francisco. The restaurants and pubs built long ago were stacked one atop another like dominoes. And there were areas that clearly distinguished themselves as gay-friendly with rainbow flags and banners flown with the flagrancy and purpose of the Jolly Roger. Other areas had the loud and rowdy English crowds we had expected of the town.

"G'day, mate," I said to Alonzo with a smile.

"THAT'S NOT WHAT THEY FUCK'N SAY HERE!" Thomas yelled in irritation without ever looking back at me as he continued to walk.

As we walked along the lively pubs, restaurants and adult shops, we crossed paths with a street-wandering dope dealer. "You guys alright?" he said smoothly as he passed, the moment broken by his Los Angeles' urban appearance and his proper English voice.

"We're fine," I said as we never broke stride. "Alright-alright," he said quickly as he disappeared into the crowd like a phantom's fart.

"What the fuck did you tell him *no* for?" Thomas asked.

"Are you crazy? You want to buy off a street vendor in the middle of a tourist town? Why wouldn't he just be selling baggies of baking powder or Drano?" I drilled. But after walking around another hour and drinking enough to make the knees and soul weak, we crossed paths with the same dealer. Only this time Thomas approached him, ready to make a deal. The two took a walk away from us, their heads down like two street demons in church as they exchanged the goods. The deal was sealed and the dealer evaporated again.

Back in the hotel room, I lay quietly on the bed, watching Thomas unravel the plastic around his bundle. Alonzo reclined on his bed as well, one foot on the floor "to halt the spins." I wasn't sure if I were going to snort that shit or not. Cocaine can be a fun ride and an instant sober from the negative effects of alcohol. However, if you are prone to addiction, you must be weary of the dust, proven by those who get hooked on the shit and give up everything for it.

I wasn't necessarily scared of getting hooked, as I have done the stuff more than once and have not craved it the next day. I suppose I just have a respect for it. You had better have respect for it because *it* can kill you. And if it isn't the cocaine itself that kills you, whatever they use to cut it with could surely put the body into a death shock. That's why I'm never the first one to snort it. I let others, those more eager, sniff it. If they are alive thirty seconds after the blast, I may take one too. Otherwise, I will be the one who calls the ambulance.

"Why the fuck did he wrap it in newspaper?" Thomas asked himself as he finally unwrapped the plastic cellophane off his bundle. And then ten seconds later, "IT"S ALL NEWSPAPER!" Thomas yelled. He'd been taken, getting just what he deserved for buying from the pusher.

"Fuck this, fuck him!" Thomas said as he headed out the door in a hurry, apparently on his way to find the guy. "G'DAY, MATE," I shouted out to him. "FUCK you!" was all he could get out as the door slammed shut. I could hear Alonzo laugh through his nose, which made me begin to laugh. My eyes shut, testing to see if I were going to battle the spins—nothing and then the blackout of sleep.

The next morning brought a fog-filtered sun and the absence of Thomas. However, he was quickly found when I entered the bathroom. He was asleep on the floor, a towel for a pillow. The stinging stench of bile was apparent, as it was evident Thomas had sung to the toilet late last night or early this morning.

As I began my morning evacuation, I glanced around the bathroom. On the counter lay several bills, several hundred pounds at least. My first thought was Thomas had found his guy and no telling how he handled it.

"What the fuck happened last night?" I asked Thomas.

"I don't know; it's a blur," he groaned and rolled to his side as if he expected to find a comfortable spot on the chilled tiled floor.

"I see, the old werewolf defense. I hope you ate the body at least."

"Huh?" Thomas asked as he raised his head and placed his hand out as if blocking the noontime sun and not just the restroom light. "The money. Did you find the hustler?"

"No," he grumbled as he climbed to his feet and looked at himself in the mirror. He was leaning forward with both hands on the counter, as if he were under arrest. "I found a casino," he said to his reflection. "I couldn't find the guy, and I wasn't sure what I was going to do if I did. I don't remember much of anything though. Just stumblin' across a small casino as I walked around."

"When did you go to bed?" I asked.

"About an hour ago, I think," he responded.

"No rest for the nefarious dude; you brought this upon yourself," was the most sympathetic line I could give him. In three hours we were destined for some puddle-jumping low-budget airline that would take us from London to Amsterdam, so we had to move, hungover or not.

We got up and worked silently as we packed our belongings and situated the bags. Somehow we were able to maneuver about the room without bumping into each other, as that would just hurt too much at that moment. My first English hangover was a let down; it hurt just as much as the ones stateside, but my head felt heavier, probably from the beer.

"I have this bottle of Silver Oak I brought for Thanksgiving dinner," Thomas said as he showed us the bottle of wine he had packed. He also waved a bottle of Patron Platinum he had purchased at the duty-free, knocking off thirty bucks, bringing the price of the bottle of Tequila to about 250 bucks.

"Not only will we never be short of booze, gentlemen, but we will be drinking some of the finest shit on the market." And he was right, as much as I would ever hate to admit tequila as a *fine* drink, I knew Platinum was hard to beat for alcohol smoothness.

A year before this trip, I was drinking with two pro-football players at an Italian restaurant in Shell Beach, California. I was in town covering a story about a football camp both players were sponsoring. One of the players asked the waitress to pick a shot for us to add to the fun. She did; she brought a round of Patron Platinum and one for herself as had been offered.

Moments later she returned to take another drink order, and the players trusted her to pick another shot, requesting she find one "as smooth as the first one." This the waitress did, close to five times, always the Platinum. This seemed okay because it was so surprisingly enjoyable to shoot, a tequila enjoyable straight—wow! Before the bill came, each player and I threw a credit card into a hat that the waitress was to draw from.

It was the player who had nothing to do with the drink order who was stuck with the dinner and bar tab. The total came to $400 for the booze alone and another $200 for the dinner. The Patron was $30 a shot, and the waitress had no problem ringing the highest- priced shot of the house up, as she saw who was spending money at her table. And I guess when it came down to it, I didn't have a problem either, since it wasn't my credit card drawn.

So, in fact, I was looking forward to drinking the tequila in Amsterdam where the beverage is relatively rare. Thomas wrapped both bottles carefully in t-shirts and strategically placed them in his bag.

Our gang headed out the door and back to the Underground to take us to the airport, certain we had plenty of time to make our afternoon flight.

"Good af-ta-noon, ladies and gentlemen, Eazy-Jet is at final boa'ding for Amsta'dam," a friendly English girl announced as we approached check-in.

"Hi, that's us; we just got in," I announced to the air-clerk. However, her demeanor instantly changed as I made my comment. She became rigid and dutiful, as if she had made the friendly last-boarding call not really expecting anyone to respond. "Hurry up, you're late!" she commanded.

"You-you have two bags; policy is only *one* bag," she barked at Thomas. He then looked at me. Apparently there was a one-bag policy with the cut-rate airline service. "You need to take your bags to window 14. Next!" she said as she motioned me to step forward.

"But where is window 14?" Thomas asked.

"Over thair," she replied, trying to look around Thomas to work with me, though she really wasn't giving any help by responding "over there."

"Uh, yeah—hi. We're sorry we're late. And I don't know if you realize this, but we're not from around here," trying to match sarcasm with sincerity, "so telling us 'over there' does very little to help and could also be misconstrued as rude or shitty service." But all his words just made her frazzled, as she stared at him with her ice-blue eyes. A co-worker, who had been close by eyeing the scene, stepped over. "I can help you, sir," she said with a warm friendly smile as she took Thomas aside.

"Don't mind him, ma'am. His baggage was lost from the last flight we took, and it had his medicine in it; and once the hallucinations start in, he becomes a bear to get along with." But she never looked up at me; she just continued to match my passport to the ticket, then placed a hard-pressed stamp on some paperwork with the force of a judge's gavel, probably for the dramatic effect of the motion, and then stuck my boarding pass out straight-armed with the thrust of a Spartan, filled with the typical customer service you can expect from Europe.

Alonzo and I headed for our gate with still no sign of Thomas. We were concerned but not willing to miss our plane. It was a pirate's code of such; and he had fallen behind, risking being left behind. As of the moment we had to walk rapidly. The temptation to run was heavy, but in these times it's probably not a great idea to make too many sudden movements in an airport. Weeks before, London police mistakenly shot an unarmed olive-skinned man who ran throughout the train station. Plus people worldwide are looking for reasons to shoot Americans; along with that Alonzo could pass for Persian, so I tried to walk a few strides in front of him.

We made our seats on the plane and fell backwards into them with relief. But as soon as we hit the fabric, an overhead speaker came on reporting a mechanical malfunction which would force us to disembark the plane and be picked up by tram to take us to another aircraft. At that the passengers unloaded like livestock in a mass movement; Alonzo and I took the time to catch our breath. "A cold beer would go down good right now, wouldn't it?" he said, almost to himself; I shook my head in agreement.

I was carrying my laptop bag with me. Attached to it I have a Playboy-Magazine press pass. A few years back, I had the opportunity to attend a Playboy Mansion party. Actually, I had the opportunity to sneak into the party when my brother found a press pass at the Playboy Scramble Golf Tournament he was participating in and subsequently won.

"Do you notice how girls act when they see that?" Alonzo asked me, never taking his eyes off the credential.

"What? This thing?" I asked. "What girls have seen it?"

"Girls are staring at it, and then they adjust their hair and look into their compacts, wondering if this is the day they become discovered."

I wasn't sure if this had actually been the case or not. Or maybe it was Alonzo's vivid imagination that drove him to notice the behavior but not realize the Playboy media credential had nothing to do with it. What kind of self-respecting woman doesn't fidget with her hair or stare at herself now and then?

But I never made the Playboy media pass abuse its power with women. However, what kind of self-respecting man wouldn't float the thought of the bullshit that could be slung with the girls who bought into the world of *Playboy*? And here was some clown with a press pass, laptop computer and an obvious eye for beauty.

Would the abuse of the credential work? "Hi, my name's Jo Hudson and I am with Playboy; obviously you can tell by the press pass. Ah-hem," I would clear my throat in order of propositioning an important business deal. "We could take a few simple and innocent photographs;

I will send them in to my people, and hopefully within a few short months your phone will ring." I would assume the pickup line would work like a voodoo charm; soon after, I'd be getting the best kind of attention from the girl.

I wanted the media pass for hotel and airport check-ins. Some hotels ask for your company name when you check in; I just write Playboy. Then I set my laptop bag on the counter where the media pass is clearly seen. By using both the written word and the visual aid to perpetrate a lie, I never need spoken words to be untruthful. And I have received several room upgrades and a first-class seat bump due to the move.

Sure enough, as the passengers slowly shuffled by us disembarking the malfunctioned airliner, I saw a young brunette whose eyes were visibly fixated on the media pass as I set my bag on my lap. Then her eyes darted to mine, and a warm smile appeared as she passed. "See, cabron," Alonzo nudged me, "you may be able to get laid one day after all."

"Yes, but if I used false pretenses to gain the action, it would only aid in the rape prosecution."

"Look at you, you're one step away from looking like a hobo; who the fuck would prosecute you for rape? There's no money in it," Alonzo said as if he himself were providing legal counsel.

"It doesn't really matter, because I will pin any crime I commit on you and instruct my attorney to move the trial to the deep South, where we will get an all-white jury to set me free and to put you away—if not to lock up an innocent man, but to get another brown-skinned person off the streets."

"Keep talkin', motherfucker, keep talkin'," he said, showing a loss of interest in the topic. This was my signal that I had won the argument... for now. You never beat a man like Alonzo or many others within the Hispanic community. You just postpone the battle. California is starting to awaken to the fact two centuries later, as the Mexicans "have taken the state back without firing a shot," just as they said they would, and the white man is beginning to squirm.

Sadly, it wasn't until Thomas hurriedly came through the door as they were about to close it that we remembered he was supposed to be with us. He was clearly frazzled and frowning as he stopped to talk with us.

"Thanks for telling me they had a one-bag policy; I had to condense my stuff and they confiscated the tequila." "G'day, Mate," was all I could get out.

"Asshole," was all he could get out as he moved on to his seat several rows behind us.

Finally, the sound of the turbines slowly, then rapidly, screamed to life and we were off. We were launching ourselves through some scattered clouds into a deep-blue sky and over the English Channel to set foot on Dutch soil for the Cannabis Cup. The Cup is the world's largest collection of potheads who come to sample the world's best weed. The event was sponsored by *High Times Magazine*.

I wrote a letter to *High Times* offering my freelance skills, as I was also covering the topic of Amsterdam drug policy for another magazine that I had arranged after planning the trip. So I figured I would throw my hat in the ring for *High Times* as well. I studied up on the various editors and found one with whom I felt a connection, a gal who had studied political science. I had just graduated with my masters in public administration, which dealt heavily in the science of politics so I wrote my note:

Dear Zena,

I will be headed to Amsterdam in November for the Cannabis Cup. I assume your magazine already has a journalist or two slated for the assignment. However, I still wanted to offer my services. I have enclosed my resume and writing sample that I find may closest resemble the manuscript run in your publication. I also have another story written about a night my brother and his veterinarian partner saved our family dog at 2 a.m., while my brother had probably a .2-plus blood-alcohol level and his partner and I had been smoking weed all night. This story serves as a further example of how marijuana isn't as bad as we have been led to believe it is, though my parents still like to argue the fact. Maybe alcohol is as bad as they tell us; but my brother, heavily under the effects, saved our dog and was the family hero that night.

I see you studied political science. I am finishing my last semester in the MPA program at Fresno State. I wonder how the hell anyone can get through those poli-sci courses without weed?

But I never heard back. At that point I felt a bit of shame for even writing to the magazine. It's a publication that promotes a vice.

A smoke-induced vice that may not be the best habit for people to have. I feel vices should be run like religion. If you enjoy it (it being games of chance, weed, alcohol, pills, powder or porn) and you can control the usage (many people can't), then enjoy your vice. But never promote or push your vice on others, never encourage, because you never know how they are going to handle the ride.

Of course, these feelings developed after the magazine didn't respond to my inquiry letter, so maybe I am just embarrassed and looking to justify why I wouldn't write for that filthy rag anyhow.

Chapter Three

We arrived in Amsterdam not with a *High Times* media pass, but as representatives of *Playboy*. "But do you understand who this man is? He is here covering the Cannabis Cup for *Playboy Magazine*," I heard Thomas telling the desk help at check-in at The Flying Pig, a popular hostel where I had *attempted* to make our reservations months earlier.

"*Playboy* put him up *here?*" the pretty blonde girl said from behind the counter with confusion in her voice, as if she knew better than what Thomas was selling.

"Yes, he is not a very good writer, and he was given a poor travel budget."

"I see. I would like to help you, but there is nothing I can do." Apparently the reservations started the next day, so we would need to find another place to lodge. The desk girl did make a call to another hostel where we could bed down for the night, so we took it.

The hostel was actually a retired hotel complex. Not very pretty, and there seemed to be a pride about the filth of the place. But our room had four clean bunks, or at least clean-sheeted bunks and a window that looked out onto an unkempt gray-stone courtyard with a giant maple tree and a view of the side of a large, Gothic, gray-stone church.

Thomas was beginning to get on my nerves, and me on his, something about two leaders traveling together. Alonzo was a leader in his own right. He has always been smart enough to not let it bother his ego when he was simply a follower.

"Whatever, man," was the response Alonzo would usually give when presented a choice on a matter. The exception being, if he had his mind made up to not do something, there was no way of persuading him otherwise.

Thomas took a piss, and Alonzo lay in his bunk with his eyes shut in a momentary re-charge; I slipped out the door to get an electric converter so I could charge my MP3 player. I stepped out of the hostel and turned in a blind direction to start walking. A gust of late afternoon wind seemed to be a breath of new life, almost as if the spirit of Amsterdam herself was welcoming me, causing the autumn leaves on the ground to scuttle and scratch at the brick walkways. I turned another corner and was instantly caressed by a tangerine mist, ignited by the sunset.

Thick beams of orange pierced through every gap in the cityscape. The moisture in the air seemed to absorb the light and turn the cobbled street into a grown man's fairytale of sorts, a Valhalla.

The air was sweet, as a result of all the canal water. It gave the place a dank scent. The surroundings were nonthreatening, and I would have been content in the moment for a long time. However, I had to keep moving; there was so much more ahead. Most of it wasn't going to be this innocent.

I found an electrical outlet converter at a small market; you won't find a Walmart anywhere close to this neighborhood, and you will pay twice as much for the item, but that is what makes Europe, Europe. So with my new hardware, I returned to the hostel, only to find a note in the room.

"Maj—go out the front door and turn left. There is a bar a half-block down. Meet us there." I grabbed a sweatshirt and headed out. The air had turned to a gray, ashy dusk with the sweet musky scent still vibrant in the canaled city. I walked along, getting to know my immediate surroundings. The cobblestoned streets were walled on each side with multi-story homes and flats built side by side. There was a tattoo place across the street from the hostel, and above it was a flat that had hung a rainbow flag from a window.

I continued my neighborhood walk and came to a lounge which had a Heineken Beer sign light in the window. I pulled the door open and stepped into a dark bar that had about fifteen shadows throughout, in small groups of two and three talking and drinking. I saw everyone was looking at me, just like in those Wild West movies when the stranger walked in. Only it wasn't happening to John Wayne, it was happening to me. And that's when I noticed the rainbow decal on the bar mirror next to the register. Those motherfuckers had steered me into a *gay* bar, into a place where I suddenly felt like the hanging Christmas ham.

I turned around and stepped out; another wind chill gave way, a cold giggle of wind, as if even the elements were laughing at me. Across the street behind a large pane of glass, Thomas and Alonzo sat in a warm, amber-filled coffee shop laughing with great joy in their eyes as they watched me. I couldn't hear the laughter, but you could see the passion in their faces. All I could hear was a muffled Right Said Fred song on the jukebox in the bar behind me. I had provided the entertainment for the two, their own goddamn dog and pony show. I turned and walked towards The Red Light District. *Fuck'em, time to be alone*, I thought.

I had visited Amsterdam a few years earlier, a day trip from a sleepier town an hour's train ride out of the city, when I traveled with a friend who had come over for his uncle's funeral. It was an innocent Dutch village that shut down with sunset with the exception of the jazz-playing pub. We were only in town for a few days, but came into The Red Light District one afternoon, just to get a look at the whore and dope show. But that was during the afternoon; the District was not very active with sin. The sun was off now, and I was alone—and worse, sober, so the District was the direction I steered.

We were staying in the Leidsplien Square area of town. The area hosts several retail shops of both tourist crap and upscale clothing, restaurants and pubs. There were plenty of coffee shops as well. These were the establishments that sold cannabis in a decriminalized form of commerce. Most were not licensed to sell both alcohol and weed, so it's tea or coffee pairings. You could also pick up hash and space cakes, which contained weed in the cake ingredients. I stepped into the first one I passed. The motif was Jamaican, with Bob Marley posters and reggae humming over the speakers.

"What do you recommend?" I asked the blond Dutch kid in his early twenties behind the counter.

"Well, what kind of high you lookin' for, bro?" he asked, trying to sound hip. "There ish da Strawberry Cush, which is a mellow high—or the Diesel, which ish a wide-awake high," he said, showing more Dutch accent as he continued. But the concept of different highs was bullshit; at least in my opinion it was. Cheap weed makes you slow and sleepy; good weed gives you a great buzz. The thought that all the various strains contain unique highs never caught on with me. The only thing different about the dozen choices of weed was price. I took a gram of the Diesel and grabbed a disposable lighter with the Jamaican flag on it. "Shweet," the kid said as he bobbed his head, looking at me almost as if I were supposed to join in with his enthusiasm. So I gave him a thumbs- up, which rejuvenated his smiley head bobbing.

"Dat will be eighteen Euro, pleash."

"Son of a bitch—that's not sweet," I said of the pricey gram, forgetting where I was. When you hear eighteen Euro, at first you are conditioned to think eighteen bucks, which isn't a bad price. But the dollar was weak to the Euro, and I was really looking at almost twenty-five bucks.

"Itch's a good deal, bro," he assured, which worried me because he was probably right, or at least now I had an idea of the going rate for weed in Amsterdam. I thanked the kid, leaving a euro on the counter. "Shweet," he said again, as I turned to have a seat to start my first joint roll of the trip. My wooden chair creaked as I sat back; No Woman No Cry filled the room with spirit, and my overpriced lighter snapped the end of my joint to life as I drew the moment into my lungs. "Shweeeet," I whispered as I exhaled.

"You like dat?" the Dutch voice seemed to appear as the Cheshire Cat.

'Yup—I like dat," I replied.

"Shweet."

I stepped out of the shop back onto the street and was walking the same direction I had been moments earlier. But things were different; the moment was lighter; it began to sparkle as I remembered where I was. A bike passed me on the left and rang its bell in announcement—I was truly in the old world; my reality at that point seemed to fleet. The bike bell rang again down the block, its toll crisply bouncing off the brick homes on both sides of the lane. I took a deep breath of the moment and exhaled the ashes of my stress.

The neighborhoods outside The Red Light District have a year-round charm that blends well with the art of the seasons. To counter the stinging spell of winter's naked chill, many neighborhoods and squares string festive lights. They are not strung American-style with loads of strung lights that vary from house to house, yard to yard. In Amsterdam, there is an order to the festive lights; neighborhoods are identified by their symmetrical light displays. In a sense an echo of lights down each street.

Caught up in the surrealism of the moment, I suddenly noticed I had arrived at the boundary of the District. Across the next canal, a stream of red-lit windows formed the boundary and a wicked interruption in the moment.

I sat on a nearby bench and pulled out my bag of weed and rolled a fresh joint. Not that I needed to smoke any more, but when entering the belly of the beast, you don't want to smoke any less.

Red Light District

I could see the activity of the area, men walking past the red glowing windows, some approaching the door for inquisitions and negotiations. Some men move on, like lost gray ghosts wandering the streets looking for their next haunt; some step through the door and are swallowed by the sin. I walked across the bridge, over the black shimmering canal water that reflected the blood of the red neon. Once across I was in the land of Sodom, worthy of dark judgment if the Savior happened to return at that moment.

I sat against the canal rail and lit my joint. I wanted to study the area more, observe the inhabitants, the whores, on both sides of the glowing glass. The red-light studios consisted of a single doorway or a line of glass-door entries, which had an adjoining studio or private room above. There were three doors, but only two entries were lit and occupied. From where I sat, I could see the appealing curves of the working women, but most detail was still vague; race and hair color were clear, but faces weren't. One woman half heartedly posed, changing positions every fifteen seconds. One leaned in her doorway and spoke on her cell phone.

I crossed the canal and started walking along the street that paralleled the glowing windows. I passed several. The women, in fact, were quite beautiful. Some would just look through you as you pass; others gave a sweet farm-girl smile, and some used glances that showed they are steeped in the art of seduction. The pointed tongue to the upper lip of an open mouth, a momentary squint of the eyes. These were perfume to the perverted. Sex is the pervert's heroin.

When you do see a man/customer/fiend exit a red-light room, you know he senses the whole world looking at him. He at that moment will sober up from his sex high. He is more than likely aware of the thoughts about him from the people who glance at him in passing. Labels, hypocritically given at times, like *pervert, chauvinist, asshole, victim, hero* will fill the minds of those who pass and look at him as he does the walk of shame. Tolerance is key in Holland, but that doesn't assure you that the filthy behaviors of society and tourist do not draw a silent scorn of sorts.

The schlep stepped from the red door in time for a dozen eyes to mark him. The John, who looked like a common New York taxi driver, didn't look directly at anyone; but he walked with what appeared to be a content tooth-filled grin of confidence, chest out proud, with apples in his armpits. But was it show? Should a man who pays for sex consider himself anything more than a whore himself? Worse than a whore? For as Christ tried to show the world, even a whore can have redeemable values as precious as rubies. But a man who pays for sex isn't really a man, at least not in the analogs of sexual conquest. He has all but taken Love from the act and replaced it with Compensation. There is not even that basic pride of the hunt.

Even in a one-night stand, with no-name sex, there is mutual attraction, an instinct to assure the continuance of the species. From mutual attraction comes Love, but that doesn't always mean the Love is not of a perverted nature. Maybe to these dark floating ghosts, the touch of a prostitute is Love; these siren types know how to put men into a trance and easily confuse the heart. Maybe Love is purely subjective and not fully understood by the *normal* of society. Sex is these men's drug of choice, their addiction. They are not worried about the continuance of the species; they are worried about getting their fix. Regardless of all these pot-induced thoughts, I still loathe the Johns and feel pity for the girls. I was witnessing the full exploitation of a vice. The actual gaping wound was right there in my face, displaying the moment like the spreading of a bacteria, propagated by feeding off the behavior.

When sex is paid for, there should be no satisfaction outside the cheap moment of orgasm. There should be no stride of victory from the conquering male. If Man was filled with the wisdom of beasts, men who pay prostitutes for the purpose of self-assurance would be attacked and killed—castrated at the bare minimum in a truly progressive society. Of course, there is a portion of the population, mostly Muslim extremists and old Republican white people, who believe a guy who wanders around Amsterdam stoned should be hanged for the betterment of society—and perhaps they are right. Though some have said certain drugs give a better high than sex, I assert they are not doing it right then.

I began to walk down Oudezijds Street to travel the main artery of the District. I walked along the glass doors, feet away from the working girls—the hanging meat. They all wore revealing bikini-style outfits. Everything but the bare minimum of flesh was revealed, which to the truly perverted is the only flesh that matters. The girls were beautiful; their bodies were their livelihood and they were tuned for profit. The first girl was the blonde you see at a Californian beach; she was also on her cell phone and carried a bored housewife's expression as she spoke, twirled her hair and looked beyond those who passed by her window. The other women searched the passersby, giving winks and smiles or a playful beckoning head nod. Each had a different hairdo. Each girl had her own bait, knowing her prey well.

As I ended the line of red glass, I came to an alleyway which gave way to a large dark cathedral of brick and glass. It sat in the heart of the District and appeared as a giant, sleeping, stone beast. The towering steeples must have been visible to the entire neighborhood like the fingers of the Almighty stemming from the ground, ready to smash the pulse of sin into the dust when the time comes, reminding that there is always someone watching, judging. And perhaps to others, the Gothic stone beast brought hope and protection, proving that God is everywhere, especially in the places She is most needed.

If I turned right, the dim-lit alley, which was brick paved and possibly just a narrow service road, curved around the church property and disappeared a hundred feet down. I could see more red glowing lights, but could not get an angle on the contents. A sign that read "Sex Shop" was clearly visible. So I walked into the area, the Valley of Death. Sin and Purity glaring at each other, like chained dogs that are kept only feet apart from each other, wanting nothing more than to obliterate each other. Or maybe like the polar opposites of a magnet, two forces of good and evil, that when placed next to each other are unable to advance. These laws are created in measures of self-preservation. For good to exist, you need the scale-balancing effects of evil. One cannot exist without the other, no matter what the level of despise.

As I began my back-roads stroll, I saw human figures stirring in the base shadows of the giant church only a dozen feet from me. I recognized them immediately—they were junkies. Scary things with wilted eyes and limbs veiled in flesh. A man sat slumped in a hooded sweatshirt; dirty vines of hair crawled from the sweatshirt's hooded mouth as the head half-hung to the ground presented no face. Next to him stood his mate. Pants high enough to expose the broomstick ankles she walked on, and her long-sleeved t-shirt hung on her like oily rags on a corpse. She had short, self-chopped hair and what appeared to be two large black olives where her eyes used to be. She stood silently over her motionless partner; her wiry arm reached across her rib cage and held onto the other arm at the elbow, either trying to keep the arm from falling off or simply for the security the posture gave her. They were gone on the drug-induced journey that they scraped every bit of pandered change to take—forgoing food for the cause. Now they stood at the church's feet, seeking Her holy protection, wrapping themselves in her shadows—or maybe the place just blocked the wind?

Still, I stood in place and watched the two. They certainly didn't notice or care; they had found their escape and nothing—bar a shot of epinephrine—would rob them of that. Soft drugs such as marijuana are tolerated in Amsterdam; however, the Dutch are well-aware of what damage hard drugs can do to a population, and these two zombies were the poster children of the cause. When it comes to cocaine, meth or heroin, the tolerance quickly and smartly weans in the Netherlands.

I felt as if I had been in the moment for longer than I should have. Or maybe it was more the weed that had delayed my sense of time—*enough of this human zoo exhibit*. I turned and continued my walk deeper into the pit.

I came across another red-glassed door, but the inhabitant was a far cry from the first girls I had passed earlier. This lady and the one in the next doorway were big or large—or girth-blessed, I should say. Large bosoms with matching-gut women, whose billowing flesh was bound only by cheap negligees. Rolls hidden under shiny sky-blue and red satin. They beckoned; but it was more of a rough motion, a slob trying to be exotic, a hog wearing lipstick. I came to the entrance of the sex shop whose sign I had seen from the safety of the open street. Inside you could see the novelties and the pornography, foreplay for a pervert—a place to get the blood going before the big deed—organic Viagra. I wasn't interested in going in—or maybe I just worried the place would close in on me, like the candy truck turned child trap in the Disney movie *Chitty-Chitty Bang-Bang*. Behind me only feet away, the dark church silently stood; a sealed church exit could open into a direct path into the sex shop—but don't count the blessed place out. Perhaps on any given Sunday, the exit turns entrance and draws upon the stained souls of the District, washing them, making them pure, if only for a moment. Or maybe it makes it easier for a priest to hold down a job at both places?

I moved on, deeper into the canyon of the damned. The next red light appeared. The woman, who clearly looked Samoan, both in feature and size, made a crude hand and mouth gesture, like some sort of international sign of a blowjob. I imagined her making the same movements on a turkey leg and coming away with a full mouth and clean bone. My only option was to smile and decline with a head shake; but before the moment could become enchanting, she made the same gesture to another who walked past me. He just looked at her and then back at the ground, hands in pockets. His body slightly slumped forward, more than likely on his own walk of shame, one with the weight across his wilted shoulders. Seeing that I wasn't the only one who received the Island blowjob gesture, I felt cheap and expendable.

The narrow street opened back up, now on the opposite side of the church. There were more red-light display windows along the street; but most, aside from a couple down the street, were dark. It was mid-week; perhaps the sin needed sleep like the rest of us during the work week? I sat down on the big church's steps to rest for a second before I walked back to the hostel. I had placed my joint roach in the watch pocket of my jeans, so I dug it out with my index finger and then went for my lighter. Just then, ominous bell tones came from the shadowy steeples of the giant church. I could only sit and listen as the somber and steady voice of the church announced its presence to the night. I could see some of the red-lit windows in the area, almost like staggered demons throughout the immediate neighborhood—frozen in fear and defiance, but not on bended knee.

I didn't notice how many time-telling tolls there were, as I started counting late, but there seemed to be more than thirteen of them. The last few hours were a tough but worthwhile ride, but it was time to return to the hostel. We had a few more days ahead of us; it was only mid-week, no use burning out too soon. I followed my earlier path home with the exception of sinners' alley. I had almost circled the giant church, and I had no interest in returning to the valley of the damned. My subconscious was certainly already working on what it would show me in my nightly dreams, stuff that turns the hair gray: sex with junkies, food fights with obese whores.

I returned to an empty, cold room. The powder-blue walls, guest lockers and steel-framed bunks didn't add a welcoming ambiance either. But there was a wall heater, the type rarely seen in America with the exception of old East-Coast and San Francisco dwellings. I twisted the handle, and it immediately ticked and creaked to life. Instant warmth radiated, and I had made a new friend.

There were four bunks in the room, two singles and two stacked. Our three bags were still intact at the foot of the beds. The room was clean, with the exception of the graffitied lockers, which were some sort of planned theme of the place; the elevators were covered in it as well. Mostly names, dates, countries, written in black sharpie, some scratched in, some written tag style. I am sure it was all in an effort to give the place a westernized theme. Europe is rarely happy with us as a culture, but they seem to embrace our wall trash.

I peeled my bedspread and sheet and climbed into my cocoon. I hoped to awaken a new man, free of sin and expanded of mind. My MP3 was charged, so I grabbed the extra pillow off the empty bunk and situated myself. I was ready to drift, but had left the goddamn light on. I tried to sleep anyway, thinking the top bunk would block enough light. But it didn't. So I got up, shut the thing off, used my music player for a flashlight and climbed back in bed; it did turn out to feel better the second time bedding down for the night. The Beatles' "Dear Prudence" was what I chose to listen to and was asleep by its conclusion.

The peace didn't last for long, or maybe it did; but that was over as the door crashed open, and I popped up and hit my head on the mesh supporting the upper bunk. Thomas and Alonzo came staggering in, laughing and trying to support each other as they walked, which didn't work with the narrow entry; but they still tried, sliding against the wall until they hit the openness of the room.

The two split, and Alonzo fell to his bunk; Thomas dove to his and overshot, sliding across his narrow mattress and falling to the ground on the other side. This, of course, started Alonzo laughing again; and Thomas, too drunk to know if he were hurt, let out a muffled laugh as his face was in the pillow he managed to grab on the way down.

"Your fucking head is bleeding, *cabron!*" Alonzo said to me and started laughing again. I felt my forehead and saw there was blood on my fingers.

34

"No, it's not," Thomas said into his pillow, as he had not risen from the floor, more than likely contemplating staying there.

"Nooo, not you—Major's head," he explained. "What the fuck happened to you?"

"What the fuck do you care? I got jumped by junkies in the District; one of them was a Samoan who tried to suck my dick— where the fuck were you?" But this just fueled another bout of laughter from Alonzo, followed by the sputtering low-toned laugh of Thomas, which could have been misconstrued for moans.

I checked my head in the bathroom mirror, and sure enough the skin was broken but just to the minimum allowing blood flow. I washed it and pressed tissue to it for a minute; the blood was done. I returned to my bed. "Where did you guys go?" I asked.

"Fuck if I know; we were all over the place, hitting pubs and rolling fat ones," Alonzo said. "You sleeping down there?" he asked Thomas.

"Yeah, it helps me fight off the spins," Thomas said. He had turned on his back, and one of his feet was posted in the air, supported by his bunk, ready to fight the spin-cycle vomit production, which is just the body trying to hurl some poison, after which you usually sleep better.

"I was dreaming of being at a Beatles' concert when you two assholes came through that door."

"The Beatles—why the fuck you dreaming about the Beatles?"
"Probably because I was listening to them."

"Oh—that makes sense—that's why I go to bed with porn on the TV," Alonzo said in a manner that was as casual as fishing, and I knew he wasn't lying—and I thought what a great idea that was.

"You're a goddamn pervert," I said, lying back onto my bunk and getting comfortable. But Alonzo was passed out cold, on his back, fully-clothed. His mouth lay open—*maybe he was dead*? AND THE

FUCKING LIGHT WAS LEFT ON!

Chapter Four

I woke feeling rested, but slowly, a result of yesterday's smoke no doubt. From out of the window I could see a powder-gray sky, mixed with the nearby skyline of old-world brick architecture. It was beautiful and a never-before-seen sight for me, red old brick and gray slate-shingled buildings; there was a pleasure about just lying in bed looking at it. I could also see some of the outstretched limbs of the maple tree that had lost ninety percent of its leaves during autumn's visit. The ten percent that fought on stood silently still, shiny copper and bronze leaves that shimmered with the morning moisture.

It was a rough night for the other two, so I kept my noise level down as I moved to the bathroom to run nature's and man's course. I grabbed my copy of the book *Scar Tissue* by rocker Anthony Keidis; I had picked it up at the airport. I stepped into the water closet, and it wasn't until I looked into the mirror that I remembered hitting my head on my bunk hours earlier. But it didn't look bad and would be a day's healing.

It's not pleasant to defecate in a European toilet. In America we are wasteful with our resources, including water. So our toilets are designed to fill the toilet bowl with water, to catch the contents, to absorb the unpleasant aromas from such dealings. Europe has always been smartly planned for conservation. So the toilets sit dry until it is time to flush. Most still run with the gravitational system of an elevated tank that brings a flush of water down.

The small room quickly filled with a scent of death. I looked at the three toothbrushes by the sink and remembered a lesson my father taught me. He said that a fart is a gas, so if it is a gas and I am breathing through my mouth to avoid smelling his farts, I am actually getting crap particles in my mouth, farticles—thus presenting me with a no-win situation if I wanted to continue to breathe.

By that rationale, the exposed toothbrushes were going to be exposed to the odors of that bathroom. I finished business quickly without any reading. I grabbed my toothbrush and left the bathroom with it; I decided not to flush, so their toothbrushes could marinate. It was a karmic retribution for the night before and the cut on my head. Aside from that, it seemed a funny thing to do, plus each would think the waste was left by them from last night. I decided to not brush my teeth that day, comb my hair or shower; I could see I was already turning into a European male. I placed my toothbrush securely in my suitcase, where it would not be exposed to any air.

Thomas never made it into his bed; he looked content on the hard linoleum floor, though he did manage to pull a blanket onto himself. Alonzo stirred and looked at me out of one eye that he was able to split open. "Where the fuck you goin'?" he asked.

"I'm goin' to the Van Gogh, get some culture out of this heathen trip." He just rolled over and was back asleep, if he were ever really awake at all.

It was 10 a.m. and I was able to catch the end of the free breakfast that was offered each morning where the basics were served. I quickly drank a cup of strong black coffee that had grown slightly cool with the late morning and refilled my cup. The only eggs were hard boiled, and there were a couple of pieces of wheat toast with peanut butter and Nutella spreads. The simplicity of the breakfast had a beauty to it. It lacked the temptations provided in the oils and fats of the American breakfast. No greasy potatoes, gravy, sausage, regrets of overeating. One of America's curses is the fact that we can eat until we are miserable; this fact is considered the afterlife to two-thirds of the planet.

Then I was out the door and on my way to the museum, which opened in about an hour. At the end of our street was a tram stop I had seen on the city map provided by the hostel. Standing at the stop, I observed the locals in action. It was Thursday morning, so even though I was on vacation, the area inhabitants were moving with purpose, starting the workday. Everyone dressed beautifully. Women wore leather riding boots and wool coats. Men had on suits and overcoats that could put them in an office or a posh upscale lounge. The most casual outfit I saw was worn by a man wearing a jogging suit with a suede and wool collared jacket. As odd a clothing combination as it was, it seemed to work; maybe he was a professional soccer coach. He walked a French bulldog whose feet traveled fast to stay ahead, though his master was not in a hurry at all.

I heard the tram's bell clang just before it appeared around the corner. A blue and white people transporter made its way towards me, traveling awkwardly down the middle of the brick-paved street;

pedestrians adjusted their walking pace to avoid it. The tram marquee announced its travel route: Central Station-Museum Quarters—this was my ride. I hopped on mid-car, only to realize I didn't know how to pay. There was an automated machine most likely used to validate a pass or a purchased ticket. Just then the train jolted forward, so I just sat down for safety's sake. Safety is more important than figuring out how to pay someone. And that's exactly what I was prepared to tell any authority who questioned me.

The tram continued through the town square, where it came to another stop. The area was the pulse of the neighborhood. It was a town square with pubs, restaurants and clubs. I could see The Bulldog Bar and Coffee Shop. I had heard of this place; it was one of the few Amsterdam establishments that could sell both alcohol and marijuana under the same roof, which for reasons unknown to me was not permitted in most cases. This would definitely be an area to explore, come the night. For now, the pubs seemed to be asleep, windows dark with only the reflections of passers by living in them. The tram doors opened and a large population boarded, each stamping something into the machine, the machine taking a bite of everything placed in its mouth. I only noticed one other rider not producing a ticket, and he looked like a hobo, which gave him more reason than safety to not pay. About twenty people boarded, enough for me to give up my seat, not only for a lady, but also so that I may leap from the door at any given stop to avoid any authority who may want to catch a freeloading American—a cop would probably get a medal back at the station for that move. Another jolt of thrust and we were off.

I stared out the window, as if I were on a city tour. We passed The American, a hotel built in the 1880s, which was dubbed *art nouveau* in the architecture of its time. The gray stone building still reeked of classical elegant features; it was kind of an honor to have the placed called American. Over a broad canal and around a curve to the left stood The Hard Rock Café and the town's casino, the Holland Casino Amsterdam. The sight of the Hard Rock threw me, something I wasn't opposed to seeing but more of an unexpected acquaintance in the neighborhood, though I had no desire to visit it. Another turn took me by a magnificent brick building and the start of the museum quarters, an area of town that highlighted the immortal arts of man. The brick building is the Rijksmuseum, dubbed "The National Museum" in the brochure I had read on local attractions. Here works by the greats such as Rembrandt are housed, but they would have to be visited on another day. Today was the Van Gogh Museum, an artist I knew very little about, other than that he was famous, half-nuts and missing part of his ear that he had cut off and mailed to a woman to prove his love. I couldn't think of a better artist to see on such a whimsical trip.

At the next stop I hopped off the tram. A sign clearly showed the direction of the Van Gogh, which was a few hundred feet down and across the road. I needed to roll a joint to get the right eyes for art. There was a bench at the tram stop, but the area was active with waiting passengers, passing pedestrians and the ever-present bicyclists, the preferred form of transportation in the city. Across the street was a strip park, some scattered street-side souvenir shops and hut-sized cafes, beyond them a long stretch of brown, dormant park grass and lonely benches. I stepped in the road, habitually only looked left for the oncoming traffic, but the crisp sound of a bike bell reminded me two-way bike lanes are on both sides of the street. Quickly I stepped from the lane and into the street, in time for a taxi to honk as I didn't look left after turning right to see the bell source. I felt like the typical tourist, like a dipshit who can't even cross a street or figure out how pay tram fares.

Finally I made the park benches; the adrenaline had worn me out for the moment, and I just wanted to sit for a second. The grayness of the sky and the emptiness of the park gave me the feeling of security I needed to carry on, so I pulled my baggie and papers from my pocket and began to roll. I finished my work and looked the spliff over. There is an art or labor to rolling a joint. It's like the simple pleasure of looking at your lawn after giving it a good mow. I rolled a fine one, slightly fatter on one end than the other, not rolled so loose as to burn too quickly and hopefully not cased so tight as to not draw correctly. There was only one way to find out; I struck my lighter and induced smoke. The joint drew smoothly, so I held the product in my lungs for a moment and blew the cloud from my lungs, releasing it to the sky. I repeated this three times, then spit in my palm and extinguished the joint with it. A joint is not like a cigarette; it's enough to get four people high, not designed in most cases for a single sitting.

I got up from the bench, did a core stretch and rolled my head on my neck. The movements seemed to knock a layer of dried mud off my bones. The air was chilled but sweet with the town's canal musk. The trees of the area were stripped clean and prominent against the sky. The surrounding architecture was model perfect, and I felt as if I had stepped into a painting. Yep, that kind of thinking can only mean one thing: I was stoned. Not to say that the area didn't harbor all the descriptors I laid out, it's just when you are high, there is another level of presence that is hard to describe to the sober.

I plugged in my headphones and pressed "random play." The song "Champagne Supernova" by the Brit brothers' band Oasis came on; it seemed the perfect song for my walk to the museum, somber but passionate and a good companion to get me to the ticket window.

The building was larger than I expected, a place with seemingly endless wall space to honor a town's favorite son. I had been told to anticipate lines at the entrance if I visited on the weekend, but this late morning only one couple was ahead of me, a young pair probably in their mid-twenties; I believe they spoke French to one another as the man said something, and his date's eyes winced with love and she stood on her toes to give him a kiss. If I weren't sure they were French before, I certainly knew it now. The couple took their tickets and disappeared into the building.

"One, please," I said to the portly blonde woman who worked behind the glass. I paid my fare to the lady, who had a natural light-cherry blush about her fleshy cheeks. She slid me my ticket. "Thank you," I said.

"You are welcome," she replied in a manner of humbled pride, as she spoke her English to a lone American, her smile now showing her perfectly-white Dutch teeth, the result of a lifetime of maintenance, not bleaching.

"You speak English well," I said, "not that Americans speak English well anyhow, but you do."

"T'ank you," her accent came into play a bit more. But I had spent enough time here and needed to move on, so we exchanged smiles; and I too was drawn into the museum, almost as if the place were inhaling me.

I didn't know much about Van Gogh, aside from the trivial stuff that most uneducated Americans knew; he had cut his ear off when a love interest gave him the request in hopes of driving his passions for her away. However, the half-mad artist obliged and hacked a large portion of the appendage off and mailed it to her. I wasn't aware of the outcome of the gesture; but it seems like the woman got just what she had asked for which, as with most spoiled women, continued to make her unhappy.

I passed by his early works, the hands of the peasants, the Potato Farmers. They were drab, dark paintings that held no warmth but captured the moments flawlessly. Exposed were the workers of the soil, operating under cold, gray Dutch skies with a meal only good for some level of nourishment, not gluttony. In another portrait was a humble farm-family meal with the ambiance darker than the evening sky. I wondered what the art subjects thought of the redheaded Dutchman who sat in the corner, capturing the dank moods of the gathering onto the canvas. No joy was displayed in the paintings, only the truth of drab lives in the moment captured, leaving you wondering, were these people in fact happy, so of the Earth in labor and life that they had achieved the Earth's humbleness? The works exposed Van Gogh's talents, but drew little gallery attention at the time of production. These early works went unnoticed and underappreciated in their time; it was fitting that I stood there and looked at them alone.

It was when I came across Van Gogh's *Sunflowers* that I realized I was viewing one of the world's masterpieces, something I had seen in posters and postcards, but rarely paid attention to.

The list of familiar paintings continued to pile up: *Almond Blossoms*, *Crows in a Wheat Field, Self Portraits*, and possibly his best known, Sunflowers, which was in fact a series with several other paintings of the flower. Along with gaining an acquaintance to the works, I received an introduction to the artist himself. A tragic character in the human drama, who died relatively unknown, though in life he was fiercely supported by a brother and a sister-in-law. The two must have had eyes that saw the future and the value of works by an immortal.

When you see the works, I mean really spill your eyes on them, covering every inch of canvas, you will see what Van Gogh did, why his work changed the face of art. The color combinations, the endless tiny brush strokes, each the size of an ant, each an insignificant speck that, when combined with the others, produced the priceless. It was like the old color-chromed television, which got its images from the countless tiny dots of color that gave life to the screen.

In the end, the artist released himself from the servitude of pain he suffered at the cold, dark hands of depression. Vincent shot himself in the heart in the womb of a wheat field. His last form of artistic expression from a man who improved art as mankind knew it.

I had gone through the display probably quicker than I should have. In America we get conditioned to avoid crowded lines, which usually appear at amusement parks. For this we are conditioned to move through attractions at a speed that makes us feel fortunate to do so—a light crowd would slow the pace, force the appreciation. Maybe that's what spawned me to extend my stay to a featured display.

The works on display were by an artist whose name didn't stick, which was unfortunate but true to my nature—my long-term memory fading—inspired to fade on a trip like this. A dozen large paintings from the Victorian era. The models were either the Misses or Mistresses of the artist or his customers. The Misses were commissioned, women of wealthy husbands, the Barons of Europe, the Titans of Industry, the early trophy wives of the world. Though in that time, a trophy wife was valued for her ability to produce shining offspring and tend to the nest. Unlike today where it is found in large breasts and high heels.

The Mistresses in his work were probably the Muses who inspired his non-commissioned masterpieces and probably a few wild nights, worth far more than money.

Waves of emotion were stirred by the beautiful works of the museum, but now another familiar feeling nagged my attention. It was hunger, the naughty cravings brought on by the weed, classified as the munchies by those familiar with its effects. I had noticed a café listed on the museum map, so I made my way toward my newest muse.

The café was large and well-lit. There was seating for over a hundred, but less than ten dotted the seating area. The food was prepared and placed out a la carte, and I spotted what I wanted immediately. It was a large, dark, glistening brownie with fudge frosting and some milk to stew it in. The milk was in cartons and half-submerged in ice, and the anticipation for the meal was almost high enough to produce some saliva in my cottoned mouth. I could swear my heart beat a little stronger in the moment. Maybe like the lioness as she comes across the herd of zebra?

There were two choices of milk; each had a colored label band around it, one green, the other blue. But the words on the bottle were in Dutch, and neither led me to know which milk was available between my assumed choices of whole milk or light. I figured, when you are eating a piece of chocolate sin, it doesn't matter the fat content in the milk; go down in flames if need be—take your chances, what an adventure.

I sat down and meticulously skinned the cellophane off my brownie prey. I sat it in front of me and moved to my milk. In my infinite wisdom, I looked for the end of the carton that had writing and easily opened the mouth of the drink, allowing the carton to spill its treasure when the time was right.

I cut into my brownie, which gave my fork a slight resistance as a respectable brownie would. The chunk I carved was twice the size the bite should have been, but I planned on stuffing my mouth with the indulgence—sensory overload was the object. I began to chew, and my brain began the slow release of endorphins as a reward for my eating habits. I swallowed the rich cake; however, my teeth, cheeks, roof of my mouth and throat were now painted in fudge frosting. This was easily remedied with the drink of milk that was on its way, the cavalry of the situation, the retribution for the chocolate dance of dominance in my mouth.

The moment was instantly brought to a halt with the comfort of a needle dragging over a record. *IT WAS BUTTERMILK! GODDAMN IT!* Only in Europe. Or more likely, only in America could you go to a café and not have to worry about ending up with buttermilk by mistake. I was doomed. I didn't take enough of the liquid to wash the cocoa mud down my throat, and I wasn't about to take another drink of the piss. I sat there defeated. There was no chance that I was going to take another bite of the thing which sat there; I could swear it was smugly smiling at me. Out of principle and fear, I wasn't going to purchase another milk, if that's in fact what was in the other carton. For all I knew and trusted, it contained tomato juice. "Fuck you," was all I could get out as I dumped the whole façade out, the full buttermilk carton celebrating with a thud as it hit the bottom of the trash bin.

Stepping outside from the museum brought crisp air that was filled with reminders to laugh at life. My discovery of the museum was beautiful; my experience in the café sucked. But the moment as a whole was bittersweet, just as the life and expressions within Van Gogh himself... *hope you got a laugh out of it all, Vincent. See you soon.*

As I stepped out from the museum, I was greeted by another quick breath of chilled wind. My high had lulled in the couple of hours I had spent in the display; the cheer of the gray day had lowered a bit as well. First thoughts were to run back to the dragon, take another drag, get lost in the mind's fog again. But this could not happen, as another few tokes would not make me stoned with euphoria again; it would just make me dull and passive. It's best to wait four hours between smoking sessions, or I would be asleep for the night sometime just before sunset. So in my quest of chemical balance, I stopped by one of the street vendors and ordered a double espresso.

My ears slightly stung from the cold, but the coffee tar taste that filled my mouth took my mind off them; and the strong java aroma gave me the urge to walk back to the hostel. A brisk walk in cold air would also serve to sober. Hopefully the guys would be waking soon, and then we could partake again and eat.

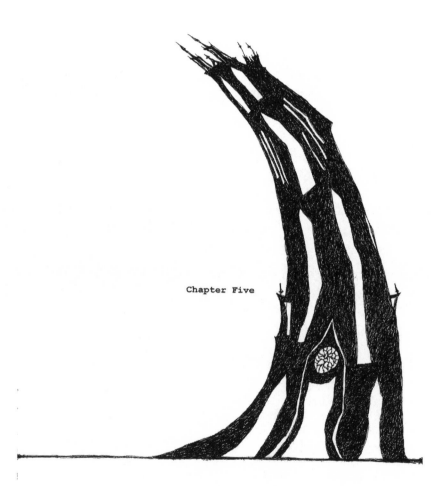

Chapter Five

I entered the room and immediately found Alonzo sitting on the toilet with the door open. Thomas was still on the floor, but somehow managed to make it appear comfortable. "You couldn't close the bathroom door?" I asked.

"And be trapped in here with the smell? No thanks," Alonzo said in a tired but determined voice.

"Well, now we are all trapped by it, 'cause it's waiting for you out here with us," I said as I made my way to my bunk. I received no response from Alonzo and wasn't expecting to. If he had suspected me of leaving the gift that greeted him at the toilet, he would have fired back at me.

"If the smell gets too bad in there, dude, just breathe through your mouth," I said. The door slammed shut; I heard the toilet flush and the squeak of the shower handle that brought it to life.

At that point Thomas sat up, looking like a prizefighter picking himself up from the canvas in the ninth round. "Man, what time did we come home last night?" he asked in a gruff voice.

"I don't know, man," I replied. "I don't remember getting in either," I told him as he squinted his puffy eyes and rubbed his forehead just above the ridge of his nose.

"Did you sleep in your clothes?" he asked me.

"Yeah, I guess so," I replied. He just nodded to me as if it were the norm to sleep in shoes all night, as he turned to his luggage to prod through the day's perspective wardrobe.

"I wonder what the weather is like outside today?" he asked, almost to himself as he looked over his travel wardrobe.

"It's supposed to be warm, long t-shirt weather," I said. He had no reason not to believe his travel partner. Without making a further decision, he shuffled his feet along to the bathroom.

"Alonzo in there?" he asked in passing.

"Yes, but just to shower."

I heard Thomas turn the bathroom door handle; and a second after, cause and effect took over. "Son of a bitch, something die in there?"

he said before continuing in and closing the door behind him. "Roll a fat one, would ya?" I heard him yell through the wall. Moments later I heard the squeak of the shower handle and the ringing shuffle of shower rings. "Goddamn, it smells in there," Alonzo said as he walked out of the bathroom, "and fucking crowded," he added as he smiled large and stuck his hand out for a morning handshake. The moment became as warm as it had been crude. But that's Alonzo, the go-with-the-flow type, always upbeat. If life forced him to eat a shit sandwich, he would end up shrugging his shoulders and asking for Tabasco. The night prior, life had given him blackouts and early morning cold sweats; but he was able to shrug his shoulders and smile the next morning—God bless him.

"It seems odd to me that you find the smell of your own shit offensive," I said to Alonzo.

"Meee? That wasn't from me; I didn't even shit."

"I saw you sitting on the can when I walked in," I reported. "Yeah, I flushed some other *cochino's* shit down and then was letting the place air out while I swallowed the aspirin and took a piss."

"Son of a bitch—that was left by Thomas last night," I said, ready to frame the helpless. "That drunk motherfucker didn't even remember coming home, and he's lucky he didn't shit his pants before. He should be ashamed of himself; that thing was a monster," I said, trying to rile the troops. "We'll come up with retribution; we still have time here. Anyhow, you don't need aspirin in this town," I said to Alonzo as he looked at me with a slight wince of confusion, and I handed him a fattened joint.

"Ahhhh, si si, amigo," Alonzo said as he bit the end off as if it were a Cohiba, spit the paper tip out and introduced the flame. He drew in his breath and with bowed chest and tightened cheeks, handed me the spliff. I followed suit, drew in my fill and walked to the bathroom, cracked the door and fogged the room with my exhalation. "Thanks, blow more in, please," Thomas said as I closed the door and made my way back to Alonzo to pass the finger baton. The shower handle squeaked again, and Thomas joined our circle, holding the towel around his waist with one hand and controlling the joint with the other. The thing circled twice more and then had the life squashed from it. I lay back on my bunk while the other two dressed. Thomas plugged his iPod into the speaker box, and John Lennon's "Instant Karma" filled the room with an upbeat vibe.

"Ready?" Alonzo said, slapping my foot as he stood at the end of my bunk, bringing me back to the moment from wherever it is one slips when smoking weed and listening to the music of Lennon. On my earlier walk, I had noticed a restaurant called Walk-to-Wok, where cooks prepared made-to-order Chinese style behind a window, where passersby could see the process, and put the meal in a to-go Cantonese container. I suggested it with no resistance from the two, and out the door we went.

"Dude, I thought you said it was supposed to be warm today," Thomas said after a half-block of walking.

"I'm no weatherman. All I told you is what the natives said. Maybe this is warm weather to the aborigines of the area?"

"Yeah, well, I'm not one of them; I'm going back to get a sweatshirt," Thomas said, as he already was walking back. Alonzo just shrugged and leaned against the wall.

"We will meet you there! One block down, turn left!" I yelled back to him. He waved a hand in the air as he continued to walk, signaling he understood.

"Let's just wait for him," Alonzo suggested. A flash of annoyance hit me, followed by a washing of shame. I had the chance to warn my friend about the weather, but I felt like being a shit to him. Now my other friend, innocent of the karma, is willing to wait for Thomas when I suggest he meet us and walk alone. I pulled the half-joint from my pocket and handed it and the lighter to Alonzo. "Daats what I'm talkin' about," he said with his smile. By the time it returned to me for the second time, Thomas was upon us with his hoodie sweatshirt and contented face. I handed it to him and we all walked together.

The ordering was simple: step up to the register, pick your noodles or rice, add your choice of vegetables and sauce and then choose a meat or tofu. We each made our selection. Thomas ordered Thai style with a pineapple sauce over rice; Alonzo ordered a spicy Thai beef; and I a sweet-n-sour chicken over pan-fried noodles. All the choices were at the same time wonderful and overwhelming. I knew the weed was working at that point. Moments later, we each had a container in our hands. "Let's walk with these," Thomas suggested.

"Where should we walk?" I asked.

"Let's either go to The Van Gogh museum or the Anne Frank House," Thomas said. "I want to make sure I do something educational here before the partying gets too heavy."

"Cool, let's check out the Frank House; I know where it is," I said. I didn't really know where it was exactly, but I had seen a sign earlier that pointed in the general direction of the attraction. Alonzo was poking through his meal with chopsticks and just looked up and nodded. The easy-to-hold container made the stroll effortless. However, we had only walked a minute before Thomas stopped. "Let me try yours," he said, handing me his container. It made sense; try the other two styles, as they were vastly different. Our gathering had grown quiet; all focus was on the food. Like a pack of civilized wild dogs enjoying the kill together—enough for all, the team rebuilt and solidified under a communal meal, all frustrations forgotten. We were Kings.

After the exchange, we continued to eat as we stood on the canal bank where we had come to a halt. The sun had broken through and the air was still. The canal water sparkled in bright strobes of sunlight. It made the atmosphere seem ten degrees warmer. I had taken my last bite when I could hear Thomas scrape the bottom of his container with his chopsticks. He licked them clean and looked at me with the big smile of a satisfied kid.

"Goood shit, huh?" Thomas said, as he reached out to take my empty container to toss in the trash can next to him.

"It was," I said. He then looked at Alonzo to take his rubbish, but Alonzo twisted his body away and pulled the container next to him, like a hobo protecting his wine.

"Yeah, it's good shit," Alonzo said. "I ain't done; I don't eat like you two filthy *cochinos*," he said with his smug smile of truth.

Alonzo put another bite in his mouth and then handed the carton to Thomas. "You wanna finish it?" Alonzo asked Thomas.

"No way, man. I'm stuffed," he said as he handed it my direction, but I waved it off too.

"I will probably want it in a half-hour," I said.

"Well, it will be here waiting for you," Thomas said as he set it on top of the trash can and began to walk. The stomachs were full and the senses heightened. We came across another sign pointing to the Frank House. "We must be close," Thomas said.

We came to the end of the street and into a large square with a giant church in the center. We crossed the road and walked past the towering cathedral. The steeple was so tall it appeared to bend at the top, as if it were looking down upon us. Just then the bells started to toll, announcing the top of the hour, and they didn't stop until we had passed, like a fenced-in dog who continues to bark until you pass the property— and then there we were, standing in front of Anne Frank's place across from the house of worship where people would have known her.

"So this is it?" Thomas said as he eyed the building. A slight creepiness crawled across me. The other two also seemed to be in their own minds about the place as well. The mind started to flow, the thoughts of fear brought on by Nazi guards who marched these same brick streets, the terror from the footsteps coming for you— with God's house across the street, silently watching it all.

"Well, we're here, may as well go in," I said as I walked up the steps into the house that was now a museum; the two followed behind. Once in, after you pay your entry, you are allowed to walk the house, which is sparsely furnished, but gets its point across with written and pictorial displays of the daily life of the Franks. Midway through the tour, an awful thought came over me as I stood in Anne Frank's bedroom. I was ashamed of the thought but still felt I needed to confide in Thomas to unload my new burden.

"Dude, this place is kind of big, at least bigger than I had imagined."

"You're right, I was thinking that too," Thomas said; Alonzo was still at the display we had passed already.

"I mean, I don't want to take anything away from these people," I continued, more comfortable now that I had a sympathizer. "No house is big enough to hole up in for two years, especially when you have to keep stone-silent every day. But I mean, I never realized Anne had her own bedroom. I guess in my ignorance I pictured the place stacked high with people in every room."

"Yeah, it's more like The Frank Penthouse," Thomas said as we both softly giggled. It's important to laugh when in the gut of a sorrowful place; it helps keep the sanity of life. Just then Alonzo joined the group.

"What's up, guys?" Alonzo said, curious to our light moods. "Shhhhh," I said, bringing him instant confusion. "Be respectful in here, Alonzo." Thomas and I turned and continued our tour. "Assholes," I heard Alonzo say under his breath as he followed—and he was right. Soon after, we finished the tour and were back out on the street where we had started.

"What now?" I asked. "You feeling educated enough for some mischief?" I asked Thomas.

"Yeah, I'm glad we came, but it's a little bit of a downer," he said.

"Let's go to the Cannabis Cup convention," Alonzo said. "It starts today, and I need to pick up my event pass anyhow."

"I can't believe you bought one of those," I said.

"Why not? It's what we fucking came here for," he rightfully said.

"I know, but we should have tried to buy an extra one off someone for cheap."

"You're a cheap fucker; let's go. We have to take a ferry to a warehouse in an industrial area just behind Central Station."

"Sounds good," Thomas said. "I need to try to get a pass too." Again, we were off on our walkabout, passing through the gingerbread architecture of Amsterdam, until we came to the dock where we would catch our ride. Looking around at the others who gathered, I noticed a trend of attendees. There were about twenty people waiting for the shuttle. Three-fourths were male, and almost everyone spoke with American accents. And if it weren't an American dialect, it was some Englishman who had visited the states enough to have bought into the *coolness* of the Cannabis Cup. The women of the waiting group consisted of four

Americanized Asian women, who wore westernized makeup, sunglasses and hip-hop culture running suits. But the overwhelming similarity of everyone gathered was a hidden geekness to their personality, almost as if we were at a Star Trek convention.

The grumble of the approaching ferry brought visions of white water rumbling behind a big boat as it reversed throttle and docked to pick us up. "That's it, let's go," Thomas instructed. Al and I followed, assuming it was our boat. Moments later, after all had boarded, the watercraft began to gurgle again and we were off to the convention.

"Jesus, where'd they move this fucking thing, an old war zone?" Al asked us as he eyed the scene. And he was right; we were navigating through an industrial area of waterfront concrete buildings that looked like they were one bad wind away from being abandoned. Multi-story concrete buildings, wheelhouses and industrial storage areas drifted past us. Some had windows intact; most had missing panes throughout, giving the architecture of the area the look of hardened faces that were missing teeth.

"Well, fellas, this is it. Now that they have us corralled on a boat, this is where they separate us and harvest our organs," I said casually. Thomas just looked at me as if he heard every word but didn't know what to do with them.

"What do you mean?" he asked.

"Don't you see? They have a boatload of foreigners, stoner foreigners. Who the fuck is going to miss any of us? And the way the Dutch will see it is, they are ridding the planet of the scourge of our kind as well as subsidizing their socialized medicine by making available to the elite of society fully-functioning organs taken from the unproductive."

"I still don't know what the fuck you're talking about," Thomas replied and turned his back to us and the wind in order of lighting a cigarette.

"You'll see," I said in a confident tone.

"I don't care if they take your guts; no one is taking my shit without a fight," Alonzo said, appearing as if he were deep into thought and planning ahead.

"Maybe I could barter my life with the promise of a return trip bringing others," I said to the two, who now just ignored me. The boat abruptly slowed, and we could see the dock we would be departing upon to places unknown.

A group of about thirty walked, mostly silent, along a path of worn, cracked and weed-webbed concrete. The path took us among more of the gray, cold, depressing buildings. It was almost like walking through a 21st century industrial ghost town. We then came to a halt in front of a large tent entrance. From through the tent, you entered the cannabis convention. The tent appeared as a lure—lipstick on a pig—as behind it lay another corpse of a building; but we were here, no turning back.

"Okay, everyone, can I have your attention, please?" a female Dutch voice called out. "Your credentials are on file in here. Step in please and find your name, which is listed alphabetically, to claim them."

Alonzo moved forward to pick up the credentials he had purchased weeks before. "You better buy 'em too, fucker," he warned me at the time, "or they may sell out, and you will be ass out."

"I'll take my chances," I told him. "I think once we get there, there will be a no-show or two and I will pay fifty Euros to buy one."

"Okay, don't say I didn't warn you," he reminded me, as he stepped up to collect his purchase.

So there we were, at the entrance of The Cup, and Alonzo looked at me as he stood in line to get his pass. He looked at me with smug eyes and a big tight smile, as if he were asking, *Well, what now, smart guy? Where's your no-shows?* And he was right; there was no one offering extra passes, and I wasn't about to fork out $200 at this fucking overrated event. Thomas stood behind me looking as well. Not so much as he doubted we would get entrance, but just wondering how.

"This is bullshit," I said to Thomas under my breath.

"What is?" he asked.

"The fact that getting into this thing is even an issue. C'mon, just follow close," I said and strolled towards the entrance of the exhibition. At the door was a guy with stringy long hair and stretched brown teeth that were on the fringe of hash and coffee erosion. His job was to look at people's credentials, and he nodded them through in a quasi-zombie state. He was baked and almost in an automatous state of function.

"WOW, LOOK AT THIS FUCKING PLACE, THOMAS! WE'RE HERE—WE ARE REALLY FUCKING HERE!" and then I hugged the guy, and Thomas just walked in. It felt as if I were hugging a straw-man. You could feel bones through his shirt, like you feel them when you pet an old farm dog. I felt odd for that brief moment of embrace, almost as if it needed to be a genuine gesture of care. I pulled back and he just looked at me and broke off a yellow tusked smile, a rare smile you could tell as the small wrinkles in his face went against the normal grain of his creases. I turned and walked in, never looking back.

I figured if the guy were that much in need of a hug, I came along in the nick of time. Or if he were just caught off guard by the moment, well, he's not going to tell his friends who will never allow him to smoke and work the door at these events again. Our only worry now was if someone noticed we were not wearing our passes around our neck, the way everyone else proudly wore theirs. Moments later it became a quick fix when we came across a table that had boxes of credential lanyards with the sponsor "High Times" printed on them. I clipped my *Playboy* Media pass on the end and hung the cord around my neck outside of my sweater. Thomas just hung the cord around his neck and tucked into his shirt front. Just as we turned to see where Alonzo was, he appeared.

"You motherfuckers," he said as he eyed our cords.

"I tried to tell you, asshole. But you insisted on being prepared for the party."

"Hmm hmm hmm," Thomas laughed to himself. But I wasn't sure if it were because I told Alonzo he wanted to come to this thing prepared, as if that were possible, or it just hit him how we got in and how much we saved by not buying passes.

"C'mon, you little fucker, we will buy you a beer later," I said. "You will buy *all* my beers later."

"Fuck you, now you're getting greedy and jealous of our good fortune."

"HEY, HE DON'T GOT NO PASS!" Alonzo blurted out, with a hefty westerner stoner accent, sounding like Cheech Marin from the comedy duo Cheech and Chong.

"Okay, shut the fuck up," I said as I was acting like I was reading an informational pamphlet on a weed vaporizer. Thomas had strolled away as Alonzo was in the middle of his statement. Only a few directly around looked in our direction, but they went back to where they were quickly as we didn't hold their attention.

"You buyin' my beer, bitch? Or should I say it louder?" Alonzo said.

"Alright. Enough. You need to grow the fuck up; I'll buy your beer."

"That's what I thought," Alonzo said as he turned and began to stroll the convention. I followed and moments later Thomas joined the group.

"They've got fuckin' everything you could want for smoking weed," he said with the hope of the Christmas-morning child. "They have rolling paper made out of hemp! How perfect is that?" he continued. They have pipes with a built-in lighter—THEY HAVE SURFER PIPES!" His eyes widened in excitement about suddenly remembering the specialty pipes. "They have a hinged lid—and the lid"—he paused and looked at my eyes to make sure I was grasping the gravity of what he was saying—"the top of the lid is a magnifying glass." He continued to look in my eyes with this big grin and nodding head, wanting me to catch on. He could tell from my stare I was at a loss about something that apparently he was clear about. "The lid concentrates the sun and ignites the weed—like we did with insects as kids," he continued with the tone of light disappointment about the fact I didn't catch on the first time. So I continued, "Why don't the surfers just use a lighter?" At that, Thomas just looked at me with no expression and walked off.

"You're kinda a dick; I'm gonna do my own thing. I'll meet you in a few hours at the High Times party," Thomas said. On these types of trips, breaks from present company are a healthy must. Thomas, like both of us, has no problem wandering strange streets in foreign countries alone—usually finding his way home sometime later, like a rogue homing pigeon. Alonzo and I continued to walk around the venue a bit longer but were unimpressed for the most part. The place didn't carry a whole lot more items than could be found at a large head-shop back home. Soon after, we bolted and headed back to the hostel.

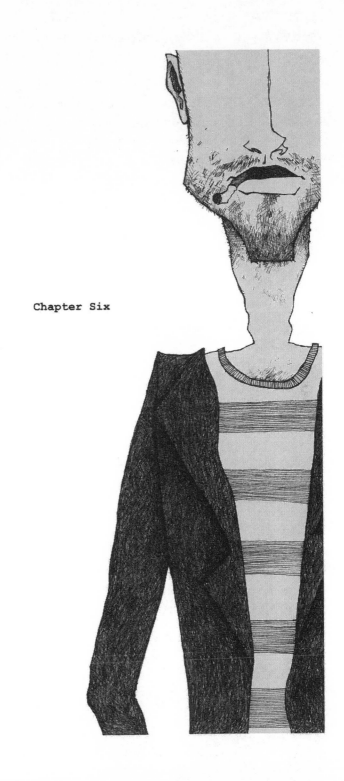

Chapter Six

"Shit, what time is it?" Alonzo asked, waking me from what started as a late afternoon nap.

"It's 6 p.m.; fuck, we've been asleep for three hours." Neither of us spoke for the next few minutes. We just got up and maneuvered around each other in the small room. I was in brushing my teeth while Alonzo got dressed. He entered the bathroom as I exited, my turn to dress; soon after we stepped out into the hostel lobby. "Stand by," I told Alonzo. "I need to take care of something; go grab a beer in the bar," I said.

"What the fuck are you up to?" Alonzo asked, knowing too well.

"Just go fucking wait; I need to square something up about our room rate." Alonzo looked at me sideways but turned and walked towards the bar, as the thought of a cold beer was better than wasting any more energy on me. I then approached the desk clerk. A cute blonde local who, like most Dutch workers who had to deal with tourists, wasn't carrying a smile, just stared at the computer screen in front of her—more than likely as an excuse to avoid any eye contact with anybody.

"Excuse me," I said.

"Yesh," was the response that came from her; she never removed her eyes from the screen.

"Yes, I'm a journalist, and I was wondering if I could bother you for a copy machine."

"You can use the business center next to the post office," she said, while punching in some sort of information onto the screen she still hadn't looked up from. She wore studious-looking glasses, which rode slightly lower on the bridge of her nose as she surveyed the work. Her hair was long and sandy and unkempt to the point that it had its own beauty; the natural locks framed a face with light eyeliner and pale lip gloss. She was certainly cute, but about as warm as a snowfall.

"Yes, but I kinda need it now, not in the morning when the center opens," I said. She still didn't look up. "Here, here is five Euro," I said, holding out the money. This got her to look up, but she still maintained her stern appearance.

"You Americans are all alike," she said, "offering money for anything that eludes you."

"Yeah, we're all assholes," was all I could think to say. Apparently it was enough because she smiled.

"What is it you need copied?" she asked. I hesitated, hoping she wouldn't ask.

"It's a copy of my credentials I purchased for an event I'm covering here, and, well, it cost me more money than my budget allowed."

"Da Cannabis Cup?" she said, interrupting my reason for the copy request.

"Yes, the Cannabis Cup," I said, happy we made a connection. "Ugh, you Americans ARE all alike," she said, almost making me feel we were now going backwards.

"What's wrong with the Cannabis Cup?" I asked. "Doesn't it promote Amsterdam?"

"It promotes Amsterdam for all the wrong reasons," she said. "If a person wants to come here and quietly experience the lifestyle, dat is one t'ing. But to promote Amsterdam as dis party place where our pride is pot and prostitutes is a disgrace."

She had a point. The Cannabis Cup wasn't put on by the Dutch, but by the Americans and purveyors of *High Times Magazine*. The Dutch do not celebrate the vices they offer. They simply offer them, freedoms for those in search of them. They do not promote or glorify the sins; they just make them available. In many ways, it's the ultimate definition of "freedom."

"Well, I see your point," I said. "I can certainly incorporate that in any story I end up creating." She was back to her cold face.

"Anyhow, I have to provide a copy of the pass to my editor through my photographer that I will see tonight, in order of getting the money back by tomorrow." She stared at me for a long second and then held out her hand. I placed Alonzo's credential that I had swiped in the room into her hand.

"Please make it in color, so there are no questions about it," I said, though that part made no sense. I hoped she would just do it and not question me further. She disappeared into an office across from the check-in desk. I looked across the lobby and into the bar. Alonzo was occupied talking with the bartender, which was good, because if he knew what I was up to, he would spoil it.

"Here you are," said the voice of the desk-girl, spinning me around in surprise at her quick return. She was holding out the two passes.

"Thank you," I said, never taking my eyes off the two small pieces of paper that were now in my hand. She had not only color- copied them in an indistinguishable manner, but also laser-printed them on thick stock paper. The second pass was also trimmed to the exact size of the original. The only telltale sign was that the back of the copy didn't have the small-print disclaimer wording, but that was easy enough to maneuver around. "Thank you," I said again, this time looking directly at her in appreciation.

"I hope it works for you," she said. I felt a little ashamed because with her intelligence, she saw through what was happening. She could have called me on it and made me look like an American idiot, but she didn't—not directly. Through her coldness and walls was a Dutch charm, ingrained in much of the culture. She was a guarded person who through enough interaction could get a read on a person. In this case, she realized though I was bullshitting, she understood why and helped me out when she could have easily not.

I reached in my wallet and pulled out fifteen Euro. "Here, for a job well done," I said, laying it on the counter.

"You don't have to do dat," she said in earnest. "I want to thank you—seriously."

Then a familiar voice sniped my ear, "What are you doing, cabron?" Alonzo asked from right behind me. "Leave this poor girl alone."

"I was just about to," I said while looking at the clerk. "What is your name?" I asked.

"It's Natalie," she responded. The cash was still on the counter, as there was a good chance she would refuse it.

"I'm Major, and this little beaner is named Alonzo," I said.

"Hello," was all he could get out as I grabbed him by the arm and tugged him towards the front door.

"You guys have a good evening," Natalie said with a smile as we turned to walk out. "For Americans, you aren't dat big of assholes."

"He is," Alonzo said as we reached the door.

Immediately through the door, we were met with brisk November air. I drew in a healthy lungful. It was medicating; it made my blood surge; it brought me new life. The moist smell of the evening air was strong. The salted air that drifts in from the nearby North Sea creates almost Holy Water for the lungs.

It brought that one-of-a-kind feeling, when the air is so foreign to you that the scent promotes a feeling of adventure. Alonzo followed suit as he drew in the medicine. He looked at me and with a smile said, "Let's go!"

We walked in the direction of Central Station. I had a good idea how to get to the party from there. "This is it; this is fucking it," I told Alonzo as we stopped in front of an Oriental massage parlor.

"You wanna go in there?" Alonzo asked, in a tone as if he knew that on the other side of the door stood a room full of radical Mormons with conversion in their hearts.

"Yeah, I wanna go in there. We have been bitching that we needed massages after our travels, and this is the first place we have come across since arriving."

"It's a fucking whorehouse," Alonzo said as he looked over the three-story, white-painted brick building.

"Bullshit, we haven't even come to the District yet."

"What the fuck are you talking about, *pendejo*? What's all that?" he continued as he pointed to the next-door building, which had several red-lit windows.

"So what, big deal, we're on the goddamn fringes of the District; that doesn't mean a thing about this establishment," I continued. "These Asian women know how to knock the shit out of you. Really bust up the knots, crack the back, punk the stress right out of you."

"Alright, but you're gonna get taken," Alonzo asserted. "Yeah?

Well, so are you because I'm not going in this place alone; they might slip me some pills, give me a hand job and then I wake up in a tub of ice minus a kidney."

"What if they do that shit to me?" Alonzo asked with concern. "Then they will be less apt to mess with me. The world's not going to miss a minority," I said as I pressed the doorbell that harshly buzzed as if I had annoyed it.

"You're an asshole," was all Alonzo could get out as the door opened, and a face spiced with the Orient appeared.

"You want massage?"

"Yes, ma'am, the best one in the house. My Middle Eastern friend here has a lot of money and is willing to pay." She tried to interrupt, but I needed her to understand the situation. "You see, ma'am, he is very stressed because he has no family or any friends who would miss him. I'm only here because he paid me to accompany him here, as he felt he couldn't completely trust the help of the establishment."

"Yes, you wan' massage?" she asked again, as if asking for the first time.

"Yes," I conceded.

"You're an asshole," Alonzo said as he stepped through the door.

We walked into the establishment and into a large living room where a few Asian pearls lounged. "Pick one," the madam of the house instructed.

"Pick one? What kind of massage house gives you a choice of masseuse?" I asked Alonzo.

"The kind that's a whorehouse; that's the kind," Alonzo replied, already predicting the mess.

"How much are the massages?" I asked.

"Sixty euro fowe half-owe'wa," which sounded like a reasonable price for the service, and there couldn't be any sex tied to such a modest fee. It wasn't only until a moment had passed that I realized the converted price put the service at close to $100 for thirty minutes. I looked to Alonzo who just looked at me with a Persian-street vendor's smile. He then pointed to a gal on the couch, who rose from the sofa with the grace of Dracula's bride.

"Fuck it, you only live once," he said, mostly to the air as he disappeared around the corner. I heard a door knock shut and wondered if I would ever see him again. Maybe I should have borrowed money from him.

"You pick!" I was ordered, though the voice now contained more pressure. A glance up, a wink from an exotic eye and I was being led to a room by a bronze jewel.

She opened a door that went into a tidy room with a freshly-sheeted single mattress sitting in the center of a wood polished floor. "You lie down," I was gently ordered as she handed me a towel and kept eye contact at a minimum. She then stepped out of the room, a move customary at massage parlors as you disrobe and give yourself a towel wrap. I knew this was going to be a legitimate massage. A hooker would have wanted to discuss business right there.

A minute later she returned and started the massage as I was lying prone on my stomach. I knew immediately I was fucked from the first rubdown contact. It was in her grip. A true masseuse works for her money. Sometimes small hands have to rub fat bodies or swollen muscles for hours on end. It's tough work; a true deep-tissue rub is a work of art. And maybe a good happy ending is a work of art for that matter, but the art of hand jobs is too pricey of an option for me tonight. Besides I could create my own art later… for free. A prostitute finds the work of sex easier than giving a good massage. It is easier work to screw a guy for twenty minutes than it is to rub him down for an hour. And the goddamn stress-relieving rubdown I was hoping for was not going to happen.

"You want have sex with me?" was then uttered only minutes into the weak massage. Not that her caressing hands didn't carry a pleasure of their own; it just wasn't what I was after, and I would end up admitting to Alonzo he was right… again. *FUCK! This costs sixty euro and as soon as I say "no" to the sex, the massage is only going to get worse and end within minutes*, I thought to myself.

"Yes! I would love to have sex!" I said, in a manner that showed I clearly didn't understand what was happening. I had such a sparkle in my eyes that she clearly would believe the schoolboy anxiety of innocent sex. In response, she looked at me with a slightly-panicked expression of confusion, just what I wanted to change the vibe of the room, to turn the tables. Now she would be uncomfortable explaining what she meant. I figured I may as well fuck with her to try to get some value for my money.

"Three hundred Euro," was all she replied. She continued to caress my body in ways that made the nerves chime, the true international language of love—or lust?

"Three hundred EURO! That's like forty-three dollars!" I again said with naivety, as she was actually requesting almost $500 for the act. "Three hundred Euro," was all she repeated as her hand brushed my scrotum, an unfair move on her part, but a great one nonetheless.

"Look, dear, where I come from, we deal in U.S. dollars; I don't understand this euro thing. What can you do for me for this?" I held out a twenty with three ones backing it with the movement one makes when he is offering something he thinks is of value.

"No. Only Euro," she said without ever changing her expression.

"So tell me, what does 300 euro get me?" I asked.

"Every t-ing," she told me as she continued to caress my flesh as my body screamed at me to pay the goddamn money.

"Everything, huh? Are there any midgets or gerbils on the premises?" I asked.

"You can lick me," was all she replied, an offer that obviously had enticed several other perverts who found themselves in this situation. And yes, without a doubt, if a girl of this beauty ever told me I could lick her, and it was after a beautiful day at the beach, or a dinner, a show or pricey drinks, it would be a done deal. No matter what it cost financially to get to that point, it would be worth it. But to receive a crappy massage and then get asked to pay cash up front for oral sex made me feel like a debased bastard, no better than a public restroom-dwelling politician.

"Now we're talking," I said, continuing the forum. "So let's say I lick you, how much do you take off the price for my part?" Just more banter on my part, I guess. I think I said it because the question sounded funny bouncing around in my pickled brain at the moment.

"You get da hell out of here!" I heard being barked loudly outside my door. My first thought was the madam of the house had gotten tired of my performance; she had been watching through some hidden camera in the room. But the expression on my girl as she looked to the door showed confusion as well.

Then a quick-passing knock on the door and I heard Alonzo's hurried voice that almost contained laughter say, "Good job, asshole, nice choice to get a massage," but the sentence seemed to fade as it was clear he wasn't waiting for me.

"That's my friend. He's ill; I need to find him," I said, rising to put on my clothes.

"One hundred fifty Euro," my girl desperately bartered, but it wasn't going to do her any good.

"Fifty Euro," I offered, assuming it would be a deal-breaker unless she was going to be willing to accept the low ball.

"No, one-fifty, no low-a." So I reached into my pocket and threw a ten-Euro note on the table and walked out hearing no vulgarities, threats or words of gratitude. I would have left only five euro had I change for the ten.

I walked out and through the living room, which had several more girls sitting around who were not there moments before; they all just stared at me as I passed. I doubt any of them would piss on me has I been on fire at that moment... unless I would have been willing to pay for it.

I opened the door with a short-lived relief as I stepped out into what seemed to be a semicircle of about a dozen people who also were not there when we entered. Alonzo was leaning against a wall smoking a cigarette. They all looked at me to see the freak who had just come out of the whorehouse door. I was momentarily frozen with guilt, or better yet embarrassment. So a nervous smile stretched my face as I stood, threw my elbows back and lightly twisted my trunk in a manner to show how coming from this place had cured my back ailments. After what seemed to be a lifetime of stares, in reality probably only a second or two, people continued on their way and so did we.

"How was that *massage?*" Alonzo asked smugly, appreciating the fact he knew it all.

"It was going awesome," I said. "She was really working some knots out until you ran by and panicked us."

"Bullshit," Alonzo said. "You should have had her work out that knot between your ears, *cabron.*" I didn't respond; I was clearly beaten. So we just began walking in what I thought would become familiar territory. Soon after though, I noticed we were in an unfamiliar area of The Red Light District. It was official; Alonzo and I were lost and making the High Times party to meet Thomas anytime soon seemed like an aborted afterthought. We knew the party was somewhere on the fringe of The Red Light District, but somehow we had gotten our directions mixed. Just then a strange voice broke our pause, "You guys need some help?" The croaked words came from a shadowy figure that approached us. Its oily hair partially covered the eyes and hung as tarred vines on the head. Its eyes were dark with withdrawal and shadows, and the sucked-in cheeks made the face look more like a skull. There was no longer any doubt; we were in the presence of a full-blown junkie. The junkie is a better-behaved creature than a zombie or any other member of the walking dead. However, if a junkie ever got the notion that a person's brain was made of dope, there would be no stopping them.

"Where you goin'?" it asked again. This poor pathetic street creature was addressing us in a voice that held both the need of pity and the angst of warning. I couldn't help wonder if we had come across the actual bloodline of Gollum, the mythical creature from *The Lord of the Rings* chronicles? He was a water person once, just as the Dutch are today.

Alonzo and I had still not responded to the creature, probably because of the pure spectacle of the thing. It continued to talk to us, its tone morphed right in front of us. It now spoke in this Tijuana street-hustler fashion. "You want sex, drugs, homosexual kicks, chicks with dicks?"

"Can you just point me in the direction of Central Station?" "I can do better than dat, my friend; I will lead you there myself." But before I could produce any protest to the offer, the creature had already started to slither forward while keeping eyes locked and throwing beckoning gestures.

"Fuck it, let's just follow him," Alonzo chimed in. So we did. As we walked, the Thing would take sidesteps so he could circle us, all the while talking to us—or at us—maybe sizing us up for the pack that awaited us around the next corner. The circling pattern would also serve well as a disorienting measure.

"You're American," our underworld guide said to us. He then broke out into a Britney Spears production, "Oh-I-did it again," he said as he bobbed in stride, looking like an off-off Broadway actor strutting to appear as a street gigolo.

"You guys have any spare coins?" the creature inevitably asked. I wasn't about to reach in my pocket for anything, nor expose anything I may have been carrying in my wallet.

"Nope," was all I said. At that he vanished, quickly just disappeared with the help of shadows and knowledge of every corner in his domain. Alonzo had stopped in his tracks and lit a cigarette, handed it to me and lit another for himself. He then just looked at me and shrugged at the past moment.

We walked to the end of the block, and it appeared as a welcome friend—Central Station—allowing me to regain my bearings and navigate us to the party spot. But first, I had to stop at a public urinal. They dot Amsterdam, usually concentrated more in areas that have heavy pub traffic. They are small, ornate metal structures that almost look like they are early phone booths. Inside is a simple, flush-less urinal. With what little light I had, I pulled the passes out to make ready for the show.

"I hope you brought your Cannabis Cup pass for the party," I said to Alonzo over the top wall of the urinal.

"Shhiiit!" he said. I left the fuckin' thing back at the room." "You goddamn stoner, you've ruined the night," I said. There was silence; he didn't even have anything to say.

"Here, dickhead, I brought it for you," I said, holding the pass over the top of the piss-partition.

"Gracias, amigo," he said as he snatched the pass from my hand. "I may have got some pee on it just now," I told him.

"Pinche Cochino," he said, though I know he was relieved that he had it in his hand.

The event took place in a local bar/nightclub that was almost visible from where we stood, just around a corner and a half-block down. "See— it all worked out," Alonzo said after exhaling from another drag, the last the cigarette could offer. He then dropped the butt and smothered it with his foot as we walked towards the party. There was a small staircase that led into the venue, with a line thirty-people deep behind it. "That looks like a healthy wait," Alonzo said, surveying it.

"Stand back and let me do the work here," I said as I took my final drag, but left the cigarette butt hanging out of the corner of my mouth, giving myself the look of James Dean's confidence. I then pulled out my *Playboy* media pass and let it hang from my neck by the Cannabis Cup lanyard.

"Hello," I said as I addressed the two bouncers at the door: one white, one black and both sizable brutes.

"Hello," responded the black one with the tone he was waiting for the next line of bullshit the American was about to give. Alonzo had walked up behind me. I addressed both bouncers as I spoke.

"Guys, I'm here covering the event for *Playboy*," I said. Their eyes both fixed on the pass I was now holding forward for them. "I am already behind on the event and would really appreciate you letting us in so I don't miss the beginning of the show," which was to be a fashion show.

"Who is dis?" asked the white bouncer as he kept his hands in his pockets and nodded towards Alonzo.

"He's no one; I mean, he's my gardener; I mean, my guest." "Dick," I heard Alonzo say under his breath.

"Do you two have Cannabis Cup passes?" the bouncer asked. "I DO!" Alonzo said with excitement as he held his out, smiling while looking at me instead of the bouncers.

"Yes, and here is mine," I flipped over the *Playboy* media and had tucked the copied pass behind it. Alonzo's smile melted into a flat look of confusion.

"Welcome," one of the bouncers said, and we were walking up the steps into the party.

Inside it appeared as most east-coast bars and clubs set up in a narrow building built well over a century ago before the public at large began the modern-day love affair of nightlife. The place was shoulder to shoulder, with the exception of a short, elevated fashion-show runway running along one side of the bar with a row of six seats behind and at the same level as the fifteen-foot catwalk. Four of the seats were taken; in one sat a white man with dreadlocks, the quintessential person for the venue. I've always sadly carried an uneasiness—maybe bigotry of sorts—for white guys with dreadlocks. I can't fully explain myself here, maybe because bigotry doesn't make sense at its core as a productive practice. Some get uneasy around clowns; midgets give some the willies; neither of those bothers me a bit. But a white guy with dreads, it's like something is lurking right under that peace and love persona, the fact I can't put my finger on it is enough for me to keep my distance from one.

Next to the transcultural, dread-headed man sat a well-put- together blonde. She had French riding leather boots with leggings and was cloaked three layers deep in fashion. A navy blue printed Hermes draped her neck, not for warmth, but for a subtle announcement of her presence. She leaned slightly to her left, just close enough to hear the words coming from a fashionably-dressed and neatly-groomed twink of a man. The fourth character was the most interesting and possibly the most dangerous: onyxed-hair and garnet-lipped, she sat with a red satin dress with a black webbed drape that wrapped her shoulders. Her bare arms were sleeved in colored tattoos and spilled out of her cape as they held a sleeping three-year-old, tow-headed boy. And as bad as that sounds, something just seemed to be okay with it—but just like my bigotry of white men in dreadlocks, I can't explain why. Maybe by the fact she was in a seat of honor meant she was a person able to make her own rules while exposing her son to a lifestyle that with any luck, he will want nothing to do with as he grows into a well-rounded human... or another blond-headed Rastafarian.

Truth be told, I could not care less who any of them were, nor would I put another thought into them. I motioned my head towards the back of the venue; Alonzo, who had been surveying the scene on his own, nodded in agreement. It wasn't so loud you couldn't speak to communicate; it would just need to be done with volume and effort. Alonzo and I slowly worked our way to an end of the bar and posted up. Drink service in Europe can be a tricky thing. Many places seem to pride themselves on slow service, whether they know it or not. At a venue like this, I could easily see a bartender not paying any attention to us for a very long time.

Alonzo worked his way to the front of the bar. I stood a few feet back, securing us a corner spot, a good perch to survey from, while keeping our backs to the wall. When in Amsterdam, you don't have to worry about violent crime, as in the town proper, it is virtually nonexistent. There are drunks about, but none looking for a fight or any kind of trouble. But such a safe area makes for rampant petty crime, performed by pussy criminals who will pick your pocket quickly and promptly apologize if you catch them in the act.

Alonzo caught me by surprise, drinks in hand. "Thanks for the help, dick," he said.

"I didn't realize you had gotten such quick service," I said loudly, leaning in towards him.

"Shit, at these prices they should be following us around and wiping our asses."

"Why, what was it?"

"WHAT?"

"What did they charge you?"

"Here, I'll tell you after you do these," he said as he pushed one hand towards me. In it he held three drinks. Because many parts of Europe have not caught up with the concept of large beers, he was able to hold a glass of beer which looked about nine ounces, along with two shot glasses of something dark. "It's Jack," he yelled at me. "A little taste of home," he said. "Salud, amigo," and he had shot the first one and was grabbing his second before I even finished my first.

As I finished my second, I was using my old college trick I learned from a Danish drunk. Take a couple of deep breaths, inundating the blood and mind with oxygen—greatest trick to stave off the gag reflex.

"You pussy," Alonzo said to me, probably judging from my face. "Here," he said, pushing his beer up for a cheer and a chase of the whiskey. We clanked glasses, and I gave him a wink to let him know I was back in the game.

We didn't slam our beers, just took about a third. "Now that we have covered that business, what do you think they charged for that?" Alonzo asked. Not that he is ever one to complain about buying a round, it just appeared the charge was just another spectacle of the scene.

"Thirty Euros," I said.

"Shit—I wish," he responded. "Almost fifty," he said, shaking his head. He then took another drink of beer and just looked around, already forgetting about what he had just said. Some house music came on, and now it was pretty impossible to speak to each other, though I motioned to the caught eye of the bartender for a repeat round—why not? We were here for what we were here for and had found good bar service in Europe, something worth the moment in cash.

The music, though unfamiliar to me in song, was much like most house music, tantric in nature, repetitive by design, with electric pulses that somehow penetrated the flesh. Just then a looming figure stepped in front of us. It took me a moment to realize that it was, in fact, Thomas.

He was in rare form. Or maybe not so rare form—just in a form. He had his large black hoodie pulled over his head and was wearing mirrored aviator glasses. His face carried no expression, but his head was lightly bobbing to the music. He almost looked like a modern version of a Grim Reaper—a more hip version maybe. Glasses indoors at night can seem a faux pas, and just about anyone I see doing it looks like a douche. But not Thomas; he somehow pulls it off. Maybe because he does it as an action of functionality, not trying to look cool. Glasses to hide the eyes, be they constricted pupil, dilated or simply bloodshot red. And a hoodie pulled up to comfort the mind, giving it some sort of protection from the episodes of paranoia it has to deal with. No, Thomas wasn't the douche who pulls his hood up and wears shades indoors. He's the guy the others are trying to emulate when they try to pull the look off. Alonzo and I just watched him; no one was talking. Thomas was facing us, which put his back to a majority of the crowd. He was looking down in concentration at something he was fidgeting with; his head continued slightly nodding to the music. Then it happened, just like Tinker Bell's pixie dust; a small white burst of powder fell across the stomach of his sweatshirt—it was a cocaine bundle he was working on. He stood motionless for a few seconds, and then his shoulders dropped in defeat when his mind caught up to him about what he had just done. Thomas gave his sweatshirt a single hand brushing, leaving some remnants still there and then simply turned around and walked away into the crowd. Though no words were spoken during the entire episode, it was good to see him. He appeared and then disappeared in a matter of a couple of minutes, letting us know he was alive and on an autopilot of sorts, which had always served him well.

"Should we follow him?" Alonzo yelled with a brotherly concern.

"YES," I replied, "but it's not as important as waiting for this next round. He won't go far—or he won't get far—and if he does, we know all the places to track him."

Alonzo nodded in agreement, already back to scanning the crowd. There is a familiar feeling abroad in large cities, when in a crowded pub or nightclub. You could be in any given pub or club in the rest of the world, and it would feel exactly the same—the hum of indistinguishable human banter and the smell of spilled beer. The dialect from the tongue is different, but the expressions on the faces spell out emotions the same way, regardless of clan.

A bartender stood at the edge of the bar hawking me, to let me know the drinks were there and ready to be purchased. I worked my way around the small layer of people between us and the bar and slapped down eighty Euro. "Keep it," I yelled, leaving him a reward for the prompt service. He curtly nodded his head and disappeared quickly to his front lines. The concept of tipping had been catching on in Europe. Though the practice is still rare, it is blooming. Though a ten-percent tip there is viewed like a twenty- percent tip in America, a five-percent tip can make a server's day in Europe still. The beauty of the European practice is, if you receive poor service—unlike in America where we demonstrate dissatisfaction in service by leaving ten percent—you can stiff an asshole European server and it's okay because that's what they expect and deserve in many ways. But when you come across good service when traveling, don't be an asshole American. There are plenty of assholes in Europe already; don't be part of the problem.

I turned to hand Alonzo his drinks. I handed him his two shots of Jack and turned back to the bar to grab his beer. When I turned to hand it to him, he had a smile and was handing me two empty shot glasses. "Jesus," was all I could get out as I made the trade with him.

I did one of my shots at the bar; the third shot of the evening always goes down much smoother than the two before, a typical side effect of the stuff. I grabbed the second shot glass and beer and turned to step back to Alonzo.

"CHEERS," he said, holding out his beer glass he hadn't taken a drink from yet. We clanked glasses and took a couple of heavy swallows. I surfaced for air and chased the ale with whiskey. I could still feel a slight wince of whiskey squint, which is probably a healthy thing. It's poison, after all; the body should never be okay with it, even if we trick the mind into liking it.

I chased the shot with more beer. "Let's walk," I said as I motioned my head in a cross-club direction, figuring we could finish our beers while we casually walked the club looking for Thomas. Alonzo followed. It was shoulder to shoulder again. As I walked, I remembered I'd put my wallet in my rear pocket out of habit, so I grabbed it and transferred it to my front pocket. European pickpockets run as thick as rats in New York at crowded tourist venues. The front pant pocket is about as secure as you could hope for without strapping things to your body.

As we drifted farther away from the bar and more into the heart of the club, the music clearly was in control. Though no official boundaries were set for a dance area, all area floor space was used by bodies absorbing the beat. As we slowly cut through the bouncing throng, you could feel the bass vibrations in the entranced bodies we passed. It was a bit tantric, almost surreal, like walking through a human aquarium.

We stepped away from the group as we neared the other side of the club. We were on the same side as the entrance, but now in the opposite corner. There wasn't a lot of action here, as all the drinks were served from across the room. But it gave us an advantageous view of the venue. The same people were seated in front of the only clear space at the club, the catwalk, though now each person was engaged in conversation with several more who had filed in behind and beside them. The sleeping child, still melted in his mother's arms, slept as if he were in the safest place in the world—and maybe he was.

"There he is," Alonzo said as he hit my shoulder with the back of his hand. Sure enough, he was walking towards the door, while being followed by what looked like security or event organizers.

"Let's go," I said. I had no idea of the pending outcome at the end of Thomas' walk, but I figured we had better be there to deal with it. On the fringe, there weren't many bodies to contend with and we were at the exit door just steps behind Thomas, though we had lost sight of him through the closing door. Once outside, Thomas was standing alone, lighting a cigarette. "What happened?" I asked.

"Oh—hey," he responded in a tone laced with gladness in our presence. I noticed the people who had escorted him out were now standing at the entrance, talking with the other bouncers and motioning over to where we were standing. "Well, I had to take a piss, and I was going to break out another bundle of coke while in the restroom," Thomas said. He then took a drag and offered an open cigarette box for Alonzo and me to grab one. He lit both for us, put the lighter away and continued, "So I'm at the urinal finished with that business; then I got the bundle open. Just about then, a guy steps next to me to pee, and though I know he's watching me and something's telling me not to, I continue to tap the contents out onto the side of my knuckle. All the while it's just running through my head, *Don't do it-don't do it*. So what do I do? I bring my knuckle to my nostril while I'm looking right at the guy next to me and I snort; and he just started shaking his head—and I knew it—he put his dick away and put his hand on my arm. I then noticed the word "Security" on his shirt, and he told me to exit the building."

"Well, at least you got your bump out of it," Alonzo acknowledged, finding a silver lining to the situation.

"Yeah, but I got us thrown out," Thomas said while looking at us.

"You got you thrown out," I said. "That place was lame anyhow," I said. "Just a High Times gathering with nothing to offer us." At that we started to walk. In doing so, we passed the security detail, but they weren't paying attention to us and we didn't really give a fuck anyhow. Amsterdam, as with many European socialistic societies, is tolerant of many things; however, hard drugs aren't something that make that list. Thomas knew this, and he tested it and proved what he had already known not to do in that restroom. But hell, we didn't take this trip to behave by anyone else's norms but our own; it was our investment of time—and we were leaning towards a good one.

"Major!" I heard my name called, which triggered an immediate confusion. The question was answered when I saw Natalie, the desk girl from the hostel in line for the party. She was standing with another girlfriend. They both had lanyards around their necks. "Look familiar?" she said to me as she held hers out for me to inspect, prideful in her wit to make a couple of extra counterfeit copies when given the chance.

"Very official," I told her with a wink. "Taking moves from an American asshole, I see," I said. Which made her laugh. The sound was music to my ears, for reasons I can't quite explain, other than it was beautiful to hear a noise so genuine. "We need to keep moving here," I said. "One in our party just got kicked out of that place, and I don't want the security to link our group with yours," I explained.

"Trouble?" she asked, regarding why we were kicked out.

"No—American stupidity," I told her.

"Ah, the best kind," she said with a smile.

"Maybe we will see you later?" I asked.

"Perhaps," she responded. "You never know," she said with a parting smile.

I met up with our group, and we started our walk again. "Who was that?" Alonzo asked as we walked.

"She's the girl from the desk at the hostel, wasn't she?" Thomas asked.

"The brunette works at the hostel?" Alonzo continued his investigation.

"No, the blonde does," I said. "She's the one who made me a photocopy of your High Times pass."

"Thaaat's how you did it—nice move, *cabron*," Alonzo said with a smile, almost proud of my move. "Anyhow, sounds like she owes me a favor for getting her and her friend in; she can repay me by introducing me to her friend," he said.

"Okay, I'll mention it to her; she said they may be back at the hostel bar later," which again made Alonzo smile. Though I honestly didn't know if or when we'd see them again.

"What now?" Thomas said with a fresh tone of enthusiasm. The one healthy bump he got in himself before being tossed from the event, the dust that can take you to death, had brought him back to life, which aside from all the negatives of cocaine, was one of the powerful positives the drug offered. We are all taught that only time can sober a person. That's because it would be irresponsible to include cocaine as the exception.

"Let's head towards the hostel pub, but cut through The Red Light District on our way," I suggested. "We can check out the circus along the way."

"Let's go," Thomas said, as he turned and had already taken a step in the right direction. Alonzo didn't respond, as he was looking back at the brunette in the venue line, who was just about to show her pass to the bouncer.

"You wanna go back?" I asked him. "I got to watch Thomas, but you can go try to hook up with her if you want."

"Fuck you! I'm goin' with you," Alonzo said as he gave a big smile. "I'll find her back at the hostel later." Alonzo was now being jolted alive by the only other drug so effective to awaken you... love. Or possibly lust—or both? I don't know, but he was sure enough he would see her again. And I was glad he had fought off the effects of the drug to see we needed to stick together tonight.

"I need to get some cash," Thomas said. "That last bindle took all I had," he said, speaking of his last coke purchase.

"I remember two machines back closer to Central Station," Alonzo reported.

"We'll follow you, man," Thomas said and we were off, walking the now more-familiar path we had covered earlier. We were on the fringe of the Red Light District, where there are more retail shops and tourist junk than sex and drugs, though their presence is made.

"Hold up a sec," I said, stopping and stepping quickly into a tourist junk store. "You have any disposable cameras?" I asked the olive-skinned clerk, who with unchanging eyes simply pointed to a back wall of the store. So I walked past the breast-shaped coffee mugs, the magnets shaped like windmills and the penis-shaped salt and pepper shakers to a shelf with a stack of boxed disposable cameras. I placed the camera on the counter; the clerk, who at this point could have been an automatous entity, rang up the purchase.

"Ten Euro," he croaked. I handed him my credit card. His eyes went from the card to mine. "You have cash?" he asked me.

"Yes," I said and just stared back at him, playing his own game. After about five seconds of this, he took the card from my hand, swiped it and placed it back down on the counter instead of handing it back to me. He then placed the receipt and pen in front of me. I signed my copy as his hand immediately came out, making sure he didn't lose another pen.

"What'd you get?" Thomas asked as he looked at my hand. "This," I said, showing him the camera.

"You needed a disposable camera?" he asked.

"I left my cell phone in the room, and we'll never know when we will need photos for evidence," I said. "C'mon," I said and we turned and continued our walk.

"Shiiit, look at that ATM machine line," Alonzo said. And he was right. There were two machines, but one must have been shut down, because all eight in line stood single file behind one machine. "Look at that *pinche* line at the ATM."

"We can keep walking and find another one," I said.

"Naw," Thomas said. "These are few and far between here; let's just wait."

"You could go to one of these tourist shops and use their cashback service," I told Thomas.

"Hell no," Thomas said. "And let one of those places get a hold of my credit card number? No thanks," he said, which gave me pause about my last purchase and behavior. At that, the two of them headed to the ATM. I noticed the reason the line was so long was in fact because one of the two machines appeared to be down.

"I got it," I said. "Wait here, I'm gonna cut the line in half," I said as I walked to the out-of-order machine. I stood in front of the ATM and pulled my wallet out of my hand in the traditional cash- machine fashion. With my back to everyone, I pulled out a few 100-Euro notes, paused a second longer and turned to face the line, stuffing the money into my wallet as I walked away. And just like I predicted, the second half of the ATM line broke off and approached the machine. I just smiled at Thomas, and he smiled back with a look of amazed bewilderment and appreciation. He and Alonzo then took their place three people back in the instantly-shortened line. "I'll meet you around the corner," I said as I walked off, not wanting to be around when the rubes returned from the discovery of what had just happened.

Alonzo and Thomas soon rounded the corner, carrying big smiles and laughing.

"That was fucking brilliant," Thomas said.

"Stick around, got plenty more for you," I said, with an arrogance of a showman.

"People were motherfucking you when they figured out what had happened," Alonzo said and then started laughing again. "Some guy tried to get back in line in front of us."

"You let him in?" I asked.

"Nope," Thomas said, "I just told him, 'bullllshhiit, get to the back of the line.'" Alonzo started laughing again.

"Nobody knew we were together?" I asked.

"Not a clue," Thomas said.

"Awesome," I said, and we started to walk again.

We were now crossing Damrak Street, and the iconic coffee shop, The Grasshopper, was lit up with emerald-colored lights. It's one of the most beautiful buildings in the area though it does have competition. But at night when it is lit up, it shimmers in the reflection of the sea marina that sits in front of it, looking like it's part of Oz's Emerald City. "Let's go roll one in The Grasshopper," I suggested. Both just shrugged and shook their heads in confirmation.

The building is split into two levels. The top plays more of a house music and has some techno lighting; below is more of a pub feel. We descended to this part of the building. Thomas immediately stopped at the weed-purchasing counter and pushed a button that illuminated the choices of smoke. One of the odd rules in Amsterdam is that the weed choices can't be in a place readily visible to the public. However, if you walk up to the counter and push the little red button, the screen becomes transparent through a heavily-tinted glass. There were about eight choices. I heard Thomas mumble terms like "White Widow" and "Northern Lights." Alonzo stood quietly and studied the selections next to him.

"I'm gonna go order us some tea," I said and walked up to the bar. "Three hot teas," I asked from the kid working behind the bar. He was a tow-headed boy in his early twenties; he didn't say a word, just turned and fetched the order. A short moment later, he returned with the first two cups of hot water, the teabags on the saucer, then turned and brought back the third.

"Nine euro," he said with the same dull and uninspired tone as the Persian clerk earlier. They just don't give a shit about customer service in most places in the world outside of the U.S. The Grasshopper and many other area retailers are predominately supported by tourists. Area employees tend to treat them as if they are more of a nuisance than a necessity. There was a tip jar by the register. But it doesn't fill because there is an asshole working behind the register too.

"I'm going to set these on a table and come back for the third," I said. The counter help just looked at me, almost as if I were insulting him explaining the obvious—fuck, politeness can be too much work. Maybe it's better when service is shitty; it can save you lots of tip money in the long run.

I sat down and had started to steep my tea when Alonzo slipped in next to me in the booth. Thomas tossed the baggie purchase in front of me. "Northern Lights," he said with a sideways grin.

"Nice," I said. He snatched the baggie back and went to work on it, like a spider spinning its prey.

"Thanks, *cabron*," Alonzo said to me as he placed his teabag into his cup. I grabbed Thomas' bag and dropped it into its bath, his eyes never coming off the fat joint he was wrapping into a tightly-enveloped cocoon. Thomas then ran it through his lips to seal it, turned his head slightly and lit the thing, stoked it with a couple of sucking draws, and handed it to Alonzo. Then he dragged his cup and saucer to him, exhaled and took a sip. Alonzo passed the joint to me, and for the next several seconds that was the routine: puff, pass, exhale, sip.

"Good shit," Thomas said in between inhaling and sipping. Alonzo, holding in his drag, looked at Thomas and shook his head affirmatively, almost looking like he was communicating while holding his breath underwater.

"Keep holding your breath; it makes your face look as swollen as it did on the plane," I said, which caused both Alonzo and Thomas to start laughing, a plume of smoke coming out of both of their mouths.

"No shit," Alonzo said. Thomas had blown his cheeks out, imitating a swollen face, and we all started laughing again.

"He... he's... he's allergic to the pot!" he forced out, making us all laugh again. It was funny stuff, not as funny as it probably really was. But drug and drunk funny, this created a hearty and welcome laughter, the kind of laughter that is as appreciated as a friend at your door.

I shifted in my seat and felt the small disposable camera pressed into my leg from my front pants pocket. I had forgotten that I bought the thing. I pulled it out and opened the foil package it came in with my teeth. I spit out the corner of the packaging onto the table. Both guys had their eyes fixed on it, not knowing what I was doing; they looked like curious dogs. I began to spin the film-advance disk with my thumb; it produced a winding noise and a click. I pressed the flash button and saw a little light turn orange—then green—and I put the eye sight up to my face and clicked on the two. The flash momentarily froze them, and then they looked at each other and then back to me.

"What's up with that?" Thomas asked.

"Memories, bro," I replied.

There were several people buzzing around the narrow streets of The Red Light District, which were largely closed to traffic in most of the area, reminding me of the streets within the French Quarter of New Orleans. There were gawkers of all kinds and makes, bouncing from one side of the street to the other. Some were perverts, no doubt, but most were just the curious from around the world, tourists looking at the local trends of sex toys in various shop windows. They were passing by the human meat, which seductively hung in the red glaring windows and passing by the sex-show theatres. Sometimes you would hear the giggle of college girls who walked in tight-knit groups of four, laughing at the "i-vibrator," a toy you could power off your cell phone. At times you would see elderly couples on double dates—probably Irish tourists— walking through the District, not so much for the sex industry novelty of the neighborhood, but to visit one of the many upstanding and respectable restaurants and pubs that dot the area. And there were also the rest of the seedy characters that always came with the territory. Here is where you will find the junkies, the pickpockets and the drug dealers that sold cocaine, ecstasy or whatever else they can convince you they can get, though chances are what you are going to get was a baggie of baking soda or a couple of colored sugar pills placed in your hand—if you're lucky. If you're unlucky, who knows what they might be trying to pass off? Trace elements of coke, cut with meth and fingernail varnish. You're getting all the damage to your heart and mind without any of the upside of the drug: the purchased euphoria, the powdered happiness.

"Let's duck into this place and have a quick beer," Thomas said. We followed and soon after, we had three pints in front of us at some dark, unassuming Euro pub. The place was beyond unassuming, reminding me of a cheap hotel lobby. There was nothing on the walls to give the place charm or personality. A one-and-done place where they stick tourists with overpriced crappy beer, not caring if they ever come back, knowing they won't anyway.

Alonzo pulled out his pack of cigarettes, tapped them to attention and offered one to each of us. Thomas took one; I passed. "The place is kinda dead," he said. Only a single bartender loitered behind the bar watching a soccer game on a TV that seemed as old as Amsterdam itself. Thomas took a look around the place, which motivated him to finish the second half of his beer in one move. "Let's get the fuck outta here," he said. "It reminds me of a failing bowling-alley lounge," which somehow summed the dive up perfectly. Alonzo and I downed our drinks, stood and buttoned up our coats. We stepped outside and each looked in different directions as to what we planned on doing next.

"Let's just keep walking in the direction of the hostel," I suggested. There was plenty of Red Light District to take in as we walked. Alonzo and Thomas fell in behind me as we started to walk. Alonzo stopped after a couple of steps to reach in his pocket and fetch another cigarette. Without speaking, he flipped the top of the paper carton open; before taking one for himself, he thrust the package towards Thomas, who took one. He motioned the pack towards me, and this time I took one for companionship along the walk. He thumbed a lighter to life and passed it to the tip of each cigarette. Then we turned and started walking again, the three of us billowing smoke as we walked like dragons on the prowl of shores unknown.

We passed a sex shop that had samples of its bounty in the windows like a pervert's Christmas-shopping dream. Next door was another coffee shop, and beyond that we passed another pub. This one appeared to be a sharp-looking place, a cross between an Irish pub and a Victorian parlor. It was alive with activity, along with a couple TVs showing soccer games with unknown—or I should say, unfamiliar to us—soccer clubs playing.

We crossed over a small lane and found ourselves on a corner with another grouping of red-lit windows. "Hold up, I need to tie my shoe," Thomas said. Just then, there was a commotion from the direction we had just traveled.

"Feuck you, you cunts, you feucking Dutch pussies." A man appeared to be speaking directly to the pub we had passed, his accent that of a drunk Englishman. It appeared he had been asked to leave or forced to leave; and the door closed securely behind him, leaving his verbal tirade witnessed by anyone *but* the people inside the establishment. "Feuck the lot of ya," he said, mostly to himself in a defeated tone.

"Okay, got it; let's go," Thomas said, as he rose from his squatted position.

"Hold on a sec," I said, keeping my eye on the drunk who was walking towards us in a manner that took effort to keep him from swerving along the sidewalk, which he wasn't completely capable of pulling off. He hadn't yet reached the lane to cross. "Just stand closer to the windows," I instructed.

"What the fuck are you up to?" Alonzo asked.

"Just fucking do it quick," I said with a plan unfolding in my head. I couldn't see the girls in the windows from my angle, but I could see the drapes were open. Alonzo and Thomas moved over to the edge of the first window; two more windows were beyond the one where they stood.

"Let's see what whores we have hanging in the windows tonight," I heard the drunk say as he walked and almost fell when he stepped into the street he was now crossing, "Whores!" he yelled. I couldn't tell if he had something against them or just liked to yell the word. I reached into my coat pocket and pulled out the disposable camera. My thumb found the film-advance dial, and it went to work advancing the film. I pushed the flash button and as he approached, the camera's green light came on, signifying the thing was ready to be fired.

"Excuse me, sir," I said. He stopped; his expression was that of someone trying to focus, as if until that moment, he hadn't noticed me standing clearly in his path. "I was hoping you could take a picture of me and my friends here." He surveyed us and then glanced at my camera I had extended.

"Are you guys yanks?" he asked, as if things were to be determined based on my answer.

"We are—though we are actually Californian," I said, hoping that would help in any way. It didn't.

"What the feuck is the difference?" he responded.

"About 3000 miles," I responded, trying to throw him into giving up the conversation and taking the camera from me. "Are you English?" I asked.

He glared at me and then looked at the guys. "Tell you what, mate —" he tried to sound official through his slurs "—if there weren't three of ya, I'd feuck you up for that accusation."

"Bite your tongue, Major; he's Scottish!" Thomas blurted out.

"Tha's right, mate," he said, as if his faith had been restored.

"I'm sorry," I said. "I'm a dumb American." Hoping the self-deprecation would be enough to gain his cooperation.

"Yeah, you got that right," he said. "I'll do it for a cigarette," he said, bartering the situation.

"Okay," I said and looked to Alonzo for a cigarette.

"Don't you have your own, you cheap fucker?" Alonzo said. "Just give me one," I said, giving him a stern look, hoping he'd go along and not mess up my plan.

"Pinche güero," he said as he tossed me the pack. I extended the cigarettes to the wicked Scot. He helped himself to two. Normally I would have said something smart to a guy who welched on a deal. But this guy was my prey, so I let him run with the hook set in his mouth.

"Perfect, now just snap a picture of us standing together," I said as he finally took the camera from my hand. I turned and walked towards the guys. Out of the small corner of my mouth, as gently as I could, I said, "Stand natural, no poses." Once I was shoulder to shoulder with them, I casually turned around. I didn't exactly point myself at him, but more cocked another direction, as if I were just a tourist looking around. Then FLASH! A second of silence, then the aggressive sound of door locks snapping.

What I knew, what no one else directly involved in what just happened didn't know, is the cardinal rule of The Red Light District— NO PHOTOS! I had read about it when doing research on the area before our trip. I had noticed small unassuming signs in random areas of the District; however, it just seems to be a known decree as you never see flashes ignite in the area. Until now.

"Mu'der fucker!" one prostitute yelled. "Give us the camera, ashhole!" another demanded in broken English, both of different accents. I figured if English were the international language of business, the ladies knew it was their best bet of communicating with the person of the photo infraction.

"Just walk off. C'mon," I said quickly to the two as we continued to walk to the hostel.

"FEUCK YOU, WHORES!" we could hear our Scottish friend yelling. We stopped when we were far enough removed from the incident to not be part of it. He had two scantily-clad prostitutes trying to gain control of his arm in which his hand held the disposable camera. His twisting movements caused his arms to flail with the fury and purpose of Medusa's cranial serpents as he turned and spun.

"GIVE IT, ASHHOLE!" I heard a prostitute yell. The other threw a knee into his thigh as she tried to pry the camera from his hand.

"Get the feuck off me!" he yelled. And through all this, he never looked for us. It was his own battle. He was fighting not for the camera of a stranger, but for the fact he was not going to lose to those he despised. He needed to despise them; they were below him, at least in his mind, a mind pickled by Scotch and whatever demons he kept company with.

"Fuck you, ashhole!" I heard the blonde prostitute say again, after they finally pried the camera from his hand. She slammed the camera on the ground and delivered the death blow with a stomp of the thick heel of her black boot.

"Up yer erse wi' it," was all he said. The girls being victorious in their quest, and more than likely not their first one, walked back to their windows and were ready for business as if it had never happened.

"Feuck," he said again as he rubbed his outer thigh, where the prostitute had landed her knee. Then he just started walking off in the same direction he was headed when we met. We were across the street now, but he never seemed to look for us. It was as if he had never even come across us. Will he wake in the morning and have no idea where the large bruise on his leg came from? Is that routine for him? As routine as picking up a drink soon after rising, to cope with the fact he has yet another bruise and sore fingers that he can't explain.

"Well, that was certainly interesting," Thomas said, just as we all continued our walk back to the hostel. It was true; it wasn't necessarily humorous. Or we weren't laughing at what we just saw; maybe because we don't know what we just saw.

"I mean that was kinda funny to witness," Alonzo said.

"You see that knee she landed? That guy wasn't giving up," Thomas said. "He wasn't going to lose to 'feucking whores,'" which did bring a group laugh, as his accent was spot on. "I'm hungry; let's grab something."

"Finally, a fucking plan that makes sense," Alonzo rightfully said, and we continued our walk towards our room. It was late, sometime around midnight, but we knew of one place we could eat. It was a small hot-food item vending shop. Different individual food items, under small heat lamps, were available for a euro or two. More obvious choices were small slider-style hamburgers. They were labeled with terms that were foreign and unidentifiable with pictures that gave an estimated idea of what they were. "Kass souffles" looked like hush puppies with cheese in them. There were "frickendels," which looked like a minced meat hotdog. And "krockets," that appeared almost like French-fried toast sticks. I took my chance with these and deposited two euro coins.

"Wha'd ya get?" Alonzo asked as he took a bite of his souffle, the hot cheese stringing out from his mouth to the deep-fried ball of batter. I had just taken a bite and as I chewed, I stared at the item, now dissected and showing its innards.

"I'm not sure," I replied as soon as I swallowed. "It… it tastes sort of like compressed turkey stuffing," I said. I took another bite and continued to evaluate. "It's like eating a fried gravy stick," I assessed as I stuck it out towards Alonzo's mouth. He took a bite and held the same expression I had moments earlier as he chewed.

"You're right—it's a gravy stick," he confirmed. "A mystery gravy stick," he followed up with.

"Yeah, you're right," I said. "Let's just hope that's cheese you are chewing on," I said just as Alonzo took another bite, causing him to subsequently chew and reexamine his food. Just then Thomas appeared with a large bottle in a bag of what turned out to be beer.

"Need something to wash that shit down?" he said as I took the bottle and a swig. As I passed the bottle to Alonzo, Thomas had dug some change out of his pocket and was feeding it into a machine. He drew a slider from the hotbox. "Good shit, eh?" he said as he took a bite and chewed while talking.

"Good shit when drunk late at night," I told him.

"Yeah, kinda like late-night runs to White Castle for steamed sliders."

"Exactly," I said as I took another bite of my gravy stick.

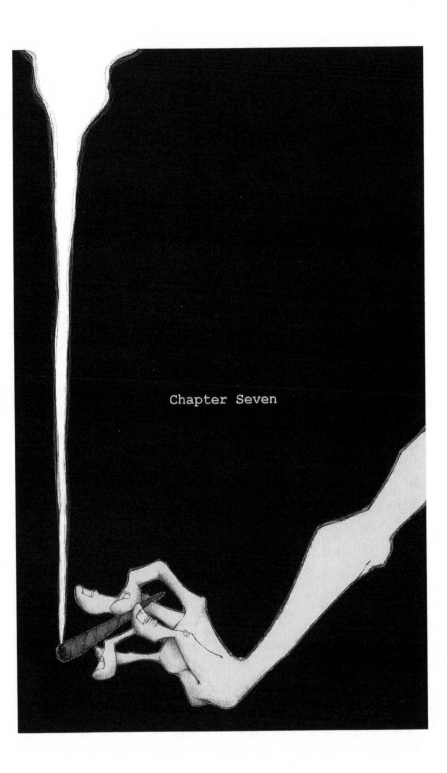

Chapter Seven

I woke the next morning at 8 a.m. which, though early, was the first time I had slept soundly through the night since we had arrived days earlier. We had gone to bed sometime around 2 a.m., I think; but I felt good, aside from my cotton mouth signaling my well-deserved dehydration from the night's drinking. I lay in my bunk for a few minutes just staring at the ceiling, with no particular thought filling my mind. That's the benefit of European travel. After a few days, the mind realizes it is so far removed from any problems back home that it doesn't even waste its energy thinking of them. So morning wakes are usually pleasant and drawn in with the hopes of a child.

Thomas lay in his bunk with one leg hanging off and his mouth partially open with a light snore escaping it. Alonzo was completely covered, a sub-waking move to block out any light that came through the flimsy blinds. I didn't have a clear view out of them, but from the framed edge of the curtains, I could see it was a typical gray morning. I wanted to open the shade and look at the large maple tree and chapel side. But it would be an asshole thing to do, and I was too sober to be mean. So I got dressed as quietly as possible and left the room. Downstairs, the breakfast spread was out. I grabbed a hardboiled egg and began peeling it as I walked out the hostel front door with no immediate plan other than getting a cup of coffee and a morning joint. At the end of the block, I stopped at a street-side vendor and bought a large bottle of water, opened it and drank about a quarter of it before capping it and continuing my walkabout.

I followed a canal, which in Amsterdam are as common as roads, beautiful waterways lined with charming houseboats and handsome stone arched bridges passing over them. The waterways passed along the canal houses of the area, enchanting structures tightly and highly built, most over three stories. Many inhabited by residents; others converted into offices or museums. Much of Holland was spared the bombings of World War II, leaving so much of the rich architecture unscathed and, for the most part, as original as it was 300 years ago. The area is the new definition of a ghost town, because those are the only souls around who have built any of these dwellings so long ago. The scene carried the look and feel of a living fairy tale.

After about fifteen minutes of walking, I came to an area where I found myself standing on the corner of Prinsengracht and Harlemmerdijk Streets in the Jordann District. I had heard of this area; it's a trendy spot in Amsterdam with lots of residents, cafes and small retail shops. What intrigued me at the moment was the bike traffic that was rushing through the area.

Amsterdam is a bike culture, the world's biking capital. In Amsterdam bikes not only have the right-of-way with cars but with pedestrians alike. A bike bell carries the weight of the law, and all who travel lanes and sidewalks are acutely aware of this fact. The bike lanes during morning and afternoon rush run as thick as blood through veins throughout the city. Where I stood, hundreds passed me, all in tune with each other, creating their own wind path as they rushed by me just feet away. I stood on the corner for close to a half-hour, never once witnessing anything even resembling or coming close to an accident. This was impressive and a good thing, since bike helmets aren't a typical option with Dutch riders. I even witnessed more than one rider pedaling along hands-free while texting on a phone. It was fascinating the way bike traffic flowed with intricacy and harmony at the same time. I'm sure adding a tourist or two to the traffic could be a game-changer; I'll have to suggest the idea to the boys.

It was about 10 a.m. and I had yet to get my coffee, so I walked toward The Red Light District to stop in at the Grasshopper. I figured it was getting to be too late in the morning not to be stoned. I only had to walk a few minutes to get to my destination. The harbor marina water in front of the Grasshopper was still; its dingy sea-green color reflected the backdrop of the Grasshopper. The scene was disturbed by a small pack of water fowl that landed and glided in the waters, rippling the scene, like when the mind loses focus of a dream right before it wakes.

I took a seat at the Grasshopper. I had purchased my Americano and a small baggie of White Widow. I took a couple of sips to pique my mind and then began rolling a joint, every few seconds looking out the window at the late morning. It was gray outside, but still beautiful. A gray day in Amsterdam has a way of making you feel warm and safe. With the right weed high, you can take yourself far away while continuing to live in the moment. Just as I started to drift to that place, someone sat down in the chair next to me.

"Can I sit here?" said an Americanized Asian kid who was already sitting.

"Sure," I said as I genuinely stuck out my hand to offer the already-taken seat.

"Do you smoke hash?" he asked. "Yeah," I responded.

"Okay, I'll roll a good one," he told me as his eyes were already focused on breaking up his hash cube into small bits to be rolled into a joint mix. He wore ironed khaki pants and a brilliant-blue North Face ski jacket, which had a shiny silver lining that looked like nickel-plated aluminum foil without the wrinkles. His jacket was unzipped and underneath he wore a merlot-colored sweater with a crisp white collar framing his neck.

"You like tobacco in your smoke?" he asked. I just shook my head *no* as I intently looked down at his fingers that methodically worked our drug fix. This focus on my part made him stop his joint production to look up at me to get his answer.

"No, I don't," I said, clarifying my position.

"Me neither; I can't stand to mix tobacco in." He then glanced back down and continued his task as focused as a hawk and as determined as an ant that carries his catch to the ant hill.

"Why do they do it then?" I asked moments after the last words were spoken by him, my eyes still locked on his manicured fingers as they twisted the ends of the joint; his nails shined and were clipped and well-rounded.

"Why do they do what?" he asked as he handed the joint to me to start; I waved it back. He slanted his head slightly and brought the lighter to the end of the rolled smoke and drew some puffs. Then he handed it to me like he was still waiting for his answer.

"Why do the Europeans mix tobacco with their pot?"

"Oh," he said with the relief of finally understanding the question. "Some say it smokes better so they don't have to keep lighting it," he explained as I drew in some smoke, exhaled and handed the joint back. The hash-filled joint had a healthy tail of white smoke that followed like an airplane skywriter until it crashed into his hand. "But I think they mix it because it is the opposite of what the Americans do."

This made sense, as Americans are viewed as a culture of wasteful excess, which was actually true; but to say so stateside would get you thrown out of the Eagles Lodge or fucked-up in an Iowa bar. But that doesn't make the fact totally false, and many of us don't realize it. The party must continue; vote out anyone who doesn't keep the giant, happy machine alive in America, no matter what the cost. On the East and West coasts, status is in style. On the East Coast, a fur coat that could be easily replaced with a replica shows how much a man has to waste. On the West Coast it seems everyone has a house, a rental house and a vacation house. They travel between homes in the family BMW or Hummer that was purchased with chrome options to never be driven off the road. But the truth also contains what much of the world may miss, that the people in Iowa have the humbleness and heart of the Bible's spirit. And you would deserve to get fucked-up in an Iowan bar for talking shit about your own country.

"Some just probably like the taste of the mixture," my smoking friend said as he leaned towards me to hand me the joint he held between his thumb and forefinger. I came back into current thought as I took the joint for my final drag. "My name is James; I am studying over here for a quarter."

"What school?" I let out as I exhaled.

"Miami," he said. "I'm getting this out of my system 'cause when I get back, I will be graduating and starting law school. I will need my head together for that."

"Hi, James; I'm Major," I said.

"Major?" he responded with the familiar expression when a person wanted to make sure they caught my unusual name correctly.

"You ever mailed this stuff back to friends?" I asked with healthy interest.

"Yeah, a few times," he said as he licked his finger and pushed a smoldering ember of hash back into the security of the joint. I was waiting for him to continue his story, because that is what we are conditioned to do in the practice of conversation. But when you have two hash smokers, you need to continually keep your train of thought going or you will answer using short sentences. James was now looking at his finger which had a small tar stain that looked like a little black mole.

"You better get that mole checked out, dude," I said, pointing to his finger.

"What are you talking about?"

"That mole on your finger, the one you are looking at," I continued, James looked back down at his finger and rubbed it with his thumb.

"No—no, that's a mark from the hash. A hash burn," he said as he rubbed it with his thumb and stuck his finger out for inspection. "See."

"Yeah, I know it's from the hash," I said.

"Then why did you tell me to get that mole checked out?" "What are you talking about?" I continued. "I told you that there was hash on your finger." He just looked down at his finger with a lost expression. It was me fucking with him though. It was kind of a mean thing, but that's what a guy gets when he sits next to a stranger and smokes hash. Take your chances; take your chances. Besides, it was harmless fun. It's not like I wanted to drag him out of there and force him into the sex-slave trade. I just wanted to warp him a little. It would be good for him as his mind was about to head into schooling for a profession where a warped mind can land you your client's settlement.

When you do hash, you need to either find a way to keep your mind active in order to get some sort of action from the drug or you can allow it to lull you into a fog, which isn't always a bad option. To build a fire on a fog-filled day and to dot a room with a few candles is a good hash-high day (just make sure the candles are well-managed). A doctor can prescribe something that will minimize stress, if only for a while. Hash can do the same thing, and the way I see it, any removal of stress from the body is healthy.

"James," I said as he suddenly broke from his trance and looked up at me with focus.

"What?" he asked.

"Have you ever mailed this shit home?" I asked again.

"Oh. Oh, yeah, that," he sputtered like an engine waiting to catch. "Yeah, I've sent it back several times." His words were now flowing and clear.

"Have you ever carried it back?" "On a plane?"

"Yeah, on a plane," I said.

"I did it once; it's not worth it though," he said. "I just took about a quarter-ounce with a small brick of hash."

"Did you get caught?" I asked.

"Obviously not; I'm headed to law school," James said in more of a conversational tone than condescending. "It's not worth it because you will be scared the whole flight home, and it's uncomfortable enough flying without that fear."

"I see."

"Yeah. I'm sure you can get weed in California, and I can get it easily in Miami. So it's just not worth taking any home." James was still for a second. It appeared he was back into his hash-haze as he stared slightly down distantly. "But," he said as if he just were zapped back into life, "mailing it is the way to go," he said as he scratched his head.

"That's a federal offense. That isn't scary too?" I asked.

"Here is what you do," James started as if he were conducting a business plan. "You send it to an address where several guys are living: a dorm, frat house, apartment or rental house. You flatten it as much as possible and use a bogus return address. You follow?" I just nodded my head yes and continued to listen to him methodically tell me how to mail pot home. "Then you don't spell the recipient's name right. Or use initials, but maybe not even the correct initials of who you are sending it to."

"And it works?"

"Not all the time," he said. "I have done it about ten times, gotten through eight."

"And what happened?" I prodded. "Do you have the lighter?" he asked. "Huh?"

"The lighter, the lighter," James said as he was patting his pockets looking for his lighter, which was on the table right in front of him. "Do you…" he started again, but then saw it in front of him. He grabbed it as if he hadn't just gone through what he went through and relit the half-smoked joint, then handed it to me.

"Tell me what happened to the pot you mailed that didn't get through," I said before I took my drag, so we wouldn't forget what we were talking about.

"The envelope came with DEA tape sealing where they opened it and took the weed out, with a note letting the recipient know the address had been "cataloged."

"That never worried you?"

"Naawww," he said; then he took another drag, exhaled and said, "They're not going to come investigate an address on a campus or college town because of $100 worth of weed."

"You're the lawyer, dude."

"That's right. I am," he said. "I advise you to hit this," James said with such a serious and professional tone that it was funny as well as impressive. I knew he would pass the bar and go on to law fortune. You could hear it in his voice. With confidence comes victory. James had that confidence. But now he was back to staring at the lighter that he was clicking on and off as he stared at the action. The future of America's law was sitting next to me high on hash flicking a lighter on and off. It made me feel warm and secure. "Well, that's that," he said as he again came to life. He was standing up and zipping up. "Gotta run, gotta study," he said, sticking out his hand for a farewell shake. "You can study like this?"

"Yeah, sometimes," he said with a bright and coherent smile; then off he went. The room seemed a little colder now, as if James were a small lantern that brought a warm amber glow to the room and now had been extinguished. Oh well, sometimes a drab room can be warm, and this place began to give its somber warmth out again. Outside was gray, naked and still. There were a few droplets of water on the window pane, though I didn't think it was rain as much as I thought it was sea spray from the harbor waters just outside the coffeehouse. In the near distance

I could see a flock of pigeons take flight; they appeared as black pepper, strewn across a gray silk sheet.

I wasn't sure how long I had been at the coffee shop. I sat and tried to estimate the amount of time I spent there. I figured it was in the ballpark of thirty minutes when I looked on my cell and noticed it had been upwards of an hour. The afternoon had started to melt onto the dawn as it neared 11 a.m. I was sure the boys were close to getting up but figured they would shoot me a text when they were. Regardless, I was going to start making my way back towards the hostel. I drained the last of what was left in my coffee cup, stood, placed the small baggie of smoke in my pocket and headed for the door.

There was a sweet pungent smell to the area, a sogginess born out of the fresh-water canal water that mixes with the sea-harbor water, which permeates the ancient wooden architecture. The wet fall leaves that gather in the gutters and upswept doorways of town buildings emit an original musk that when all is mixed together creates the perfume of autumn.

I started my walk just as the tram rounded the corner and came to a stop feet from me. Passengers disembarked and I stepped on. The doors closed behind me, and the tram lurched forward. By paying the fare, you get a small, printed receipt ticket. This ticket would need to be produced if ever requested by tram security. But if you're only going a few blocks, you can usually get on and get off before anyone approaches you for proof of ridership.

The sun broke through a split in the clouds. I looked out the tram window from where I stood. As the train gently rocked with forward progress, the outside scene was brought to life with the instant spotlight of the sun. We were approaching Dam Square where the old Dutch Royal Palace now stood. I pressed the "halt" button and hopped off at the next stop. No sooner had my feet hit the ground than the sunshine recoiled, disappearing almost instantly like a sea anemone in the presence of a sea slug. But it doesn't matter because Amsterdam remains fairytale-like in the bright shades of gray too.

It was now late morning or early afternoon, based on your productivity level or wake time. The large, brick-paved square in front of the palace could host much of a football field and was heavily scattered with foot commuters. Within the area, I was surprised to see four or five street performers. It only took a second to recognize they had stolen their "art" from the front of Hollywood's Chinese Theatre. Each performer was dressed in a costume, recognizable by various Western entertainment genres. I decided to grab a double espresso and a seat on a nearby public bench to observe the behaviors.

More times than not, back in the States, I'm inclined to give spare change to a panhandler. I understand the reasons we're told not to: "It can be enabling; it only exacerbates their addiction," so on and so on. But they are also a person who is on the street or in a situation where they have to beg for money. Sometimes I don't blame them if they use my money to buy a beer; their life must suck. However, in much of Europe, there are endless and effective social programs available to citizens, so panhandling isn't really necessary. Yet some still do. Who knows these guys' stories? Just college-age kids trying to make an easy euro? Junkies who haven't found a program that supplies their fix? I don't know, but it didn't take long to see they already have added the European twist to American street art. One was standing in a Batman suit, probably a sound investment to obtain as it was a nice detailed replica of the costume. This thought was furthered by his European tell; he had spent so much money on the suit that he wanted to protect it. So, in the misty rainfall that had started, the kind that evaporates almost as soon as it touches the forehead, Batman stood holding an umbrella. He stood looking rather silly—a superhero afraid of the rain. The Dark Knight held a large umbrella, shielding his plastic, Lycra and rubber suit from the elements, just as his practical mind has told him to do his entire life. But taking a picture with an umbrella'd superhero just kinda robs the photo's moment of worth.

Behind and to the right of Batman was another familiar character; it was someone dressed as horror star Freddie Krueger. The performer was dressed very similar to the monster, complete with the mask of the twisted and burned face, but in place of the movie nightmare's bladed glove hand, he carried what surely was a plastic butcher knife. The only problem here was the artist was being a little too convincing. As people would pass and glance at him, he would thrust out his arm and point at a passerby, then point quickly and purposely down at the tip bucket; this was then followed by a rapid downward stabbing motion with the prop knife. It was his clever way of being spooky by letting the person know, *YOU! Give me a tip, or I WILL GET YOU!*

It was as if this Euro performer was forgetting he's dealing with Europeans who are, in most cases, timid or keep-to-themselves type souls who don't want to be a part of anything outside their norm. Tipping a street performer is oftentimes out of their realm; approaching a person who is making menacing and violent movements at them generally inspires the pedestrian to look away and pick up the pace to gain separation. I then made the most fun discovery looking at another pair of street impersonators. The one in front was cloaked in black cloth and was wearing the contorted ghost mask from the movie *Scream*. He would beckon pedestrians as well, but in a calmer, slower, ghostly manner, which was softly encouraging people to approach and take pictures and drop coins. His problem was the neighboring performer who was set up about ten feet behind him.

Behind the ghost was an unrecognizable figure dressed like a banshee in white, wearing a robe of flowing and tattered materials. He was a hooded character, hidden with a black, impervious mesh veil. This guy moved a little quicker, with sideways sways, like a mental patient in the refuse of a hospital corner—or a curious chimpanzee. Whenever someone would start to approach Scream, the Banshee would shake a loud tambourine-style instrument at the potential patronage. More than once, people would look up at his distraction and then approach him over Scream as he disrupted their initial plans and gained their attention. Over the next few minutes, it happened again. What looked to be a pair of twenty-something-year-old female Japanese tourists with big, tight toothy grins walked leaning shoulder to shoulder towards Scream; just then the Banshee rang his chimes as loudly as possible. The girls giggled and walked past Scream onto the Banshee's turf. Scream turned around and watched it happen. He made a hand motion to his competitor about the move and then went back to his perch.

The hostel was not far from the square, so I decided to head back to see if the boys were up. I tossed my espresso cup in a trash can and walked across the square towards home. I was approaching Scream with my hand in my pocket, making it appear I was digging for change. As soon as he saw that move, he started with his gentle beckoning moves towards me. When I was fewer than five paces from him, the chimes rang out and the Banshee waved his arms. I turned and looked in his direction as if it startled me and turned and walked towards him with my coins in my hand. I dropped my coins, and it was enough to break him. Scream came towards us, shouting muffled words through his mask and pushed the Banshee. The Banshee responded with a standard Euro kick that didn't land, but just looked good—or maybe good isn't the right descriptor for a Euro kick. It looked a little silly and effeminate, but was enough that Scream stopped advancing and just threw his hands up. The Banshee returned the move in almost an identical fashion, and they both went back to their spots to continue their day. I wish the boys could have been there to see it. It was worth the two euro I dropped.

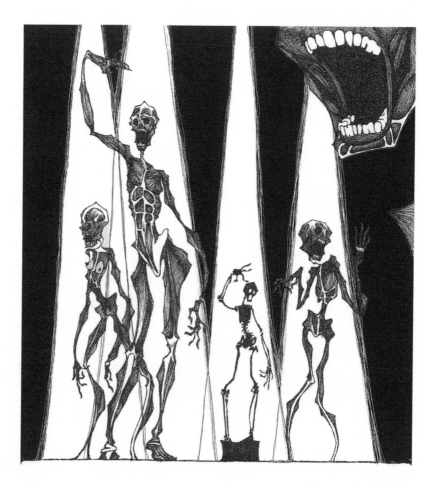

Chapter Eight

I got back to the room; a light steam seeped from an almost- closed bathroom door. Alonzo was on his bunk, bent over tying his shoe, hair wet from his waking shower. "S'up, *cabron?*" he said with his signature smile.

"You guys apparently—at noon, nonetheless," I said.

"Hey, man—what is it, 3 a.m.-4 a.m. back at home?" he said. "Dude, that excuse wore off a couple of days ago with the jetlag," I said.

"I know," he said as he reached to tie his other shoe.

"What's up?" Thomas said, appearing from the bathroom, wrapped in a towel and cleaning his ear with a cotton swab.

"Hey," I said. "I just came back from walking around town a little bit. Didn't want to wake you guys up," deciding not to tell them about what I did at the Square. I just didn't think it would sound as funny retold.

"Cool. I'm starving," Thomas said. "You guys?"

"I could eat something," Alonzo nodded in affirmation while looking at me, waiting for my response. I pulled a joint off the windowsill, lit it, inhaled, held and blew. "I've got the munchies," I said.

"Right?" Thomas said nodding.

"Right on," Alonzo said. And though everything we said was amusing to say, it wasn't particularly funny. But we all laughed. Probably because of a combination of stuff accumulated in our blood, as well as being mixed up in our sleeping cycles.

We spent the next several hours like the other days: walking around, eating street food, drinking espressos in between coffee shops. In the late afternoon Thomas found us a Thai restaurant he had passed before and was curious about on Zeedijk Street; it turned out to be a good call. After we finished the meal, we went into a pub and had a round of beers.

"I saw they are displaying 'The Bodies' exhibit in town. You guys familiar with that?" I asked.

"Isn't that the display that uses human corpses or something?" Thomas asked.

"Yeah, something like that," I said.

"You've got to be kidding me," Alonzo followed with. "Get the fuck outta here."

"I don't know a lot about it," I said, "but it looks interesting."

"Yeah, we should check it out," Thomas said, in a fashion of agreeing it might be fun, as opposed to really confirming that was the plan. We finished what we had in our pints and stepped back out onto the town.

"Let's step into that mart there so I can grab some cigarettes," Alonzo said. Thomas and I both stood outside and waited. It was late afternoon, and the winter sun had already settled deep enough to turn the area purple-gray. There were lots of people walking around and riding bikes. The Dutch dress nicely in proper yet comfortable clothing. The women who would coast by on bikes in their leggings, leather boots, woolen coats and flowing scarves carried with them a unique Euro beauty. In America lots of effort goes into the face. Here the entire package is wrapped, and the face is only dusted with paint.

"Jesus, what took you so long, you grocery shopping?" I said when Alonzo surfaced.

"Nope, I just wasted forty euros," he said. "On what?" I asked.

"A good time, that's what," he said, as he pulled a bottle of beer from a paper bag.

"Wow, you gonna drink that whole thing by yourself?" I asked. "No, we are all going to drink it—actually, we each have to chug our portion."

"Sweet," Thomas chimed in, always willing to do his part. Alonzo popped the cap off with the use of his lighter butt and handed the bottle to Thomas, who started to drink, then pulled it away and coughed. "Fuck, that's horrible," he said.

"Drink up; you already put your lips on it," Alonzo said and Thomas abided. He finished his few ounces and handed the bottle to Alonzo. His face was a little contorted with squinted eyes. This surprised me because Thomas was a seasoned drinker. Without saying anything, Alonzo handed the bottle to me. I sniffed at the bottle. "It's not wine, *pinche güero*; drink up," Alonzo ordered. So I took my drink. I was able to get my third of the bottle down with some effort; Thomas' reaction had prepared me for what I was about to drink. And it was awful-tasting, like tar and gasoline mixed. I finished and handed the bottle to Alonzo as I looked away trying to focus the mind on something other than my gag reflex. Alonzo drank his,, and though he could not remain expressionless, he handled it the best of the three. "You know what that was?" he asked.

"Napalm?" I said.

"That shit was 120-proof beer. The highest in the world, brewed right here in Holland."

"No shit?" Thomas asked, his interest piqued by the prospect. He reached out and took the bottle from Alonzo and started reading it. "I'll be damned, says so right there, 60-percent," Thomas said, looking at the label like a doctor studies a chart.

"What was it you bought that you wasted money on?" I asked. "That shit right there. I spent thirty-five euros on that bottle," he said.

"Are you shitting me?" I asked.

"I believe it," Thomas said. "That high-level specialty stuff isn't mass-produced usually."

"I also bought this," Alonzo showed us an ugly, neon-green Velcro wallet.

"Did you lose your wallet?" Thomas asked.

"Or are you going to an 80s ugly wallet party?" I said, which sounded funnier to think rather than to say, but too late for that. Thomas and Alonzo chuckled still, which was proof what we had just chugged was doing its magic already.

"Yesterday when I was in the Red-Light, I squatted down to tie my shoe," Alonzo explained. "Within seconds I had two gypsies on me, acting concerned; but I knew they thought I was drunk and were going to take my wallet," he continued as Thomas and I stayed silent to hear the full story. "So I stood up real quickly and startled the shit out of them."

"Did they get your wallet?" Thomas asked. "Nope, but they are gonna get this one," he said. "I don't get it—am I that fucked up?" I asked. "I don't get it either," Thomas said.

"C'mon, when the time's right, you'll get it," Alonzo said. And we continued our walk. "I'm feelin' pretty buzzed," Alonzo said.

"Me too," Thomas said.

"Should we slow down and go in and roll one?" I asked. "Slowing down is the last thing we need to do right now," Thomas said, as he dug around in his pocket. He pulled out a little bundle, and I knew immediately what he had.

"That's what I'm talking about," Alonzo said with a wide grin. "This will help us put it in another gear," Thomas said as he split the bundle open. "Here, give me your knuckle," he said to Alonzo. The request left me momentarily confused, but Alonzo immediately produced his curled index finger to Thomas, who tapped out an aspirin-sized bump on the side of his finger. Alonzo took it straight to his nose and gave it a chase snort to take it all in.

"You?" Thomas asked, motioning to the baggie.

"Why not?" I said, sticking my knuckle out as Alonzo did. "He put a little more on my knuckle than Alonzo's." "You're a bigger guy."

Alonzo just looked at me and shrugged. Thomas followed suit. We each did one more bump and moved on.

You could feel the drug come on quickly. That's the benefit of the narcotic, a quick fix. Downside, the high doesn't stick around long. The more you do, the more chance you're taking with the drug. It's a dangerous dragon to chase. We did bumps, not lines. It's the responsible way to do it. Enough to wake you, even sober you, but not enough to give you the grandiose thoughts that those seek in fat lines of the stuff. If the world of coke-snorters could resign to the notion of coke bumps, not lines, we could cut out a lot of the problems the drug presents. At least that's what rare users like me tell ourselves to feel better about what we are doing.

"Alright, let's head to the Red Light District," Alonzo said, with the rare leadership side of him clearly showing. We fist-bumped each other and were on our way.

"How're you feeling?" Thomas asked Alonzo.

"Fucking good—you?"

"Yeah, this stuff is better than what we typically get stuck with when buying off the street here," Thomas said. "It's still heavily cut, but it works."

"How're you feeling, Maj?" Alonzo asked me.

"I'm good… awake," I said.

"That's what this shit is good for," Thomas said. We carried on with small talk as we walked; and, before we knew it, we were back at the old church in the heart of things.

"Okay, so here is the plan," Alonzo said in a manner that drew us in. "I'm going to put that cheap wallet in my back pocket and walk ahead of you guys like I don't know you. When the street narrows,

I'm going to walk with a slight sway. I will then squat down, like I'm catching my breath or trying to balance. When the pickpockets come, you two walk behind them; and I'll jump up, and we'll scare the shit out of them." Thomas and I both sat still for a second. There was a slight shock to Alonzo's plan. Not that it didn't sound amusing to attempt, but just that he had become so assertive in coming up with a pointless, semi-dangerous, exciting plan.

"What do you want us to do to them when we catch them?" Thomas said, as if he felt he needed to be vigilant about anything Alonzo planned, for Alonzo's sake.

"Nothin', man, nothin'," he said. "This isn't worth getting a blade pulled or anything. Let's just make them jump. Gypsies aren't used to getting the other end of the stick; that's all we are giving them. It's going to be fucking funny." I looked at Thomas, and he looked back at me. "Plus, I left a little note inside the wallet." Alonzo opened up the wallet and where the bills would typically go, he had left the receipt of the beer and wallet with the words "FUCK YOU" scratched into it.

"Nice touch, hope they can read," I said.

"Alright, let's do it," Alonzo said and started to walk ahead of us.

"Wait-wait," Thomas said. Alonzo returned to the group. Thomas pulled out his baggie and untwisted the cellophane. "Good idea," Alonzo said. This time Thomas dumped the powder on his own knuckle, and held it under Alonzo's nose. He did the same for me and himself.

"Okay, let's go," he said as he twisted the substance up again and returned it to his pocket. And we were on the move again. A strange but intriguing feeling came over me. It was tough to explain but felt powerful. We were a stalking pack. Most humans don't have what we had to offer. We were our own gang. Our own pack. Loyal alpha males who do what they want. What we were on was a mission. An objective. The fact that the objective was pointless gave even that much more royalty to our presence.

Behind the church, the road goes narrow into walking-only paths. We turned down Annedwar Street and stopped. Alonzo had stopped and put his real wallet in his front pocket; he left enough of the neon wallet hanging out of his back pocket to attract the pickpockets like the wormed hook to a fish.

He started walking again; we kept a couple of tourist buffers in front of us, making it appear he was on his own. The stretch of street was a little shorter than a block. We weaved through a crowd that wasn't shoulder to shoulder, but the next closest person was always within an arm's length away. By now there had been a few who had moved between us and Alonzo. He wasn't dangerously far from us but had separated himself by twenty feet. Halfway down the street, Alonzo slowed his pace and just looked at the ground as he walked. The flow of tourists now went against us as we made our way to him. He was squatting down by the time we got close to him. He had found a small area where a few bikes were lined up by a pub. And just like that, two people were walking close to him. A gypsy couple, the woman approached him and put her hand on his shoulder and leaned over to talk with him; her partner, a small younger man looking in his early twenties moved behind him.

"Look at that shit," I told Thomas. "There he goes, his hand is moving to the wallet," I said. Alonzo had a quarter of the wallet hanging out, well-placed to attract the slime that would drool for the easy mark.

"Should we go over?" Thomas asked with a little angst. "Look, look," I said and pointed. The way Alonzo was crouched made the thin fabric wallet hard to pull out. The woman continued to talk to Alonzo with her hand on his shoulder; he stayed crouched in position, as if he were teetering on passing out drunk. Thomas and I walked over to join in. "You okay?" I asked Al.

"NEVER BETTER!" he said as he quickly rose to his feet with a big smile. The gypsy woman fell away in confused surprise— something tough to do by the street-smart breed. Her accomplice provided the show though. He had been pulling so aggressively at the thin wallet that when Alonzo stood up, the thing came free and sent the pickpocket flying backwards into a line of four bikes that were lined up side by side. His eyes were stretched wider than they knew they could. The neon wallet was clearly clawed into his hand, and he tried to stand and retreat at the same time, looking like a crab making a rapid escape. But he had a puddle of bikes spread under him, and the panic in his movements made it all seem like a Charlie Chaplin skit on meth. The woman had vanished, and two men appeared quickly over the top of the pickpocket. I figured they were just helping the guy; but as quickly as they appeared, they vanished in two different directions, and the wallet was gone. The two shadows were part of his crew. The wallet was left to the fate of a wounded fish in a school of piranha. The thief was able to get his footing, made a quick turn and vanished too. They were all ghosts of the underworld, and we treated them like hunting trophies. We were left there standing, looking at each other; we were then suddenly, and simultaneously, washed over in laughter at what just happened.

"Dude, you couldn't have played that any better," Thomas said of the gag.

"No shit," Alonzo said. "They thought I was drunk and were on me quick," he said. We just started laughing again. It felt good; the laughter was the drug of the moment, and we were high on it.

"That was awesome," Thomas said. "I didn't think it would be that funny, but the way you sprang up and he fell back was classic," he said as he fist-bumped Alonzo again.

"Yeah, I feel like I've served some pointless karma to these fuckers," Alonzo said.

"Probably the first of its kind, dude," I told Al.

"Let's go get some 'shrooms," Thomas said out of nowhere. "Let's fucking do it," Alonzo said, and just like that we were off again.

We headed into a Smart Shop, a place known to carry mind- opening items, in search of some magic mushrooms. Not your normal mushrooms, but the strongest they could give us, no more of this fucking around. It was time to trip, and what better place on Earth than right here, as long as it was a good trip, God-willing. Maybe Amsterdam wasn't the place for this ride. But they provided the ticket, and we stepped right into it with free will.

"Take *dees* den," said the Dutch hippie chick behind the counter when we described where we wanted to go. "What are these?" Thomas asked as he held and eyed the mushrooms like a child ogling a shiny Christmas ornament.

"T'ese are Ha-waian, t'e highest of dem all," she said. "Psilocybe cyanescens—strong as acid," she followed with, letting us know clearly what we were getting into. I purchased the mushrooms with my credit card, as we were low on cash. Doing so meant I was tempting the lords of Credit Theft Karma, but what choice did we have?

Outside we each took our portions of the Amsterdam Acid. The taste was like flavored chicken-shit and aspirin, but you couldn't just swallow. You needed to grind, pound and drive those spores out. Get 'em all, see the colors, taste the sounds.

"Let's go see some bodies," Thomas said. And at that we were headed to the Beurs van Berlage exhibit hall, a large, red brick cathedral-sized building on the fringe of the Red Light District's glow. The building housed "The Bodies" exhibit. This was a controversial exhibit to the fullest, displaying the outright beauty and the grotesqueness of the human body, all the while capitalizing on the dead. Organs, skin, muscles and teeth, all exposed and plasticized. Actual human beings posed and dissected in morbid poses. It was the underlying logic behind beauty only being skin- deep in physical form right in front of our eyes.

I tried to read the numbers that showed the entry fee for the museum, but they seemed to swim slowly around on the page, appearing as Alphabets cereal and milk. Alonzo, recognizing my frustrations, pushed me aside and paid my fare. The mushrooms had me; and Alonzo saw that, so in the interest of time, he slapped the money down, and we entered the traveling tomb.

The realness of the situation hit immediately as we came across the first glass case, which contained an entire human skin. It was laid out as if it were a deflated love doll. The flesh was lightly posed with legs crossed covering genitals and an arm draped over the face, as those who nap during the day do to block the sunlight.

There was no talk within the group, aside from the hush of Alonzo's "fffffuuuuuck," which seemed to echo quietly long after he uttered it... or did it? We turned the corner to see more of the display as it opened into a larger area. At that point we drifted apart, not intentionally but more methodically, as the 'shrooms put us in our own worlds.

The corpses were dissected in every possible way. Entire human bodies were stripped of flesh, exposing muscle, veins and tendons. Some corpses were posed frozen in various physical activities such as a tennis serve in full-bloom; another looked as a quarterback may look as he surveyed the field before him, ready to pass. The problem was, the damn things were watching me. I could see their eyes follow me through the exhibit; I could see their fingers wiggle in their uneasiness of the situation.

I walked over to Alonzo and asked, "Hey, are the eyes of these things hooked up to watch us?" Alonzo just looked at me and responded with a loud "Shhhhhhhhhhh!" not because I was loud— I was too mortified to be loud—but because the other forty people at the exhibit all turned to see who the gesture was aimed at. That did it; now I had strangers and corpses looking at me. I didn't know what else to say. With some sort of low-level thinking, I replied to those close by, "Sorry a-boot the noise. I am from Canada and my Iranian friend here feels I am being loud, which I am not; I just hate Americans." The last part seemed to be the magic words for forgiveness.

I wasn't sure if Alonzo thought I was being too loud because of our heightened senses, or if my voice were truly loud and, because of our senses being dulled, I just couldn't hear myself. More than likely, he did it because he knew I wouldn't react well to the stares of both the living and the dead. But in any case, I needed to get away from him, if for no other reason than that he looked more Persian now than ever and through my bigotry I no longer trusted him.

Probably the most disturbing display (outside of the fetus and baby exhibit) was the man who was sawed in half and propped up in a position that appeared as if he were high-fiving himself while exposing every gut in his body. That's when I got *the sweats*—a cold sweat, cold to the skin that wasn't hot enough to perspire in the first place. It was the body trying to repel whatever the fuck it had been forced to eat.

I felt weak, strange, filled with hamsters and sparks. And then the man who was sawed in half began waving at me, both raised hands waving at me as if we were old friends. Or perhaps it was his way of tormenting me with the fact that sooner rather than later, I would be joining the lifestyle of the corps. I would become just another skull in the endless piles of some catacomb or graveyard.

Sweat, more goddamn sweat, and then a sigh to my left from a corpse positioned as Auguste Rodin's *The Thinker*. A giggle from another corpse and then another from places unknown. I wanted out; I needed air to calm the skin. But where, how do I exit? Plans as this become much more complicated when hallucinating. And then the smell of smoke. More than likely the drift of a cigarette from an open door. But you can't tell the mind this in these situations. *What the fuck, what if this place caught fire? My mind started to pulsate; every one of these goddamn corpses would point me in the wrong direction. Some sort of sick and hilarious practical joke the dead like to play.* I tried to slow down by reminding myself that I was on drugs, but that doesn't work any more than telling the schizophrenic the voices were not there. The mind goes on vacation and plays with the body for fun. "Time to go time to go time to go," I softly repeated in a manner that seemed to soothe my mind. Thomas was exiting another part of the exhibit, a portion of the show that was hidden behind a black curtain. He looked pale and almost carried an expression as if the Pope himself learned there were no God. "Uh, there's babies and shit in there," he flatly told me; and that was it, I wasn't about to look at a fetus in a jar exhibit. "Yeah," he kept talking as I walked, hoping to find a way out of this hell. "They had a jarred fetus from practically day one all the way up to an infant," Thomas continued.

"Don't say shit like that to me right now, man," I said, more pleading than asking. I then heard several corpses giggle, almost as if I had my own laugh tracks. Perhaps if I had come sober, my mind could appreciate the science of the exhibit, but it was too much right then. Maybe eating those mushrooms before looking at this wasn't the best idea, but it seemed like the reasonable thing to do at the time.

Finally a door out, at least out into the lobby which held a souvenir shop where Alonzo paced with a cigarette and a look of confusion. "Let's bolt," he said; we followed without a word.

"How'd ya like that ride?" Thomas said moments later, the first to break the silence—the first to emerge from the fog.

"Worth every fuck'n penny," Alonzo answered.

However, I didn't feel so fulfilled by the journey. I somehow felt as if those corpses had gotten the best of me.

"Sons of bitches," I said in the direction of the display, with the same passion a man uses whenever he gets his ass whipped.

"Who?" Alonzo replied, looking as if he thought there were someone in particular that I cursed.

"Never mind," I said. "I'll deal with those fuckers some other time."

We now headed towards the hum of the Red Light District. Not because it was necessarily a good idea to walk around in that part of town in the state we were in, but because the shelter of our room was on the other side of the District.

As my mind swam in the colors of neon and moon glow, we headed to our hostel seeking some unwritten safety of the place. Maybe I just wanted to get behind a door that locked, just in case one of those prankster corpses tried to follow us. We wandered some side streets in the District. These were not wide avenues but more like alleyways. The brick-lined streets were very level at times and in other areas the bricks had settled into the sand underneath them, creating potholes of sorts. Sometimes the level street would meld into a sinkhole, trying to trip an American.

You had better pay attention where you walk in a socialist country. In America you can choose to walk out of a bar drunk; and though you have an entire street to choose from, you can pick the one spot to cross that has you stepping into an open manhole and then sue with impunity. But here the judge will simply tell you, "Watch where you are going next time." But at least he will say it with a smile.

We hung out in the safety of the room until the trickle of drug-induced paranoia wore off. Wore off enough to let me unlock the door and look out into the hallway, which by the sound of it teemed with life or some other activity. Alonzo and Thomas eyed me from their beds as I made my way to the door.

"What if it's one of those de-fleshed bodies coming to force us into their ranks?" I asked. They each held a look of curiosity as if they too believed I could open the door and see some corpses wandering around, looking for some undead payback. They both contained a morbid curiosity about what lurked in the hallway, but neither of the bastards tried to stop me or at least back me up.

Alonzo had a bit of a tight smile, as if he hoped something would drag me off. "You take up too much room anyhow," he said right as I opened the door.

But the well-lit hallway stood empty. "There's nothing out here," I reported back into the room, as if there were some rationale to the action. Just then two olive-skinned male residents from two doors down stepped from their room into the hallway.

"I didn't vote for the fucker," I said, trying to make friends by using the slogan. But they just nervously smiled. "The other two in my room DID vote for him," I said, giving a wink and a thumbs-up. They too were now doing a version of the Euro head bob while walking backwards with the same nervous expressions, as if they expected me to leap at any second. They reached the hall's end and side-stepped around the corner.

I turned around and went back in the room. Thomas had his bedspread pulled taut over his head and tucked around him, appearing as a big blue mummy. Alonzo was sitting up. His hair was messy on one side of his head which matched his perplexed face. The scene made me start laughing because he looked like the kid who gets off an amusement park ride that went too fast and is now locked into a balancing act of fighting off the feelings of nausea while attempting to bring back some sort of equilibrium. He looked like a confused baby bird.

From here I felt like wandering around. Not too far, but to stay in the confines of the hostel. "Come on," I told the guys. "Let's head downstairs to talk politics with the world."

"Not me," came from the mummy. "I'm fine right here." Alonzo moved to the bathroom to fix his hair.

"Come on, what's wrong with you?" I asked Thomas. "Just a little paranoia, that's all. Just give me a minute."

"All this over a little paranoia? Paranoia is good; it shows we are getting a bang for our buck. Yes sir, store-bought fear. Where else can you purchase such a fun emotion? PARANOIA! Wow, what a spice of life, a drug-induced addition of mystery to an everyday boring life. The fear someone larger than yourself is out to get you, something out for you and it could be around any corner."

"Just give me a minute. Come back and report on the situation. Besides, you have got *the rants*." And he was right. The rants, the condition when the mushrooms shift on you, making you no longer paranoid, but filled with the answers of the world. Your mind expands, though chances are your intelligence doesn't. However, it is possible to say profound things, as the user has the tendency to say so much that something of value has to slip out in between otherwise pointless phrases. "Alligators had a million-year head start on us; if they didn't want to be turned into shoes, they should have developed opposable thumbs."

Alonzo followed me out of the room and to the elevator. The elevator was filled with four players from a South African rugby team. As soon as the door closed, I asked out loud, "Is anyone else nervous about being on this thing with this Iranian?" Alonzo just stared at the ground, shaking his head side to side.

"Pardon?" I heard one thick accent respond, but the door opened and we stepped out onto the lobby floor before I had to answer any questions about my statement.

"You better cut that shit out," Alonzo said, "or I'm gonna punch you in the nuts," which he indubitably would, had I pushed him too far.

"Yeah, well, you're only saying that because your racial shortcomings have left you feeling guilty. So let's get a couple of pints and forget about all this." Again, he just shook his head and walked away towards the bar.

The common area of the hostel was alive tonight. Low lighting, but still enough to see around the common room, which seemed warm as the ambient light reflected off the amber wood tables and floor. The activities of our surroundings provided entertainment as we sat and drank our beers and listened to various foreign tongues. There were about four different groups in each corner of the place; God knows where they all stemmed from. But it seemed we were in the famed Star Wars cantina: different skin tones, different tongued dialects, lots of energy confined to various tables, different galaxies. In one corner what appeared to be seven or eight Germans, mostly guys, seemed to drink and cheer with the gusto I have seen them express in the movies. A small party of coffee-with-cream-colored girls sat in another corner. One girl's brown eyes warmly glowed from the reflection of the mood lighting birthed from a tabletop candle. She was exotic, stemming from Egypt or Monaco. It isn't wise to provoke the Germans; the world has learned two important messages about that in the wake of two world wars. Regardless of their win/loss record, they aren't afraid of a go if they feel "right."

"Want a beer?" Alonzo asked, bringing me back.

"Yeah... please," I said. "I'll grab a table." I had just sat when Natalie and her friend came through the door. She saw me immediately, as I was in view of the entrance. She smiled and waved. I did the same, but motioned them over. She held up a finger letting me know she would be over momentarily. Al appeared at the table with a couple of Heinekens.

"Salud," he said as we clinked bottles together.

"You like that brunette from earlier?" I asked. "The one we saw outside the High Times party?" "Yeah," I said.

"Yeah, she's cute," he said as he took another drink of beer.

"Cool, I made some calls; she's going to come down here," I said casually, then took a sip of my beer as I appeared to be interested in looking around the room.

"Wait... what?" was all he could get out just as Natalie and her friend approached the table.

114

"Hi, guys," she said in a very warm and happy way. "Hi, Nat," I said. "This is my friend Alonzo." "Nice to meet you, Alonzo," she said.

"Likewise," Alonzo said with charm.

"Dis is Ashley," Natalie said, introducing her friend Alonzo was interested in.

"Hello," Ashley said to us, her accent clearly British. "Hi," I said.

"Pleasure to meet you," Alonzo said, locking eyes smiling. I knew his senses were being hit from every angle during this encounter, but Alonzo had always been a respond-to-pressure type guy. The mushroom peak had already occurred, and his intrigue in this girl overpowered anything that could rob him of confidence.

"Can I buy you ladies a beer?" Alonzo asked.

"I actually have to go to work behind the desk," Natalie motioned to the hostel front desk. "But Ashley may stick around," she said as she looked to her friend.

"Sure, I'll stick around for a pint," she said.

"Done, I'll be right back," Alonzo said and disappeared to the bar.

"Late night shift, huh?" I asked Natalie.

"Yes," she responded, "kinda a bummer."

"Yeah, I bet," I said, continuing the small talk.

"Here you go." Al reappeared with the beer that he handed to Ashley.

"Well, I'll leave you to it," Natalie said. "I have to tend to business." She excused herself, leaving us three at the table.

"Where are you from?" Alonzo immediately took the lead. "London. However, my father builds ships and does a lot of work out of the Netherlands, so I spend a great deal of time here," she said.

"Wait, wait, wait a second," Alonzo said with curiosity. "Your dad builds ships? Like he does actual construction work on them or…"

"Oh, yes, he's more of a designer-engineer type," Ashley said. "That's cool, impressive. I've never met anyone who was a shipbuilder," Alonzo said. He always had a way of making the person supplying personal information feel good as he took a genuine interest in the conversational topic.

"Well, you still haven't met one," Ashley pointed out. "Just the daughter of one," she continued, followed by a cute laugh.

"You're the closest I've come," Alonzo said as he raised his beer.

"Cheers," Ashley said.

"Salude," Alonzo followed with and we chimed the glasses.

It was easy to see Alonzo had found a connection and my presence wasn't really needed. So I excused myself. I was coming down from the ride, though I could still feel the subtitles of the drug. Colors and light were more vibrant; sounds still peaked. It was a good time to go put in the earbuds and drift off to that other place, far beyond here, to an untouchable place through sleep's doorway. Natalie was at her place behind the computer monitor. Her face shone smartly in the blue electric light that came from it. She had on studious yet fashionable spectacles. One long blonde lock fell forward from the others that were swept back. She was a beautiful girl, sweet eyes hidden behind a poker face. A big heart, guarded. A gem to be discovered. I wanted to stop and chat, to get to know her better, but she looked busy.

"Good night, Natalie," I said. She looked up and instantly smiled at me. "Ashley's in good hands," I said.

"Have a pleasant evening, Major; perhaps I'll see you in the morning?" she asked.

"Hopefully, but you never know. I'll see you again though, I'm sure," I said, believing the statement. Though I never did see her again.

I walked into the room. Thomas had fallen asleep. He looked at peace, which can be tough to accomplish when you try to sleep with 'shrooms in your veins. Sometimes the mind takes over. Like on those sober nights when a person lies in bed and can't get the mind to turn off. Only with the end of a 'shroom ride, sometimes you deal with that times ten. Not tonight; he had his earbuds in, listening to something that had lulled him to sleep. I was anxious to join him in his venture.

I glanced around, looking for a joint or a roach to draw from before going to sleep. The room was cluttered. The contents of all of our suitcases had spilled or crawled out onto the floor, cot posts, corners. The only place clear of our belongings was the ceiling. A few food wrappers lay in various spots, thrown down after late nights, only to be forgotten. The mess was an honest testament to the previous days' efforts. Then I saw what I was hawking for to begin with. On the windowsill next to a Coke can and a pack of cigarettes was a half-smoked joint. I cracked the window open and lit it. I ended up taking three hits of it before I licked my fingers and squished the life out of the cherry tip. I then climbed into my bunk, put on the *Sergeant Pepper's Lonely Hearts Club Band* album and drifted away.

Chapter Nine

I woke to the gray room the next morning. I felt good. I had slept soundly. Thomas was snoring, but it was a lighter snore, a morning coo. A softer snore than the all-out drunk snore that is more like snarls. I looked on my phone clock; it was 9 a.m. That was the latest I had slept the entire trip; the body's clock had adjusted. I got up to take a piss and was happy how good I felt. Maybe I didn't even feel all that good, but I felt better than had been typical on this trip, probably because I didn't go to bed completely drunk.

I twisted the cap off a bottle of water I had by my bed and walked to the window to look at the weather. The courtyard looked the same as always, but as always, it gave me an unknown pleasure to look upon. The morning hosted a thick cloud cover, but no rain.

"What's up?" Thomas asked as he slowly blossomed with life. "Hey, just woke up, looking outside at the weather," I said. "Cloudy, I'm guessing—like most days here," he said, as he maneuvered into a sitting position, his feet now on the floor.

"Yup," I said. "How'd you sleep?" I asked.

"Lights out," he said. "Only woke up when that girl walked into the room." Then it hit me like a rediscovered dream you forgot awakening. A girl had walked into the room last night.

"That's right, I remember seeing her. She walked out as I was trying to focus on her," I said.

"Yeah," Thomas said. "At first I thought it was someone with Alonzo," he explained. "She must have been a late arrival, and the cheap-ass hostel tried to rent out the fourth bed. She walked in with her suitcase in tow, looked around this pigsty and turned right around and walked out."

"Probably left the entire property after that move," I said. "Right," Thomas said, as he rubbed his eyes with one hand, using the thumb and side of his index finger, so he could lean on the other arm as it was planted on the bed.

"Al ever come back?" I asked.

"Not as far as I know. He still has clothes on top of his bed, so it doesn't look like he slept here," Thomas said.

"He must have hooked up with that girl last night," I said. "The one who walked in our room?" Thomas asked.

"No," I said, just as it dawned on me that that was certainly a prank from Natalie, who was working the check-in desk. A prank from her, on us—and also on the girl she sent up to rent the fourth bed. A good one, a good sense of humor, another of her hidden charms. "He has had his eye on some gal the past couple of days. She's friends with a girl who works here."

"Here at the hostel?" Thomas asked, which showed we obviously had been on separate ventures on the trip.

"Yes, a blonde that works the check-in," I said. "Natalie?" Thomas asked.

"Yeah, that's her."

"She's cool," he said as he rose and headed to the bathroom. "Yes, she is," I said more to myself. "You wanna go downstairs and grab breakfast?"

"Yeah," I heard over the sound of a healthy piss stream. Soon after, Thomas entered the room. "I'm starving, slept quite a while last night," Thomas said as he pulled up his pants and grabbed for a shirt. I planned on coming back to the room to shower after eating. I threw on some sweat pants and a thermal long johns top and slid into my Chuck Taylors, and we were out the door.

The elevator door opened into the lobby; my eye went immediately to the check-in desk. But Natalie wasn't there. She was replaced by some young guy, who appeared in age and appearance like most the residents of the place—a Euro-granola look. It was close to 10 a.m. and there were a few scattered guests eating. I grabbed a few pieces of toast, peanut butter, Nutella, cheese slices, cold-cut meat and a couple of hard-boiled eggs and made my way to sit down.

"You want some tea?" Thomas asked as he walked by the station.

"Yeah, grab me some Earl Grey," I said. That flavor is a very common breakfast blend in Europe, though it was recently discovered by me to be a good wake-up drink. He set the hot cup of water down in front of me and tossed my teabag in front of me.

"I'm gonna grab some grub," he said as he headed to the spread. I dipped my bag in the water and steeped it, more so for the amusement in the action than the purpose.

Thomas returned with twice the food that I had on my plate. He sat down, never taking his eye off the plate. I knew he was hungry and focused. I left him to his work, and I started on mine.

After breakfast I was craving a cup of coffee. There was none offered at the meal, so I told Thomas I was going to run down the block and get a cup to go and bring it back. "You want one?" I asked.

"Naw," he said as he stuffed the second half of a boiled egg in his mouth. So I got up and went out the door. As I walked, I couldn't help but notice a couple of people looking at me with a peculiar expression on their faces. When I passed the gay bar, I heard a faint whistle from above. I looked up and there were two gays smiling me, each sitting in a window smoking. They were apparently very happy with me; but, just like with the others who had looked at me, I had no idea why. I just kind of smiled in acknowledgment and moved on.

"I'll have an Americano," I said to the barista.

"You got it," she replied, sounding very Americanized. "Your English sounds American," I said to her.

"Probably because I spent a couple of years there," she said as she started my drink.

"Oh yeah? Whereabouts?" I asked.

"NYU," she replied, talking about the prestigious New York University.

"That's impressive," I said. "What did you study?"

"American history," she said, as she mixed hot water into my cappuccino.

"Impressive," I said. "You probably know more than many Americans do on the subject." I subsequently realized I was putting my own country down or putting it down with a sad fact.

"Thanks," she responded. I didn't want to prod any further as a couple had entered the shop.

"Hey, quick question," I said. "Sure," she responded.

"I'm staying down the street, and on my way here people have been looking at me as if something is odd about me," I explained. "Do you notice anything out of the ordinary? Do they take messy hair that seriously here?" I asked.

"Well," she said with a small smile, "it could be the top you're wearing." I looked down at my shirt, wondering if I had spilled something on it or if a bird had shit on me or something. I didn't see anything out of the ordinary, just my gray thermal.

"I don't understand," I said.

"In Europe, a thermal top is kinda looked upon as underwear of sorts," she explained. And it was clear by the reactions of the two twinks earlier that I had made the bold fashion move to walk down the street in my underwear.

"Ahh—I see," I said, nodding to myself while I mulled over the situation. I pulled out a two-Euro coin and slid it to her. "Thanks for the information."

"Thank you, any time," she said with a smile. "Don't worry about it," she said. "Knowing Europe, you'll probably start a trend here." I gave her a small courtesy laugh and walked out with my coffee. I walked back to the hostel a different way. I didn't want to put on another burlesque show for the locals I had already passed.

I got back to the room, ready for a day of adventure or napping; both were beautiful options. I was surprised to find Alonzo packing his clothes. "Cleaning up, Romeo?" I asked. Thomas was sitting on his bunk.

"Hey, dude," Alonzo said with a warm smile. "I'm splitting on you two," he said, as he scooped a couple of shirts off the floor and folded them.

"What the fuck are you talking about?" I asked with confusion. We still had a few days left on the trip.

"She goes to Oxford, Maj," Alonzo said, "business graduate school." And that was enough. He'd fallen for her, and she had the world to offer.

"You fell kinda quickly for this one, didn't you?" I asked. "We fucked in the hostel stairwell last night," Alonzo said. "I didn't want to disturb your beauty sleep." "I see; she stole your heart," I said.

"And apparently she stole his balls too," Thomas added.

"I met her dad this morning; they are staying at the Amsterdam Waldorf Astoria. They are headed back to London on his jet, and I'm going to go with them, guys."

"You fucked her in the stairwell?" Thomas asked, the fact just coming to reality for him.

"Well, shit, I couldn't bring her in here with you two *cochinos*, now could I?" Alonzo said.

"Where'd you stay?" I asked.

"At her dad's place. It was a suite, but we couldn't fuck there either. Got to bed at about 5 a.m., then up at 6:30."

"Sounds like you all hit it off pretty well," I said.

"I like this chick, Maj," he said, and I could tell he did; and more than likely she was a good find for him. He finished with his bag, turned and stuck his hand out for a handshake, which turned into a hug.

"Have fun, amigo, it's why we came on this trip," I said.

"Yes, it is, bro. Yes, it is," he said, as he gave Thomas a hug too.

"I'm still confused," Thomas said.

"Maj will fill you in, bro," Al said, grabbing his bag and disappearing out the door. And that was that; Alonzo was gone. He was following his heart—or his dick; each prospect was romantic, depending on the person judging it.

"You want to go grab a smoke and tea?" I asked Thomas.

"G'day, mate!" he said with a fresh smile. Making me feel that the trip was in a rebirthing of sorts. Our last few days will be a renewing of adventure.

On the way to get tea, I explained to Thomas the best I could about the girl Alonzo had hooked up with and how she seemed cool. "Good for him," he said about it all, and that was all that was said.

Thomas and I sat sipping our tea, which was too hot to drink. He sat his cup on the saucer, which made a high-pitched clink sound of china or porcelain; I wondered if there were a distinct sound between the two. We were in the Dolphin, a coffeehouse that was decorated between tackiness and impressiveness, appearing like an underwater scene. Corals and sea plants made of hardened foam were created and painted in the blues and greens of the sea. The entire scene appeared as if you had stepped off the street into a Jacques Cousteau wet dream—or nightmare.

Coffeehouses, as opposed to pubs, are much quieter. Those in them who are fetching a fix tend to transcend into the surroundings. Most become lost in the escape of thought that they came seeking. Thomas and I were both here, sitting across from each other at a small table, and not a word was spoken.

Thomas pulled out a small baggie and some rolling papers that he tossed onto the table. "Let's try this shit," he said, almost to himself as he eyed the weed he had begun to break up into rollable fill. I didn't answer; I didn't need to. While he continued to roll, I picked up the honey bear on the table to sweeten my tea. I watched it drip and then stream into my drink. It looked like beer pouring in slow motion. I noticed the words "pure honey" on the bottle once I set it back down on the table. And the words made me think and appreciate the fact that I was enjoying something pure, a magical rarity in life. Though in reality, it was bee barf.

"Got it. Here," Thomas' voice brought me back. He was handing me the freshly-rolled joint, an act of class in the stoner world.

"Do we need more of this shit? Can we get higher?" I asked. "Find out," was all he said as he re-offered the joint. A click of the lighter, a drag of the dragon's breath and then a slight wonderful cough to wake the spirit. I looked about the room as Thomas took his drags. There was a sleeping jukebox across the room. Thomas again was at my door with the joint. I took it, dragged it and passed it back.

"You know what bothers me, dude?" I asked as he held his breath and an expression of anticipation of my answer crossed his face. "Fucking Fonzie," I said.

"From 'Happy Days'?" Thomas asked as part of his exhale. "Yeah, from 'Happy Days,'" I said with confidence as I took another drag. Thomas didn't say anything; he just waited on my words. "He goes into Arnold's, and his signature move is to bash the jukebox and get free music—that's stealing; that's not cool."

"Are you done?" Thomas asked.

"Yeah," I said, slightly defensively.

"Pull your head out of your ass," he said, delivering me a proverbial slap of insubordination across my face. I waited for his drag and exhale. "Fonzie brought the crowd. Fonzie brought the girls. He established an entire social food chain, with him on top, of course, but why not? The owner was making money off the persona." I sat quietly amazed that the concept had not occurred to me. "Yeah, so he got a few songs; it's a fair trade."

"But don't you think the owner of the place had to replace—or at a minimum, constantly repair—the jukebox from being hit and kicked and assaulted so often?" I said, trying to keep up some sort of argument.

"It doesn't matter. The Fonz is good for business, and he pays for himself—easily."

"But two Fonzies wouldn't be good for business," I added.

"Absolutely not," Thomas said with a stern face of authority on the matter. We then simultaneously started to laugh. "I was thinking about heading to the Van Gogh today," Thomas told me. "Wanna come?"

"I actually already went a few days ago," I told him.

"Ah man, you did?" he said, making me for the first time feel bad I went by myself.

"Yeah—sorry, I just wasn't sure you would want to go, and I didn't want to miss it," I said, trying to justify my actions.

"You coulda asked," he rightfully said.

"Yeah, yeah, I know, I just—"

"No big deal, dude," Thomas cut me off, letting me off the hook. "I could go again," I suggested, trying to make up for my inconsideration.

"What for?" Thomas rightfully said. "It's no big deal, dude," he said, now showing no regrets for anything. "I'll go check it out. What do you think? A couple hours?" he asked.

"If that," I replied.

"Cool, go walk around or send some postcards or something. I'll catch up to you later today," he said as he stood and put on his hoodie.

"Cool," I said. "I'm gonna stick around here and drink a little more tea," I told him.

"Cool," Thomas replied and stuck out his fist for a fist-bump; then he was out the door. A slight loneliness came over me at that moment. Alonzo was gone, and I had come to the point in the trip where I was enjoying Thomas' company again, and now he was gone. I sparked the lifeless joint back to life, drew in its cargo and blew out towards the ceiling, even though I didn't need to; no one was sitting close by or would have cared anyhow. Maybe I was just exhaling a prayer of sorts.

I finished my tea and took the cup back up to the bar for a hot- water refill, as I was going to try to squeeze another life from my teabag but was told they do not give free refills on hot water. Of course, they don't; I should have known better. Cheapness or frugality, depending on how you look at it, is a strong part of the European service industry. You want a package of ketchup at a Euro McDonald's, better be prepared to pay for it. You won't be getting unlimited refills on your Coke either; you're gonna pay four Euros for one, though. And when you want a refill on hot water in an Amsterdam coffee shop, be prepared to basically buy another cup of tea. But hey, like I said, depends on how you look at it. In America we consume too much and pay too little to do so. Naturally we have an overweight society. And truth be told, a Coke is something that should be enjoyed, sipped and with its sugar content, be treated almost as a dessert. In America we replace water with it and make it less expensive.

I left the coffee shop and out to Leidsestraat. This was a main artery through Amsterdam proper. I could turn left and walk through the high-end shopping the area offered. Not that I was interested or capable of shopping in the area, but it's a cool place to people-watch. Maybe grab a cup of espresso and sit on a canal rail and just watch the people as a child watches ants. Or I could turn right and head into Leidseplein Square. For some reason, a shot of whiskey sounded really good, so I turned right and headed for the square's pubs.

As I walked along Leidsestraat, I heard the clang of the tram bell coming from behind me. These people-movers seem to coexist well with the pedestrians of the area, always noticeable by the bell and the electric hum of the tram in movement. It travels down the middle of the street, which is usually cluttered with walkers and bicyclists rather than cars. I took a couple of side steps to make sure I was clear of the tracks which are subset into the ground. Moments later the giant blue and white train passed me, without even enough speed to create an accompanying wind rush.

I could see the square open up about a short block ahead of me. Public squares are a dying breed of commerce in America. In most European towns there are several squares, depending on the size of the town. In Amsterdam proper, there are many spread out throughout the area. For the most part, residents support their square. They patronize the markets, shops, restaurants and pubs within their square and surrounding neighborhood. In America, our loyalty lies with product price, many times. We drive across town to buy a bag of charcoal from Walmart for three bucks instead of paying five and supporting our neighborhood privately-owned market. We drive across town to eat at trendy restaurants, forgetting the ones in our own neighborhood. In this local town square, citizens keep their businesses in the same spot for decades. We are Americans. We don't consume smart; we just consume. I reached the square which opened up almost like a park; but instead of grass, there were cobblestones, bare trees, benches and a perimeter square of pubs, restaurants, shops and markets. It was late November, and the square had been decorated with holiday trimmings. Small, portable huts were set up selling seasonal treats like Oliebollens, similar to American donut holes, a deep-fried ball of sweet goodness. Another hut hosted traditional warm pretzels, and another had a large, almost wok-looking pan with a fire underneath and long coiled sausages and onions cooking on top. This spiced scent filled the air more than the other delicacies. And though I had smoked and had the munchies, I didn't want to fill up on street foods just yet; I didn't want anything heavy in my stomach to slow down the progression of the whiskey.

127

I looked around at the various pubs. There were different themes; one was a sports bar, which had a TV outside showing a soccer game. Through the windows I could see a couple of other TVs streaming different games. No American football though; most in America were bedded down for the night. Another bar looked high-class. Large glass windows gave view to an inside pub filled with shiny wood furnishings, mirrors and polished-brass fixtures and accents. Next door to that one was a traditional Euro/Irish pub-restaurant. Through its windows, you could see a smart, warm Christmas-decorated establishment. Lots of greenery accents and shiny glass green, red and blue globe ornaments. It appeared to be a warm, inviting place. A good place to order some grub and an Irish coffee. However, that wasn't my mood. A couple of doors down from there was a place simply called The Roadhouse. It was clearly a lure to give people the "all-American" experience of a honky-tonk, juke joint, whiskey-spilling place. It seemed kinda tacky to me, but it was almost cute. I figured I'd go in there, see how they captured a feel of home.

I was immediately caught off guard when I came across a doorman at the entrance. Not only surprised that the place needed a bouncer so early in the day, but more taken back that I was greeted warmly by a six-foot-five bald Hell's Angel.

"Identification, please," he said with a smile. "Sure," I said and presented my driver's license. "Ahh, Cal-i-fornia," he said, nodding his head.

"Yeah, the original home of your… club," I said, not wanting to use the word *gang*, not that I necessarily thought the word would offend him, but it just wasn't a moment to test cautionary words.

"Yes-yes, it is," he said, appreciating the statement. "Would you like to leave your coat?" he asked.

"Yes actually, thank you," I told him, appreciating his welcoming nature. He seemed like the right man for the job in this place. He wasn't trying to be intimidating, not in the slightest, and in fact quite the opposite. But as my father once taught me, it's these big, quiet, genteel types who can flip a switch and take care of business when needed. I gave him my jacket, and he handed me a piece of paper with a number on it.

"Welcome," he said, as he opened the door for me to step in. The place had worn wooden floors and a long saloon-style bar, backed by a double-shelved row of booze bottles. A large mirror framed in thick wood centered it all. They did a decent job of capturing what they wanted to. On the far end was a lonely medium-sized stage, hosting a few bar stools and a couple mic stands. There were several tables, mostly empty, but not all. There were three groups in the place, spread out almost mathematically in space among each other. Two tables had three to four people at each. One table of three stood out, and through their talk and laughter, they made themselves known.

The bar had several neon beer signs, but I noticed one that stood out, the Budweiser sign. The word had been shortened to "Bud." I looked in the beer cooler behind the bar, and all the neatly-rowed lines of the same beer had the moniker "Bud" on them as well. I thought a moment and came to the realization that words ending in "weiser" were European in origin, not very appealing to someone over there who wanted to drink the beer from the land of Ronald Reagan. As I looked over the beer list, I also noticed Bud was an import beer and priced accordingly.

"What can I get ya?" the bartender asked, a guy in his twenties wearing a plaid shirt, maybe the outfit taking a stab at being Western in theme.

"I'll have a Guinness and a shot of Jamison," I said.

"You got it," the bartender said, doing his best to sound like a surly roadhouse bartender.

"Shouldn't you be ordering a Jack Daniels, mate?" I heard from the loud group behind me. At first I worried I would turn around and have some British roughneck hooligan types waiting for me to choose the wrong response, to turn the scene into the real deal. In much of Europe, the men are passive, not willing to let an ego lead to a challenge. The Brits are different, every bit as tough as American bar crowd counter types. As I slowly turned around to acknowledge the remark, I glanced at the door to see if the bouncer were looking our direction. He was sitting on a barstool reading a book.

"Yup, having a little of the good stuff while I'm over here," I said.

"Cheers, mate," one in the group said, raising his pint.

"Cheers," I said as I took my shot.

"Come have a sit with us, mate," another said in the group. So I picked up my Guinness, pulled up a chair and joined the group.

"Hi, I'm Major," I said as I introduced myself.

"Cheers, I'm Craig," the one who appeared to be the leader of the group said. "This is Brian and Mark," he continued as he introduced the group. Brian was the smallest of the group and appeared to be the puppy among the dogs. Mark was the strong, quiet type, nodding as we shook hands, but not saying anything.

"Whe'a ya from?" Brian asked, as he leaned forward to hear my response.

"California," I said, then took another drink from my beer.

"California, eh?" Craig said. "Know any movie stars?" he continued in a typical, but good-natured Euro's question about the state.

"Just Arnold Schwarzenegger," I said with a straight face.

"Seriously, mate?" Brian said, giving me his full attention.

"Naw, I'm fucking with you, man," I said.

"Awe, you cheeky bastard," Brian said with a smile. Craig chuckled and drew his pint to his lips. Mark looked at Brian and smiled and then took a drink of his beer too.

"Craig was just tellin' us a tale," Brian said. "Go on, Craig, finish the story."

"Naw, our friend here has better things to listen to than this story," Craig said, trying to throw Brian from his request.

"Doubleback Hog Growla', Doubleback Hog Growla', mate!" Brian continued pleading. "Seriously—you gotta tell us."

"What's that?" I asked, as I was now intrigued by the term.

"It's the Doubleback Hog Growla'," Brian said, never taking his eyes off Craig. "It's the fuh-king funniest thing, mate," Brian explained with the excitement of a Christmas day child.

"All fuck-ing right, Brian, you're breaking my heart; belt up and I'll tell it." Brian's anticipation was contained to trembles as he awaited the story.

"Do you remember Doti, Mark? Big tits, brunette."

"Oh, the bitch?" Mark answered softly.

"Yeah—that's right," Craig responded. "That's how I referred to her usually."

"I remember, Craig," Brian reassured quickly, trying to keep him on track.

"But those tits—they were bloody huge." Craig held his hands out in front of his chest to mimic the size. He didn't appear to be doing it to show us, as much as he appeared to be reminding himself. "But I'm a tit man, and the sex was great, mate, and that's why I put up with her shit for so long," Craig said and then took a sip of his beer. He then looked at the ground at an angle that looked as if he were staring a million miles away or trying to focus on something on the ground that wasn't there.

"The Hog Back," Brian whispered timidly.

"Oh yeah," Craig said, snapping back to reality. "So whenever I would stay over at her house, her mum would walk into the room unexpectedly, no knocking, no nothing. You got a cigarette?" Craig asked Mark, who pulled a pack from his coat pocket. He opened and pushed the box towards Craig, who in one single move swiped the thing, put it in his mouth, leaned towards Mark's lighter, drew the flame and nodded in appreciation. Mark motioned to me.

"No thanks," I said, making a waving-off motion.

"Cheers, mate," Brian said as he took one.

"So you were sayin'… " Mark prodded, doing so more for the benefit of Brian.

"Yeah, so she would just barge right in. She knew we were shaggin' when I stayed there, but she never caught us. But it never stopped her from doing it. She would always come in asking some dumb question like, 'Have you seen your father's dress socks?' or something to that effect." Brian stopped for a second, took a drag and exhaled.

"Maybe you should have fucked her mom?" Brian said, causing Craig to wince.

"Towards the end of our relationship, all three weeks of it, I was getting pretty sick of both of them so I hatched my plan; I would give the mum a Growla'." By now Craig had all our attentions. He took another drag, exhaled and looked around the area.

"Well, fucking go on," Brian said.

"Mmm," Craig said in the middle of his next drag. "So I heard her mom doing her familiar creep down the hallway, which was what always gave her up. I moved to the foot of the bed, took off my boxers and started to position myself on all fours with my bare arse facing the door. And Doti is getting all nervous, 'What are you doing? What are you doing?' she kept saying. Just as the door opened and the hallway light formed a rectangular spotlight on my arse, I went face-first into a pillow, had my cock and balls pushed back towards the mum with my legs together so they would stay and I pulled my ass cheeks apart, so I was, in a sense, staring back at her."

"No fucking way," Mark said, just as Brian burst into laughter. Mark and I started to laugh too, and the mental picture finally caught up with the humor of the story.

"No shit, mate; that's how it happened," Brian said.

Then what?" Brian asked.

"After the shock wore off, her mum started yelling for me to get out, so I picked up my belongings, got dressed—sort of—and went out the door."

"What did Doti say?" Mark asked.

"Nothing, I think she was in shock over the matter," Craig said. "I don't blame her," I said.

"Cheers to that, mate," Brian said as we all clinked pints and took a drink of our beers.

I bought the group another round in appreciation for them bringing me into their fold to tell me their interesting story. I found out they were linemen who had flown in that day and were expected to travel south to the Hague to work on some power lines. Tough, dangerous work, but somehow I felt these roughnecks were the right men to get the job done. We finished our round, and I got up to excuse myself. I didn't want to get stuck in a pub for the day; I had had my fill of beer, whiskey and conversation.

"Don't forget your jacket," the doorman said to me as I approached the exit. "It's cold out there," he said in such a warm and caring way that it was as confusing as it was comforting. I was clearly seeing his best side, but I knew he was hired for a reason and I wouldn't want to see that reason at work. I gave him five euro for his service and appreciation.

Leidseplein Square was a good-sized area, split by a street and a couple of bike paths. Maybe that's why I hadn't noticed the temporary ice rink they had set up in one area of it. A simple square set-up, roughly the size of a tennis court. It had lights strung across it that glowed white in the gray day's atmosphere but would be functional at night by allowing skating to continue. There were only a few people skating now: a mother and her two kids. They laughed and smiled and moved across the ice straight-legged and awkwardly, but they were clearly enjoying every second of it. I then began my walk back to the hostel.

I stepped off the street and into the warmth of the hostel entry. I nodded to the girl at the desk; she put little effort into smiling in acknowledgment, but it didn't bother me as it reminded me of Natalie. I heard a round of celebrating voices and random claps from my left in the large common area. Thomas sat at a table with a half-circle of people in front of him as he was dealing cards.

"Hey, I've got another game I can teach you," he said to the group of four around him. "It's called Texas Hold'em, just picked the game up myself. I've got a rule book I've been reading right up in my room; I'll fetch it after this hand." I could see now they were playing 21; each had a coin, more than likely a euro in front of them. Thomas's eyes were intensely excited, but only I saw it. Subtle shows of excitement at a card table were rare occurrences and a *tell* of Thomas. No one would see another of his tells that evening, as he wouldn't want to scare off the prey. Like a well-behaved shark in a pool of koi, the fish would be too dumb to see what was coming and too slow to recognize it when it happened.

Thomas dealt the last hand of 21; he dealt the players' hands face-up and turned his dealer card face up, an ace. The table collectively melted at the sight. The best hand dealt was to an Australian—or a New Zealander—probably not a South African chick who I could already tell Thomas was into. The worst hand was dealt to an Israeli kid I recognized from earlier in the trip, when he had sat and rocked for a couple of hours in the hostel's great room while on 'shrooms. He didn't bother anyone or make any noise, just quietly rocked himself in self-soothing movements and stared 1000 miles away. But now his cards showed a 16 total. Two others at the table were unfamiliar to me; but as they spoke, it was clear they were Americans. One small guy appeared a cross between a stoner and a hippie: a slight roughness, coupled with his shoulder-length curly blond hair, softened his appearance. The other guy was built like a college football linebacker. He appeared like an American Islander with tanned skin and a tight haircut.

"Tell you what," Thomas said. "I'm gonna flip these cards; and if it's 21, I will treat it like an 11 and will hit on it." Everyone at the table got smiles of hope as they looked at each other for reassurances that all was not lost. "But if I lose doing that, the table pitches in and buys me a beer. If you lose, you lose," Thomas said with a sporting grin. "Yeah?" he asked.

"Yeah-yeah" and a delayed "yes" from the Jewish kid were the responses. He flipped his cards exposing a suited blackjack. "Eleven," he said loudly and officially as he laid the next card. "Sixteen," he said as all eyes were focused on the felt where the next card was to be laid. "TWENTY-SIX," Thomas said loudly, as if he were happy for the loss. "There you go, Rebekah," Thomas said as he paid her money, doubling the euro coin she had wagered. She eagerly hugged herself and appeared as giddy as a child right before opening birthday presents.

"Thank you," she said, looking Thomas in the eyes that filled with a warm return expression at her attitude.

"And for you and you," he said, laying down money for two other winning participants. "And you, Mikhail, you're gonna take my money?" Thomas said in a playful tone. Mikhail, who was the only one who had not quickly picked up his money already, looked at Thomas with a boyish naiveté and said, "But you made the rules, Thomas."

"I'mmm kidding you, Mikhail; take your winnings, good job," Thomas told the Jewish player while patting him on the shoulder in a positive gesture. It was then Mikhail smiled with relief that his pittance was won with honor.

Thomas approached me. "Gonna have my trip financed tonight," he said with a smile, adding his arm around my neck in a brotherly embrace. He guided us away from the room and towards the elevator. "HEY!" he yelled over his shoulder, "you guys owe me a beer; get me one. I'll be back in a minute."

"Cheers, Thomas," someone yelled behind us as we entered the lobby.

"What's your plan?" I asked as we stepped into the elevator. "You heard me... I'm gonna arrange a Texas Hold 'em game," he said in between steps.

"Arrange?" I asked as we arrived on the third floor.

"Yeah... why?"

"Nothing, I thought I also heard you say you were just picking up the game yourself?"

"Why do I have to divulge how long I've played? Where's the advantage to that?" And at that, I realized he was right. When you pull your money out with the hopes of gaining more quickly, you're asking the stars to align and take your money; and they almost always appease. Thomas was simply a facilitator for the cosmos. A Lord of Karma at work.

Thomas picked through his bag and found his Texas Hold 'em rule book. "What do you need that for?" I asked. "Don't you already know the rules?"

He stared at me for a second, almost as if he were questioning if I were being a smart-ass towards him, or if I didn't know the answer to my own question.

"I take this everywhere," he said. "Not only does it make me look like a beginner, it also allows me to show someone the rules as I take their money. It's not like I need to cheat at this game to win," he said, almost defensively.

"Take it easy," I said. "I'm just asking."

"I know," Thomas said, while he looked around the room. "I'm just a little tense—or excited."

"What are you looking for? This?" I asked, holding up a joint. "Naw," he said as he briefly looked up and then back down, raking his eyes over clothing that littered the floor. "Ah—there it is," he said, holding up an airplane-sized booze bottle. "Tequila—I got at a mini-mart last night," he said as he twisted the cap off, its clicking sound announcing the bottle had just been opened. He sucked down a little more than half of it, made a winced face of bitterness and stretched the bottle out to me.

"No thanks, looks like you can use it more than me," I said.

"Yeah, you're probably right. I need to find a liquor store and find us a proper bottle of this shit," Thomas said as he tossed the bottle into the corner of the room. "Let's go. You gonna play?" he asked me.

"Naw, I'll watch you operate," I said.

"Probably a good move on this one," he told me as he winked. We exited the room and returned on the path back to the common area and Thomas' waiting riches.

"Oi, here's your beer," said Rebekah.

"Thanks, Beck, I mean it's the least you could do after taking advantage of me," Thomas said, then took a drink. "Hey, have you met my friend Major?" he asked.

"I have not had the pleash'a," her accent apparent as she stuck her hand out for a shake.

"Major, this is Rebekah; she's Australian," Thomas announced. "Oh, well, g'day, mate," I said, thinking it was the perfect time to use the phrase.

"Hello," she said with a warm smile.

"Don't they say 'g'day, mate' in Australia?" I asked, slightly disappointed I didn't get to hear it authentically uttered.

"No. I mean some people probably say it," she said, trying not to feed my failure.

"They don't really say that *anywhere*," Thomas said with the biggest smile of the trip. And why not? It was perfect timing for the moment.

"Let's grab a table," Thomas said, and we followed and sat down. Just as I sat, I realized I should have grabbed a beer up at the bar, so I excused myself and went to fetch one. Upon my return I saw that Mikhail had joined the table, along with the other two Americans. Thomas had the cards out and was snapping them alive through a crisp shuffle. Mikhail watched him with boyish wonder. Rebekah glanced around the room and didn't pay too much attention to the shuffle.

"Are you from the same town as Thomas?" she asked me. "Yes," I said. "We were both born in different places but ended up in Visalia," I told her.

"Vi-salia," she repeated. "That's fun-sounding. Vi-salia." Her Aussie accent made our town sound more exotic than it was, but it sounded fun to hear. "What do they do in Visalia?" Rebekah asked.

"Cows," Thomas said, looking at me with a sideways smile; the cards applauded again in shuffle.

"Yeah, we're surrounded by a lot of agriculture," I said. "Thomas grew up around the ocean and movie stars and had to move away."

"Isn't all of California next to the ocean?" Rebekah asked. "Yeah, if you look at it from a globe—but we're actually a few hours from the beach," I said.

"Ohh," Rebekah replied as she glanced around the room, losing interest in the geography talk.

"I figured you must be American," Mikhail said to the other two Americans at the table. He was so quiet I had almost forgotten he was sitting at the table waiting to play.

"Why do you think that?" Thomas asked.

"I don't know," Mikhail said. "The big guy isn't from this side of the world; they just stand out enough to give themselves away," he said. "Americans hold themselves a certain way—with confidence or arrogance. I figured they were either American or French," he said.

"My name is Frank," the big guy said with a warm smile. He stuck out his hand for Mikhail to shake. "This here's Bob," Frank said, introducing his friend.

"Hi," Bob said to the group quietly.

"I'm Major," I said, shaking both of their hands. They seemed like cool guys.

"Where you two from?" I asked.

"I live in Hawaii," Frank said. "I'm a sushi chef there." "Very interesting. How'd you get into that line?" I asked.

"I've always been into cooking," he said. "I played a couple of years in junior college football, then enlisted in the Marines."

"What position?" Thomas broke in. "Fullback," Frank answered.

"I'd hate to tackle you," Thomas said.

"Aahh, you look like you can take care of yourself," Frank said to Thomas. "Anyhow, I was a cook in the Marines. I won a national mess-hall competition in the service and ended up cooking for President Bush for a stint."

"Wow, that's fucking cool," I said, earnestly impressed with the story. "They taught you to cook sushi in the Marines?" I asked.

"Prepare," Frank said.

"Prepare?" I asked.

"Yeah, bra, you don't cook sushi—you prepare it."

"Ahh, touché," I said.

"I learned to cook in the CIA," Frank said.

"The intelligence agency?" I asked, slightly confused.

"No, it's the Culinary Institute of America," Thomas interrupted.

"You got it," Frank said.

"Yeah, they have one in New York aaand… ?" Thomas was trying to think of another location.

"Napa," Frank said, with appreciation for Thomas knowing about the culinary school. "Yeah, used my GI Bill to pay for schooling and took a gig in Maui."

"Preparing sushi," I said with a smile, showing I learned something.

"You got it," Frank said and gave me a fist bump.

"What about you, Bob?" I asked.

"Me… uh… I farm out in Colorado," he said. His demeanor was as shy as a withdrawing snail, and I didn't press the issue any more.

"What are we going to use for chips?" Mikhail asked. The question snapped Thomas into a frozen pose of thought.

"Hmm, can't believe I didn't think about that," Thomas said. "At home we always have them available."

"I thought you said you were just picking this game up yourself?" Frank said, half-joking, but half-serious.

"I am," Thomas said. "You can't pick it up if you don't have chips."

"Hmm," Frank replied. Telling the truth about your poker experience isn't a must before a game. It's just an angle. But if you get caught bluffing, then part of your game is exposed. Several days of smoking and drinking had allowed a small slip, but the harm was minimal. At best, Frank caught on that Thomas knew more about the game than he had let on.

"We need to get a bunch of coins," Thomas said. The denomination doesn't matter. He sat quiet for a second, hoping someone would have a suggestion.

"Hold tight," Rebekah said and got up from the table. "Be back in a moment," she affirmed and walked off towards the lobby. "Well, the wait is killing me; how about a round of drinks?" Frank asked. Everyone agreed. Mikhail asked for a hot tea instead of a beer, which is a slight hassle when it comes to drink orders. "You got it," Frank said with a smile, though.

We sat with our beers. Mikhail sipped his drink; it was the most noise he made while the rest of the group chattered. About ten minutes passed and Rebekah returned; she was clutching something in each of her hands. She set three rolls of coins on the table. "Got these from the office," she said. She had euro coins broken down to pennies, nickels and dimes, representing fifty cent, euro, and five-euro denominations. The group decided that a thirty-euro buy-in was agreeable, which made the pot around $175 U.S. I decided to sit out. Not that I can't play cards, but this was Thomas' brain child. He set out to claim the prize. I figured I'd stay clear and more than likely save some money.

"Does everyone understand the game Texas Hold'em?" Thomas asked.

"We've played some," Frank answered for the pair; Bob nodded in agreement.

"I picked it up about a year ago; it's caught on quite big in Australia," Rebekah said.

"I've played video poker before," Mikhail said. Thomas stared at him for a second, either thinking how best to explain it to him or to guess if he were being bullshitted. He went on to explain the game, and Mikhail listened intently. "I think I understand," he said. "Are there any wild cards?"

"No," was all Thomas replied. Then he paused, "Just watch a few hands until you're comfortable with the game," he said, more than likely because his conscience got to him for believing he was being hustled, when in fact he was the one attempting to do so. "I have this rule book if any of us get confused about stuff," he said. Mikhail reached out for the book, and Thomas handed it to him. Moments later each person had cards in front of them.

"Not playing, Major?" Rebekah asked.

"Naw, I know even less than Thomas about this game. Go ahead and take his money," I said. The group laughed, except for Mikhail who never looked up from the book. He swiped through a couple more pages as others studied their cards. He immediately folded his first hand and kept thumbing through the book.

"Ahh," he said, "the odds." Mikhail had found the page that explained hands and odds and followed the words quickly with his finger. Thomas took the first hand's winnings with a pair of tens; all but Frank had folded so the pot was small, but still symbolic to him. He passed the sloppy deck to Frank, who picked them up and shuffled them back to life.

"Anyone need a drink?" I asked the table before I headed to the bar. Thankfully there were no takers. I didn't want to be cheap, but the concept of Happy Hour had never really caught on in Europe and a large round can leave a person unhappy as a result. I left the table and headed up to the bar and ordered another Heineken. Heineken has been a favorite beer of mine for some time. Its distinct dank taste has always appealed to me. However, something I learned about the beer on this trip was that it had a different taste in Amsterdam than it did in California.

As I said, there is a distinct taste about Heineken; maybe that's why it's the world's most popular beer. It doesn't appeal to many Americans; and what they don't know, what I didn't know, but what everyone who drinks it in Europe knows, it is much smoother there. I don't want to say it tastes watery, but it just goes down as smooth. It dawned on me, the Heineken we drink in America—in California especially—has traveled from a half-world away. It ages in that time. It goes through different storage handling, more than likely through temperature change. It's been through just enough variables to tweak the taste just enough for it not to be true to its original taste. But I will forever drink it now, especially for the nostalgic feelings I will carry for it after this trip.

An eruption came from the table, causing me and the scattered few in the great room to take notice. I walked back to the table to see Thomas raking in a pile of chips. Frank was looking at Bob with a smug smile, shaking his head. It appeared Bob had gone all in, and Thomas had called him. A pair of aces were in front of Bob, a hand known as "bullets" in the poker world. In front of Thomas was a pair of 2s, a hand easily beatable in many cases, but not when the flop in front of you contains the other two 2s in the deck. Thomas had flopped a four of a kind. The third card in the flop was a 7, it didn't help anyone but had given Bob the courage to go all in, thinking he had the strongest hand.

"That's rookie," Frank said to Bob about the way he had played his hand.

"Fuck you," Bob said, managing to somehow not sound offensive in his words which were soft-spoken and beaten, but with just enough edge on them to let Frank know he probably shouldn't add any more salt to the situation.

"Want a beer now, Bob?" I asked.

"Naw, I'm going for a walk, gonna go buy some cigarettes," he said as he rose from the table. Mikhail and Rebekah's chip stacks appeared untouched. Frank had clearly won a hand along the way, but Thomas had doubled his money early. His plan was well on its way.

About that time my attention deficit began to nag me, along with a hunger pang. "I'm gonna go grab a bite; I'll be back in a bit," I said, stopping short of offering to grab something for anyone else, as I didn't want to bind myself. I knew where I was going before I announced I was leaving; I was craving Wok-to-Walk, only a couple of blocks away.

When I entered the store, the Pavlov effect took hold. The line was only three deep. It gave me the time to look over the menu and watch the food being prepared. The cooks stood behind their wok ovens and mixed the brew. You could hear steam, wood utensils on an iron surface, a sizzle and the sound of meat popping as it cooked. When I reached the register, I placed my order: egg noodles with shiitake mushrooms. I added pineapple and peanuts and choose Bangkok sauce, which was yellow curry and coconut.

They packaged it up in my Canton carton. I grabbed a set of disposable sticks and found a seat in the seating area. Seating in Europe is usually handled differently and more efficiently than in America. In the U.S. if a party of two sits at a table that can accommodate six, well, that's it; they keep the table. It's almost territorial like in the animal kingdom; the lions can't eat in peace with the jackals lurking. And so goes it at the American restaurant table. In Europe, the party of two would sit at one end of the table, and another two or three would sit at the other end. And if need be, someone would sit at the last remaining place at the table. However, why it works in Europe, for better or worse, is because people keep to themselves. In most cases the only exchange would be a curt head nod from the person taking the seat. In America we feel, for better or worse, compelled to talk to each other. "How are you?" we ask in passing. The opportunity usually only presents enough relative time to say "Good," though that isn't always the truth. So a European can sit across the table or next to you on a train and not say a word to you, and everyone is comfortable with the silence.

My food, just like fresh pizza, was tortuously hot, forcing me to tolerate patience. It's funny how that scenario alone makes hunger grow by the second, making the moment of consumption that much more satisfying. On a Paris trip a few years before, I had learned about how the French practice a meal ritual. At a restaurant or a dinner party, each individual in the party doesn't just look at the menus—they discuss menu options. Then when they decide, they discuss with the group just what they are ordering and why it appeals to them. All senses are used for the meal. The service is slow to arrive at the table; Americans would call it bad service. In France and other Euro areas, the wait staff isn't there to interrupt the dining experience; they are there to make it happen... be a part of it, but not an unnecessarily intrusive part. When Americans sit down, often times it's simply to get the food to the gut as quickly as possible. And sometimes that makes culinary sense too.

I finished my meal and scraped at the paper side of the container with the tip of my chopstick, getting the last specks, a peanut chunk and a bit of mushroom. I was hungrier than I thought, proven by the fact I easily finished the order. Europe can do that to you. Much of the continent is fit. Not so much from diet, but from the everyday modes of transportation, mainly by bike or foot. The body can take on more calories because it will put them to use.

I left the restaurant and crossed the street to a small market. I needed deodorant and shoe powder if they had it. Shoe odor can grow quickly and take over a pair of shoes; and in tight quarters, if it's not your shoes that stink, you'll want the stuff handy. Our shoes have worked overtime for several days now, best be prepared. I paid the clerk, a friendly older man with white hair. He said, "Oi'" for hello, thinking I was a local.

"Hello," I said.

"Ahh, American," he said with clear English. "I met Americans during World War II."

"You're a vet?" I asked, surprised that though he was geriatric, he seemed young for a war vet.

"Yes," he replied, "but not of World War II. My big brother Michal—Mike—fought the Nazis," he said with an expression of pride and sadness. You could almost see the child inside him through his eyes at the thoughts he was running through his head. "He vas part of the exiled Dutch military—a captain." He paused for a second but I didn't intervene, as I knew it was important to him to get the thoughts out. "He vas not happy vith the lack of resistance our country put up when the Germans invaded." I wanted to ask questions but felt I should just let him tell what he wanted to tell and not prod. He continued, "Looking back, perhaps the pacifists' road was all we could do at that point against such a dark machine. But that never set vell vith Mike, so he joined a resistance group—and got himself hanged."

I wasn't ready for that. We both sat silent for a second, almost as if we were talking about something that had happened last week. "Vhat part of America you from?" the clerk asked, smiling and bringing us back to the present. "California," I said.

"Ahh, do you know any movie stars?" he asked with genuine interest.

"No," I said with a smile. Though I probably should have just lied to him. "I did see Arnold Schwarzenegger walking down the street once," I said, recalling a day at Venice Beach.

"Ter-mi-na-tor," the old man said with an attempt at a tough, strong voice.

"Yup, that's him," I said. "You had mentioned that you had met some Americans years ago. Has it been that long since you have come across another one?"

"Oh, heavens no, I've met several Americans over the years, but I met my first when I was seven. They were impressive, the type of people the world should have strived to be," he said as he glanced off in memory. Then he came back and looked at me, "Though no self-respecting European would admit such a thing," he said as he laughed at his own joke.

"Americans are probably different today than they were when you admired them so much," I said, "though no self-respecting American would admit to such a thing."

"Ahhh!" the shopkeeper said, his eyes looking gleeful with the play on words. "That's funny—the American sense of humor," he said, almost beaming with pride at the fact he had grasped it. "Well, you know, people are people. If the world called on America for a cause, like stopping a rolling tyrant, America would answer." Those weren't the typical words you'd expect to hear in modern Euro descriptions of America.

"Sometimes I think the world has forgotten what we did with Hitler. I mean, the French oftentimes seem to despise us for it," I said.

"But that is where you are wrong," the shopkeeper said, looking down his nose and over his bifocals at me with an expression that would be followed by something that needed to be understood.

"Listen to me," he said. A customer approached the register. "Oi," the clerk said to the lady. "Oi," she repeated in greeting. He got a couple of pieces of fruit and a cut from a cheese round. They spoke a couple of words in Dutch, and the customer moved on.

The clerk came back to me. "There are a couple of things Americans need to remember," he said, sounding like a lecturing professor. "One: the Russians have just as much right to claim that their efforts ridded the world of Hitler. They suffered gravely on the war front which came to their front door." Then he stopped all of a sudden. "Forgive me; what is your name, son?" he asked in the charming Dutch way, realizing we had been in deeper discussions than the ones he was typically prepared to engage in.

I smiled and felt warm. "Major," I said. He stuck out his hand.

"I'm Rob," he said. The name was pronounced sounding somewhere in between rope and rob. "Can I offer you some tea?" he asked.

I accepted, though typically I'd be inclined to pass, but the moment seemed too sweet to pass up. Rob nodded and slipped out of sight in the back of the store. I could hear the clang of tea cups as I glanced around the store and outside to the gray, late-afternoon weather. "Ahh, Major," Rob announced a moment later as he set a cup of hot water on a saucer in front of me. He then pulled up a wooden box, opened the top and presented me with a half-dozen tea bags of various flavors.

"I'll take the Earl Grey," I said, announcing my selection. "Good choice," Rob said as he continued to pick his selection.

"I'll have a Pickwick." "Pickwick?" I asked.

"Sure, it's a popular Dutch tea," Rob said.

"Well then, let's make it two," I said.

"Ahh... better choice," he said as I exchanged my English tea bag for a Dutch. We sat silently for a minute while we opened up the tea envelopes, setting free the bags to be steeped. "Okay, where were we?" Rob asked.

"Russia's war effort," I said.

"Yes, yes, okay. As I said, that population was exposed to human savagery; everyone over here was. If it weren't for that tough Russian rage—and winter—Hitler might have very well taken it all." He pulled his tea bag from the water and placed it on his saucer; I did the same. We both slurped a small sip of the tea, its temperature still too hot to drink.

"What's the second thing Americans need to know?" I asked as I had grown intrigued by the conversation—or lesson, I should say. "Americans need to know, many of us remember and most of us know that if it weren't for the United States' efforts, Hitler might have very well taken it all. And your country sacrificed much too," he said and took another sip of tea. "However," he continued, "for it to be continually flaunted in the faces of, say, the French, begins to almost become rude."

"Yeah, I understand what you are saying, but there are frustrations in America about how the French rolled over," I said, trying to defend the crude behavior of Americans abroad.

"There was a lot of frustration by all of us about how the French and other nations laid down their arms to the war machine," Rob said. "But that is over and done. Much of the French realize things should have been done differently. They weren't, and it's tough enough to live with that knowledge than to have to be reminded of it, usually by an American who is too young to have fought in any war."

I took a larger sip of my tea. It was at a manageable temperature to get down, where you can enjoy the warmth and taste simultaneously. "I see your point," I said to Rob.

"And remember, Major, had it not been for the French in your Revolutionary War, you wouldn't have had your country at all." Another point made, not really driven home back home. "Yes, Europe's debt to you is fresh in the timeline of wars, but nobody is perfect when it comes to war."

The tiny bell above the door rang out another entry. An elderly lady walked in. Rob greeted her as a friend more than a customer, a sweet-looking old lady with white hair and a navy-blue scarf on her head. Rob approached her gently and took her hand. He spoke warmly to her, and she smiled and returned the gesture of kind communication though I couldn't understand what was being said. Rob picked up a basket and took the old lady by her arm and gently walked with her. He would say a single word and motion in the direction of produce and then on to dairy. I heard him say "brood" just as they walked to a shelf that had bread. And then "bier," which sounded a lot like what it was. To my surprise he opened a refrigerated cabinet and grabbed a large bottle of beer with a resealable porcelain cap, then rearranged the basket contents and placed the beer away from the bread, so as not to crush it. They then headed to the register. As they passed me, Rob stopped and said what turned out to be an introduction; I recognized it as such when I heard him end the sentence with "Major" and "American." Her eyes squinted and sparkled with a kind smile. "How do you do?" she asked with some effort in the foreign tongue.

"Goed, dank je," I said. I had picked up the Dutch words for "good" and "thank you." She and Rob looked at each other with smiles, as parents might do when their toddler speaks a new word. She then took her items that Rob had loaded into her worn, reusable grocery bags and shuffled out the door.

"Ah, you've picked up on some Dutch," Rob asked.

"Not much, a couple words—like 'bier,'" I said with a smile, as I had just picked that up while in the store.

"Ha!" Rob let out. "That's an important one."

"Yeah, I heard you say it to your customer," I said. "It's a little surprising to see an old lady buying a big bottle of beer."

"It's not uncommon for the elderly to drink, but it's not to get *messed up*," he said, taking on an American accent while impersonating the youth. A laugh escaped me, as the words looked so unnatural coming from him, it made the moment comical. Rob laughed at himself too. "No, she and most others do it for nostalgic reasons," he said. "Her husband died a couple of years ago. That was his beer—she drinks it for him—for the memory the taste brings back." I understood what he meant… the way a smell, a color or the weather can instantly take you back decades. The closest thing to time travel that there is.

"Do you know why it is good to pick up a few words of local dialect when traveling?" Rob asked.

"So one can always find a beer?" I responded jokingly.

"Ha," Rob said, again. "No, and it's another travel mistake Americans make."

"What's that?" I asked.

"When Americans travel abroad, let's use France as another example," Rob said. "Americans land in Paris, far from home, and go around asking everyone, 'Do you speak English? Do you speak English?' Now why do they assume everyone has the potential to speak their language in a place where English isn't the official language?" he explained. "You know?" he asked, sounding like a drinking buddy instead of the gentle shopkeeper I had just met.

"I get what you are saying. The people who come from the country that says, 'This is America; speak English,' want people who live in France to speak English."

"Exactly," he said, as he took another drink of his tea. I followed suit. My cup was over half gone and just warm enough to take a mouthful without a burn.

"But you can't expect foreign visitors, which are a blessing to local economies, to pick up enough of the language to communicate," I said, defending the American practice.

"Yes, you are absolutely correct," Rob said, agreeing with my point. "But if you learn basic words—'hello' and 'thank you'—it will take you far."

"But then what?" I asked.

"Then, after you have shown the humbleness of showing respect for the local language, they will appreciate your effort and in many cases begin to speak to you in your language."

"I see; that makes sense," I said, and it did. We walk around expecting everyone to speak our language. When was the last time you were approached by a European tourist in America and asked, "Tu parles Francais?" *No! Why the fuck would I speak French! This is America!* In Europe you learn the languages of your neighbors; it makes sense. In America, it's almost considered treason to push for another language. Love thy neighbor; just don't learn to communicate with them.

"Oops, I almost forgot," Rob exclaimed. "Here… here," he said as he opened a tin full of tea biscuits, thin waffle-style crisps Americans would call cookies. "You can't have tea without one," he said. I took one from the tin and broke some off with my teeth. "Good, eh?" Rob said.

"Yes," I found myself answering, at first out of courtesy, but immediately after as the flavor of the biscuit took hold, I said "yes," again. It was a magical encounter. I meant to go into a store, get in and out as quickly as possible, because that's how we are programmed. Instead I had an incredibly entertaining and enlightening conversation, which I can carry with me back to the New World and be broader in thought for it. The feeling gave me a beautiful inner value, as if I had just picked up a ruby and put it in my pocket.

I finished my tea and figured it was time to get back. It had only been a bit over an hour since I had left the poker game; I doubt much had changed in that time, but with Thomas' skill for the game, you never know.

"Rob, it was an absolute pleasure to meet and talk with you," I said, wanting as much earnestness in my voice as possible to drive the point home. "But I have to get back to the hostel to meet up with friends."

"It was very nice to meet you too," he said with a smile and eye contact. He stuck his hand out and I took it. I then leaned over to give him a hug. "My boy," he said. I think my presence served as a nostalgic reminder of the American servicemen he had met as a child. I was his proverbial bottle of beer at that moment, and he was a lantern for me of sorts, shedding light on dim areas.

149

I stepped back outside. The area shop and strung Christmas lights had been turned on, as the gray afternoon had been milked of its absorbed light and saturated into dark. I felt good about the dark and the cold. The market conversation had given me a new inner courage about things. The lecture was like a refresher course in mortality: the fear of death giving courage to live, the reality of life giving peace about death.

I walked back to the hostel to check in on things. I walked through the door and glanced to the check-in desk, hoping to see Natalie; but it was the same grump staring at the computer screen, not even looking up to see who walked through the door. I took a left and stepped into the great room. There were people scattered in their groups, but no poker game. *Had they moved?* The game couldn't have ended that quickly, could it? I've seen my share of card games move at a rapid pace, but it's certainly not the norm.

I headed to the room to see if I could find Thomas, which I ended up doing. He was lying on his back, headphones in, staring at the ceiling. He turned his head to look at me with the movement of a bedridden hospital patient, making me wonder if he had hit the hash pipe.

"What happened?" I asked, knowing I was going to ask again as soon as he pulled his earbuds out.

"Huh?" he said as he pulled his earbuds out.

"What happened? Did you take 'em?"

"Nope," he said, as he got out of bed and walked past me to the bathroom. I wasn't quick to press him because a poker wound is like a wound in body or heart, as there is a lot of agitation involved. He turned the sink water on, met his wet hand to his face and repeated the motion. The sink handle squeaked as he shut the water off. He turned and dabbed his face with the towel that hung behind him. He walked out, passed me again, walked to the window and picked up a joint, then lit it and drew deeply. Still holding his breath, he extended it to me. I took it and drew in as well.

He exhaled and stared at me for a second. "I thought I had it; my plan was working, faster than I could have imagined," he said. I didn't say anything to just let him decompress slowly. "With Bob out quickly, we were down to four. Frank was feeling 'proud and good,'" he said, mocking the KGB character from the poker movie Rounders. "So he was leaning on the table a bit and had bullied Mikhail out of a couple of hands," he said. Then he reached out for the joint I had forgotten I was holding. He relit it and took a drag but didn't hold this one long.

"Mikhail came back on Frank's third attempt to bully him and went all-in with pocket jacks, to Frank's king-ace. The river was all number cards aside from a queen. Frank stood up with such force I thought he had blown a gasket. But that was the extent of it. He smiled and said, 'Good play' to Mikhail and joined Bob at the bar." He handed the joint to me, and I relit it and inhaled.

"So play remained fairly level for about a half-hour. I wanted to create a little action, and I was big blind, so I stayed in with a 5-7."

"Suited," I asked, making sure I got the whole picture.

"Nope," he said. "The flop read 6-8-king, and he comes at me with a small bet, so I figured he had something to play with and was baiting me. The small bet was his mistake because the next card was my 4."

"Nice," I said.

"Right?" Thomas replied. "So he ups his bet, figuring he would attempt to buy the pot. I pause a bit and say, 'Okay, I'll pay that to see what you have.' The river gives another king, and he goes all-in."

"Wow," I said, wishing I had seen the showdown.

"Yeah, pretty intense," he said. "I figured he either had a king—or a pair of them. But—I don't know what it was, and I've only experienced the feeling so strong one other time—I knew I had him, and I knew it was a perfect opportunity to take him down, so I went all-in too, which didn't match his chips but would take three-fourths of them if I pulled it off."

"And what? He had cowboys?" I asked, the term used to describe a pair of kings.

"Nope… he had a king-8," he said.

"Awesome," I said, excited for him.

"Didn't matter," he said. A few hands later Rebekah took the rest of his stack and then on back-to-fucking-back hands, she cleaned me out," he said, his eyes looking past me. "I've never seen anything like it before."

"You're shitting me," I said. "Nope," he responded.

"Was she a legit player?" I asked, looking for an explanation. "No... at least I don't think so," he said. "I mean it happens—fuck, I mean hardly ever—but I guess today was ever."

I sat on my bunk and was hoping the loss wasn't going to put too much of a damper on the rest of his trip. "Where is she now?" I asked.

"She left for Central Station to meet some friends," he said. "They were going to head to The Hague for the night. She invited me, said she'd pay my train ride."

"Shit, why didn't you go, dude?" I asked. "You seemed a little into her."

"Fuck, dude—go and leave you?" Thomas asked. "G'day, mate!" he said, his eyes springing back to a man with no regrets. "I got her contact info, bro," Thomas said. "I'll be going to Australia soon enough; I got to win my money back somehow!"

"Cool, dude, I'm glad you didn't go but wouldn't have blamed you if you had."

"It's all good," he told me, "plus I worked out a good deal for us."

"What are you talking about?" I asked, wondering what he got us into.

"You know Bob and Frank from poker?" he asked. "Yeah."

"They rented a houseboat for the next couple of days in the Jordan District," he said.

"So?" I asked.

"They said we could go in on it if we want to get out of the hostel," he told me. "We can check out in the morning and spend our last couple of days on the boat."

"What's that cost?" I asked, wondering what we were getting into.

"It's only fifteen more euro a night each," he said with enough excitement in his voice for me to see he was looking forward to the offer.

"Alright, dude, since you hung back, we'll do it," I said. The offer sounded pretty cool and would put us in a new environment for the end of the trip. The Jordan was across the District about a mile-and-a-half away. It was an area with a little more artsy and fashion vibe to it. Cafés and retail, cheese and wine shops, trendy dinner spots. It was close to the intersection where I had enjoyed sitting and watching the morning rush of bikes a few days earlier. A lively area of the District with more locals' presence than tourist. The prospects of houseboat lodging started to become exciting as well. Lots of boats docked along a canal that runs through the heart of the District, a far cry from hostel lodging.

Chapter Ten

I woke the next morning to Thomas packing his bag. He shuffled around the room, picking up clothing like he was picking up litter. The room looked like a tornado had hit it, and much of our clothing was mixed. I felt pretty good because we had fallen asleep early the night before, and for the first time on the trip, I had slept the night through. It was almost 9 a.m.

"At it early, huh?" I asked, still lying prone in my bed.

"Yeah, I wanna get this stuff packed and get over to that boat," he said. I lay there and rubbed my eyes, then dropped my feet to the floor and sat up.

"What time we need to be outta here?" I asked.

"Eleven," he said as he bent over and picked up a shirt he half- assed folded and tossed in his bag. The good thing about the hostel was you could just check out and leave. There were no cancellation issues like in a hotel, so as long as we were out of the room by checkout time, we were good to go.

We got to the front desk; it was tended by a girl I hadn't seen there before. Thomas said we were checking out, and I asked about Natalie. "Natalie is on holiday," she told me, as she printed out our paperwork and charged our credit cards what we owed for the days we had stayed there. I didn't ask any more about Natalie; she, like many of the other European discoveries, had come and gone and vanished like a good dream you hope not to wake from.

We finished our business and headed to the other side of the District to our new declinational lodging. At the end of the block we caught our tram. As had become our custom, we didn't purchase a fare, just stood by the door in case we wanted to hop off quickly at any random stop where transportation officials might be stepping on to check for stowaways.

"Get off here," Thomas said.

"But we have one more stop before we need to get off," I said. "I know," he said, "just do it. I'll explain why." At that we quickly hopped off the tram, an eighth of a mile from the stop we needed.

"What's up?" I asked as soon as I could.

"I've been noticing rail officials waiting at the Grand Central Station stop each day during the lunch rush," he said. I had to stop and think what he was saying.

"Just come on," he said and we started walking. I carried my case at times; the round plastic wheels on my luggage announced us as tourists as they clacked along the brick paved street as I towed it. Thomas had his stuff in a large duffle that he carried. As we approached Central Station, I realized just what Thomas was saying. In front of the main stop at the station, police-looking officials were checking people's tickets, making sure the fare had been paid.

"Ahhh?" Thomas asked at my *ah-ha* moment. He had picked up on the routines of the rail staff operators. We had outsmarted them—this time—but I had heard the penalty was stiff if caught. Thomas's move may have just cut down the ultimate cost of the trip by hundreds.

"Nice move," I said and stuck out my fist for a fist-bump. He gave me one and then looked down at the map.

"This way," he said, and we started our walk again. According to the map and the address Frank had left with Thomas, we could walk a few blocks to the boat. So we set out.

"Let's get an espresso," I suggested.

"Good idea," Thomas said so we stopped at a small sidewalk café. I went in and Thomas stayed out front watching the bags. I returned with the coffee, and we just sat silently and sipped them. The late morning air was still fresh with promise.

We finished the drinks, discarded our cups and began our walk again. After a couple of blocks, we began walking along a canal. Boats were docked on both sides of the waterway. Thomas was looking at the posts that showed addresses. "This should be it coming up," Thomas said, while he was walking and keeping his eye on the slip numbers. "Yup, here it is," he said. We studied the boat silently for a second.

"It's kinda small," I said as I eyed it. Many of the other houseboats were bigger crafts; most had an appearance of charm and several were built on old low-decked barges, now decorated in ways that added beauty to the canal, rather than distracted from it. Ours was visibly smaller, but still a solid-looking boat. It was more of a traditional houseboat, a rectangular housing structure built on top of a floating platform.

"It's bigger than our hostel room," Thomas said, which was a great way to look at it. We approached the door and used the doorknocker. In America, doorknockers are more ornate than functional. In Europe, many doors are as solid as slate and tough on the knuckles. The knock on the boat door sent vibrations through the wood at our feet.

"Heeeeyyy, guys," Frank said, opening the door with a big welcoming smile. "You find the place alright?" he asked, as he sidestepped the door and motioned for us to come in.

"Yeah, no problem at all," Thomas answered as he stepped in first. Once inside, like most trailer space, the boat looked bigger. The living room, which was smartly decorated, was a studio set-up. A sectional couch lined the corner, a TV on the wall, a large area rug, small dining table and kitchen all fit by intelligent design in a twenty-foot by ten-foot section. The other ten feet of housing held the bathroom and the single bedroom, which had two comfortable-looking cots.

We looked around for where we should put our stuff. "There's actually a small basement in this place," Frank said.

"Yeah?" Thomas replied.

"Yeah, check it out," Frank said as he walked into the small kitchen area and opened a rectangular door that had a stair ladder descending into a five-foot-deep area, complete with enough storage to stack a few suitcases and a washer/dryer in one unit.

"It doesn't work," Frank said, answering my question before I could even ask. "But it's a great area to store your shit," he said. "There is a closet with enough space to put some of your clothes in; we left some in the cases down there," which was all good planning if four guys were going to coexist on the vessel.

"I was just about to go to a farmers' market to pick up some food to cook," Frank said. "Anyone want to come with me?" he asked.

"Naw," Bob said from the couch.

"I knew your lazy ass wasn't getting off the couch," Frank said. "I actually saw a laundromat a block down," Thomas said. "Seeing that machine reminded me I need to take care of some tthings."

"Hey, if I pay your laundry fees, will you do a bag for me?" I asked Thomas. He looked sideways at me, not too excited at the prospect, but agreed.

"Thanks, dude," I said and pulled out fifteen euros and handed it to him.

"I doubt I'll need that much," he said, "but if I gotta be this close to you, I'd better help you out."

"Can you help me out too?" Bob jokingly asked from the couch.

"Don't push it," Thomas said back to Bob, playing along. "What about bikes?" Bob said from the couch.

"What about them? Oh, yeah, renting them," Frank answered, figuring out his own question in the process. "Hey, guys," Frank said, addressing us now, "we were thinking about renting bikes for a couple of days just to have for transportation."

"And to see the city with," Thomas broke in, already grasping the value of the move. "Yeah, let's do it," he said, looking at me, making sure I was in.

"Sounds good," I said.

"Good, let's go get them now," Frank said. "Our first usage will be to ride to Albert Cuyp," he said to me.

"Where?" I asked, having no idea what he was talking about. "Albert Cuyp, that's the name of the farmers' market I was talking about."

"Oh yeah, cool," I said. There was a bike rental place at the end of the block. Thomas and I had walked past it without noticing it on our way to the boat, but now it stood out as we neared it. We rented four bikes from a Dutchman who had a white boxer. I took it as a sign of sorts, being I had owned a white boxer named Blu on account of his having one blue eye. The owner of the place was a large guy, both in height and weight. But he wasn't a soft heavy, just a large man as many of the Dutch are. I told him about my dog; he seemed unimpressed. Sometimes the Dutch come across like assholes. Usually they aren't; they are just a culture that takes small talk for what it is and don't usually feed into it. For example, it irritates the Dutch when you ask "How are you?" in passing. They wonder why someone would ask a question that can't be honestly or fully answered in most instances. They are critical thinkers, which leaves them lacking the ability to recognize or appreciate sarcasm—for better or worse.

I didn't think having the same rare-breed dog was small talk. But maybe he just didn't give a shit. It was no matter; we were out of there a few minutes later, sent to the back of the building where the bikes were stored in the bike-repair area of the building.

We stepped through the door; a small bell announced our presence. A salt-and-pepper-haired man wearing oval spectacles appeared.

His hands and apron were black with bike grease and tire rubber, though somehow he managed to keep his collared blue shirt clean. "Hi, guysh," the repairman said, "do you have an order receipt?" he asked. Frank handed it to him. "Thank you," he said, as he then dutifully started collecting the bikes, picking each according to our sizes. He then handed each of us a bike lock. Being Amsterdam is a biking community, one of the most active on the planet, bike theft is high. Violent crime is almost non-existent, but bike theft is rampant. So rental bikes come with two locks. One is actually a heavy-duty bike chain and lock. Then, built onto the back wheel was a small contraption that would actually lock the wheel when activated. When you park the bike, you push the wheel lock in place and then the key is released from the lock. This key also operated the chain lock. This was important information, as it was explained to us that as long as we have that key in our possession, if the bike gets stolen, it proves the bike was actually locked and we would not be responsible for the loss. So there wouldn't be any *leaning the bike against a tree to quickly run into a store*. That's the exact behavior bike thieves wait for—just like jackals.

"You guys sure you don't want to go to the market with us?" Frank asked Thomas and Bob. "Naw, thanks," Thomas said, "gonna do that laundry."

"That's right, I forgot you said that," Frank said.

159

"I know your ass is just gonna go back and lie on the couch," Frank said to Bob.

"You got that right," Bob responded, affirming and not shying away from Frank's comment.

"Let's go," Frank said to me, and we were off. Very soon after my feet hit the pedals, I realized what a great idea bikes were. Though it was late November, even Amsterdam is susceptible to a late dying gasp from the mild weather of autumn. It was a sunny day, though that could change at any time. For the ride we wore shorts and long-sleeved tees; it was a comfortable outfit. I followed Frank, as he knew where he was going. "Turn left up here," Frank instructed, giving me several yards' notice before the turn. Houses passed us quickly as we made our way, covering two blocks in what would have been a half-block walking time. "Right," Frank said as we made another turn. The sound of the tires and the clank-clicks of the bike sprockets turning were the prominent noises heard, along with the pedal momentum wind that swirled the ears. We came to a stop in Leidseplein Square. Frank pulled out a small paper map.

"Okay, we're on the right track," he said, as if talking to the map. "How ya feeling?" he asked me.

"Not bad," I said, "but I'm sure tomorrow I'll have sore legs before this is over."

"Nah, we're just gonna cruise," he said. "We have less than a mile to go."

"I can handle that," I said.

"Alright, cool," Frank said and we were off again. We pedaled in line on a bike path that led us by The American hotel and then along a canal. On the other side of the canal was the Holland Casino and next to it a Hard Rock Café. Amongst the old, Gothic-charmed buildings, there were always signs of the West. "You see that?" Frank asked me over his shoulder.

"What? The Hard Rock?"

"No, the casino," he said, as he spun his torso the other way and pointed at the building.

"Yeah, saw that. I'm sure Thomas has found it, and if not, I'm sure he's going to," I told Frank.

"I wouldn't mind checking it out later either," he said. "Then again, you need money to go into those places," he said, and then he let out his now-familiar laugh. We continued to pedal, past the iron sign that signified the entrance to Vondelpark, a large area with ancient trees. We rode by the Heineken brewery, which was actually the old brewery we found out when we stopped in front of it. It now served as more of a Heineken museum, as the plant had moved and been updated some time ago.

"I think it should be right down this street," Frank said, and a block later he was right. We parked and locked the bikes, using both bike chains as we locked them together, and began our walk. The market took place along the street. Vendors were on both sides of the street, with the center walkway open for foot traffic.

"Looks cool," Frank said, making an early assessment. "Yeah, let's check it out," I said, and we began our walk.

"I'm looking to get some specific items to cook a big meal tomorrow for us," Frank said. The comment reminded me that he was, in fact, a trained chef.

"That will be awesome," I told him, excited about the prospect. "What specific items are you looking for?" I asked, as we walked and maneuvered around people.

"Maybe I shouldn't have said 'specific,'" Frank said. "I just meant local flavors to incorporate into our Thanksgiving feast," he said, which stopped me in my tracks. I had forgotten that tomorrow was Thanksgiving. When we planned the trip, I knew we'd be in Amsterdam during Thanksgiving, but I hadn't given it another thought since touchdown.

"Dude, I completely forgot tomorrow was Thanksgiving," I said to Frank.

"Man—you've been over here too long," he said, smiling big at me about the moment.

"No shit," was all I could get out, as we started walking again. A small excitement grew inside of me, though, as I realized we had a chef for Thanksgiving—and we were in a Dutch farmers' market getting supplies.

"I just kinda want to walk along and see what kind of stuff they have for me to work with," Frank told me. We walked along; most of the tented tables had food items: vegetables, some fruits, cheese and in a trailer behind glass, various meats were displayed. Some set-ups had electronics or clothing displayed. I stopped at one that had leather jackets hung on display, though it wasn't the clothing that caught my eye. It was a rust-colored puppy on a leash, secured next to the cash register. It was clear he was from a large breed dog; his oversized paws on his small body lent him the clumsiness of a puppy, but the forewarning of size.

"I got to check out this dog, dude," I told Frank.

"No problem, man," he said. "I'm gonna go over to that meat truck and see what they have. I'll meet you back here."

"Cool," I said as we split paths. I walked up to the pup; his master stood close by, tending the register. "May I?" I asked, motioning my desire to pet the dog.

"Sure, sure," the middle-aged man said to me with a smile. "Pepe," he said to me, giving me the pup's name.

"Hi, Pepe," I said as I kneeled down to one knee and began lightly scratching under his ears. He held still for a moment, enjoying the rubs, but then he turned his head up towards my hands and playfully nibbled on my fingers. "What breed?" I asked the clerk.

"Bordeaux Mastiff," he said.

"Ahh, he's beautiful," I said as I continued to let him play-bite my fingers while I scratched his chest. He was careful not to bite too hard, though his puppy teeth were characteristically sharp and I'd retract my fingers at times to avoid too much of their piercing. He made a funny breathing sound as he would open his mouth and swirl his head in different directions trying to catch a part of my hand.

"Nine weeks," the clerk said to me, as it was clear I had taken an interest in Pepe.

"He's gonna be a big boy," I said as I looked up to the clerk; I rose to my feet to talk eye to eye with him.

"Yesh, he is," he said, his Dutch accent coming out in his conversation.

"Is this your shop?" I asked, wondering if he owned it or worked for someone. Some of the market items were displayed out in front of the permanent store behind the tent set-ups.

"Yesh, dis is my place," he said. "Been here eight years," he told me, as he motioned to show me his shop behind him.

"Okay, so you're well-established here?" I asked matter-of-factly about the amount of time the shop had been there.

"Yah, pretty much," he said, "but it's business; you never know," which was true. He went on to give me some interesting information about the Albert Cuyp market. The street, Albert Cuypstrat, was named after a 17th century painter, and the market carried the same name. It's arguably Europe's largest open-air market, created at the turn of the 19th century.

It was all good info, but in the end I slipped back down to a squat and loved on Pepe. He absorbed every bit and made me feel the moment had value for both of us. I let the shopkeeper show me a couple of jackets. I'd compliment each of his choices, but luckily my outstretched arms proved to be too long for the jacket's cut. I didn't want a jacket in the first place, but I thought it might be rude to not act interested.

Just as I turned to leave the place, Frank appeared. "What's up, buddy?" he asked with what was rapidly becoming his recognizable smile.

"Hey," I said, slightly surprised to see him. "How'd your shopping go?" I asked.

"Goood," he said, with a satisfaction that sounded like he got what he was looking for. "The butcher hooked me up—hooked *us* up!" he said.

"You find some of the stuff you were looking for?" I asked.

"Some? I found all of it," he exclaimed with his continued excitement. "I bought a couple of Cornish game hens and a small slab of pork belly and started talking to the guy. He turned out to be really cool, took me straight to another guy who had the produce I was looking for."

I was excited to see Frank excited because it sounded like we were going to have a meal to remember. "You need anything else?" I asked.

"I need to stop at one other place to pick up some spices, butter and bread," he said. "The butcher told me where I can get them in one place. Then we kinda need to bolt. The meats I bought will save for a little while, but I don't want to push it." It then dawned on me; Frank's hands were empty.

"Where's your groceries?" I asked. He twisted his torso, and there on his back was a bulky stuffed rucksack.

"I needed one anyway," he said about the purchase. "I was so excited to shop here that I got ahead of myself on how to transport the stuff," he said, laughing at himself. We made the final stop at an actual market that was just around the corner from the Cuyp. There wasn't enough room in Frank's pack, so we purchased a reusable cloth bag, and I carried it back strapped to the carry-all on the back of the bike. The trip back to the boat seemed quicker than the original ride out to the market. Probably because the surroundings were becoming familiar, and the second pass of the same drive always seems quicker.

"Hi, guys!" Frank announced on our return visit as we stepped through the threshold of the boat's door.

"Find some good stuff?" Thomas asked.

"Oh yeah," Frank said, "gotta start prepping it today for tomorrow."

"Yeah, I was wondering what we were gonna do for Thanksgiving," Thomas said.

"I fucking forgot it was tomorrow," I said.

"Jesus, you already fry your brain?" Thomas asked.

"No shit," I said. "It's just getting over here, you totally lose track of days and times."

"Yeah, I hear ya. I forgot too until a day or two ago," Thomas said, affirming my reasoning for forgetting. It was a big culinary day, so there was no way Frank was going to forget.

"Hi, Bob," I said to him, as he sat quietly and unassumingly on the couch.

"What up?" he said. "Cool market?"

"Check this out," Frank interrupted with an announcement. He was holding up a cut of meat I couldn't recognize. It was the size and shape of an average Bible.

"What is it?" I asked.

"Bacon," he said, "pork belly." The foreignness of it was explained, as in America we usually see the cut sliced and vacuum-packed in plastic, not the whole cut of pork.

"This is the shit," Frank said of the meat; you could see he was excited about the preparation ahead. He went on to pull out a couple of gourds, two half-circles of cheese, a loaf of bread and other vegetables, with two freshly-cleaned game hens. "I figured the boat's oven wasn't big enough for a turkey, but these will work," he said as he sprinkled some kind of dry green herb on them, rewrapped them in their butcher paper and set them in the refrigerator. It looked like we were heading for a memorable meal.

"I'm gonna lie down for a bit," I said. "Mind if I take the bed, Frank?" I asked.

"Be my guest, bro; I'll be in here a while," he said.

"Let's go out and hit the bars tonight," Thomas suggested. The group agreed to the plan. I went to nap. I turned onto my side in the bed; it gave me a view of the canal's beautiful brackish waters and the neighboring boat across from us. It was a retired barge turned houseboat, with flaking gray paint with black trim and a rear deck that had red flowers in planters within green leaves. The contrast of the peeling paint and the beauty of the flowers summed up much of the artfully decaying beauty of Europe herself.

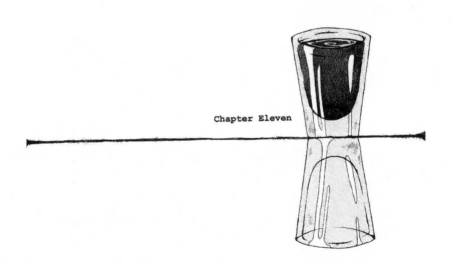

Chapter Eleven

"Here, drink this; it will wake you up," Thomas said to me as I sat up and tried to focus on him. He had a shot glass extended. I reached out and took it, and the recognizable smell immediately woke me up. It was tequila, and I knew that meant a storm was coming. So against my better judgment, I took the poison and downed it, as it would be better to arm myself rather than run from it.

"Feel better?" he asked with a tone that expected the answer to be "yes," but I just ignored him, handed the glass back to him and placed my feet on the wooden floor of the boat. He was right though, the shit woke me up—maybe not pleasantly, but it worked. My concentration was not on the grogginess of the moment, but on the concentration of taking deep breaths through my mouth to stave off the lingering taste, as well as to overload my lungs with oxygen to take the mind off the gag reflex.

I walked into the living room; it was teeming with life. The television was on with the volume down, some female weight clinging event was on Euro Sport. The Doors played on the stereo, and Frank was standing in the frame of the open double doors with a joint loitering on his lips.

"Good morning, sunshine," he said.

"What fucking time is it anyway? Don't you people have any decency?" I asked.

Bob just sat quietly on the couch and chuckled to himself.

"It's 8 p.m.; the night is young—here, take this," Thomas said. As I turned around, he was standing with another poured shot.

"Goddamn it, no," I said; but he was frozen with the shot extended, so I reached out to take it. The Rolling Stones' "Sympathy for the Devil" now came from the stereo play list; it was going to be a good night.

After my shot, Thomas poured two vodka red bulls and handed me one as I passed him on my way back to the bedroom to get dressed. Moments later we were stepping off the *Santa Cruz*, which we learned was the name of the boat. We had discovered it etched in the brass of the doorknocker. We started walking through the Jordan toward the

Red Light District. Bob handed Frank a freshly-rolled spliff, so we stopped and waited. Frank bit the tips off, rolled it in his fingers to even it out and lit it with a lighter he pulled from his pocket. He drew, inhaled and then exhaled the blue smoke that showed against the black sky. We each took a turn; the joint made two circles within the group, and then we continued on.

We walked in semi-silence for a while, just taking it in: the cobblestone streets of Amsterdam, looking at the centuries-old brick stacked homes and the graffiti, even the small amounts of litter that collected in doorways. It all had its beauty, its own art; it appeared to be choking with culture, a culture that a young America lacked for the most part. The Dutch in blood and culture are beautiful. We stand out because we wear baseball caps and T-shirts with thermal sleeves below; they dress with purpose. The men wear dark-blue woolen coats with earth-tone scarves. The women were beautiful, but not in the American way. In California the women strive for overt marks of beauty: make-up, high-dollar hair, nails and breast implants. When done right, it can catch the male eye—and penis, in an instant.

Here the women grab the eye, the heart and the spirit. They too wear woolen coats with sash belts, tan leggings tucked into leather riding boots. They have pinned hair and a light dusting of make-up which gives more of a look of innocence. They look like wildflowers as they ride by on their Old-World bikes, alerting you of their presence with a handlebar bell.

In no time we were in the District, which was less than a mile away from us. The area is fascinating; it has its own beauty and charm, with a twisted feel about things as you walk past a sports pub with ordinary-looking people who live in the neighborhood and then past a sex shop with a window display of graphic DVD boxes or pink dildos. Another door down is a coffee shop and then a Thai restaurant. The business pattern then repeats itself with revolving street cuisine and vice to fill the Sodomite instincts that still plague man to this day. The intriguing part of the neighborhood is how senior citizens and even children will run through the streets unfazed, healthily-desensitized to the garbage on display; taking the taboo out of something takes part of the fun away as well, which the Dutch have figured out is a good way to minimize vice's appeal.

We had already ducked into a couple of random pubs and drank our pints with a mission when we came across The Rock Planet. Europeans have a funny way of advertising to attract a certain crowd. I don't know if it is Americans specifically they think they are pulling in, or if it's those who want to experience something tied to the great spirit of the West, but a bar called The Rock Planet is clearly the mind genius of some over-educated Euro nerd who has traveled to the States and brought back wild stories about the famed Hard Rock Café or Planet Hollywood's star-studded clientele. "Listen—Americansh love thish kind of shit, man; they see thish sign, and dey will want to come in here."

"Four pints, my friend!" I told the bartender. Then I slammed my hand on the bar and shouted, "ROCK PLANET!" just to prove how well Americans reacted to the name of the place and threw up a hand for a high-five to Thomas. The server just kind of looked away. But hey, we were who they wanted to attract, the *cool* American patrons—or other foreigners who thought Rock Planet was a *cool* place to see *cool* Americans.

We continued to drink at the same pace and no sooner had we spent a moment in a place, we would spill onto the streets again. When we exited a pub, we each had to yell, "Rock Planet!" because we were *cool Americans*. Only a block later did we pass the Remember Café—where inevitably some Dutch guy told his friend, "When these Americans want to *remember* where they were, they will look at each other and shay, 'Remember Café, it'sh in the name.'" And the ownership would be so happy with themselves, figuring out Americans so easily.

As we wandered the crowded narrow streets of the District, an occasional small commercial van would force its way through the crowd along the narrow lanes, especially the canal side ones, that are about the width of an average alley. These commercial vehicles weren't the typical-sized vans you find in America, but more like modified smaller ones. The current one we were dealing with was aggressively advancing at a slightly faster pace than that of the pedestrians. It's funny, in Amsterdam, a town of pubs and coffee shops and rush-hour bike traffic, you hardly ever see a crash or collision. Obviously when you live in a country where you cannot sue someone blind, you have to pay attention to where you are walking. But this van was too much. I could hear the driver angrily talking to himself, "These fucking people don't know when to get out of the way."

Something had to be done. So as everyone else wisely cleared his path, I didn't. I acted as if I were preoccupied with something, and I let his front bumper slightly brush the side of my leg. But I made it appear it made me buckle and fold onto the side of the hood. "MY GOD!" I yelled as I rolled away from the vehicle. I could hear concerned banter coming from the crowd, mixed with the laughter of friends. The driver, who had a large pink shaved head, became flushed with red.

"Think he got your point?" Thomas asked.

"Fuck if I know, for Christ sake, that guy almost killed me!" "Oh yeah?" Thomas asked in a casual tone. At that, we continued our walk along the canal, which shimmered with red-light reflections that were rippled when a group of swans swam through them. As we passed a long line of Red-Light windows, I got lost in thought about the purveyors of the strip. Who were they? What were their hearts made of? Rage, pain, sorrow, tragedy, loneliness, hate, survival? What brought them here? Has love been melted away from their heart's wick? Did any enjoy what they did? Could they still love? Has sex become a chore? Could it be differentiated when they were with someone else, someone they cared about?

The Red-Light ladies appear as any stretch of used autos might. You have something for everybody, from the Ferrari to the Buick. You can find some of the most beautiful, sleek women on the planet behind a window, and a block later you will pass some plump Filipino woman who you would think could starve in the profession, but her girth and ability to pay rent proves someone is paying to drive. Some just look past you, making you the ghost that you are. Others talk on their cell phones with the typical look of bored phone chitchat. Some wink at you, sensually beckon you with a finger or a soft shoulder throw or a tongue point to the side upper lip. And even though some playfully beckon a man as he wished they would in pubs, couldn't these sirens be some of the planet's meanest creatures? To toy with love for profit, to pervert the emotion, to believe the lifestyle will not haunt them one day if they live to old age. There is tragedy here, masked with the happiness a vice can provide, the very representation of the Drama Masks.

Could they be some of the planet's purest? In their profession there isn't much room to be a hypocrite. Maybe that's why Jesus loved Mary Magdalene. She was who she was, did what she did, condemned no one, judged no one just as the Bible instructs us. In reality, perhaps being a used-car salesman is far worse than being a prostitute. Preachers are pimps of another color.

But no time for the world's problems; we were here to join the party, to contribute, to feed the beast whose only existence is to drag us down to Hell—to turn us into donkeys. But no time to worry about that either; if we were destined for Hell, we may as well earn our spots. Personally, I've always lived a life that would get me to purgatory, and I would be satisfied with that outcome.

We were on the edge of the Red Light District when a pub window-dressing caught my eye. There were a couple of iconic artists painted on the large glass pane. One was Bob Marley; another was Jim Morrison, singer for the classic rock band The Doors. The window was also displaying different tag lines that, once again, some Dutch kid was asked how Americans speak. Things like "Double Reggae" and "Come in, but don't fuck around" were neatly painted on the window backed by the red, yellow and green of the Rastafarian flag.

"Wow, not single reggae, but *double*," Thomas said, giving me a sarcastic flash of impressed wide-open eyes. "Let's go in and have a drink—but not fuck around." This made us all laugh.

"Irie, mon," Frank broke in with a Jamaican accent, "let's get us some double-dose of reggae, mon." Which caused us to laugh just as we had recovered from laughing at Thomas' joke. Thomas was holding the door open and we walked in. The place was a medium-sized bar and wasn't quite half-full. It was fairly dark with the concentration of the lights coming from above the bar. The other lights in the room were dimmed to barely give off a glow. In the back corner of the bar were a few slot machines, of all things. I'd seen them in other establishments, but not in many… probably places that had once had a permit that grandfathered them into being allowed to have the gambling devices on the property.

We walked back to the corner where the slot machines were. Not so much to play them, but because there was some open space back there.

"I'll get this round," Frank said, stepping up to the bar. Bob joined him to help him carry the drinks. Thomas and I took a couple of stools and slid them up to two more so we had our own spot set up. Moments later,

Frank and Bob were approaching us, and I could see they had shot glasses in their hands with dark liquid inside.

"Jagermeister, boys," he announced. I felt my throat squeeze, the physical reaction to my body understanding what I was about to put into it. I looked at Thomas and gave a stressed-face look. He understood what I was getting at. The first time I ever had Jager was years before. The first taste of it somehow seemed enjoyable—reminding me of black licorice. That all ended the night I drank until I puked it all up, instantly losing any taste I had for it. But shit, Frank spent a pretty penny on the shots; sometimes you've just got to have balls and swallow what you get.

"Cheers, fellas," Frank said as we clanked the shot glasses and took our medicine. A couple of noises of struggle escaped from the mouths of the group after we had downed them. I was surprised, though; it went down much smoother that I had anticipated—clearly a sign I was already more drunk than I realized and a good sign I'd be barfing my contents later that night.

"Ahh, smooth," Thomas said with the same sarcastic vigor he had showed for the term "Double Reggae." Frank and Bob took their seats. "I'll get us a round of beers," Thomas said, stepping away and towards the bar. Frank and Bob were talking about something I couldn't quite hear. I looked around; the slot machines caught my eye. There were two, side by side an arm's length away from me. They were the older-school video style, and I noticed one of them was registering with twelve credits, roughly three euro or four bucks American. There was no one around, so I reached over and hit "spin" and won a few more credits. I hit it again and a couple more rang in. I stopped and looked around, and there was still no one around to contest the machine. By the time Thomas had returned with the pints, I had it up to about twelve bucks.

"Hey, check this out," I told Thomas.

"Huh, yeah?" he asked, not quite sure why I was telling him to look at a slot machine, something he's looked at a thousand times in his life.

"I started out with a couple bucks in it… of some credits someone left behind."

"Cool," he said with a mixture of genuine and false excitement. "Hit it a couple of times for me for continued luck," I told him. He reached over and casually hit the "spin" button. Bing bing, the machine signaled another two-credit winner. "See," I told Thomas, affirming we were onto a strategy.

"It's all yours, bro," he said as he went back to drinking his beer, not interested in playing right then. Over the next few minutes it went up and down, and I was on about eleven dollars up when an Asian kid approached me.

"I was on that," the twenty-something guy told me. His voice wasn't stern or challenging, but he also didn't exactly sound like he was trying to sell me the story either. I was a little dumbfounded, like when you go to the bathroom and come back to your bar stool and in those couple of minutes someone has taken your seat. But it had been longer than a couple of minutes.

"Wha'd he say?" Thomas asked, leaning over to me so he could hear my words, while keeping his eye on the guy.

"He said he was playing this machine," I told Thomas, hoping he would respond with something that reaffirmed my feelings of telling the guy to *fuck off*.

"Cool, man," was all he said; then he lightly bumped me. "Let's split anyway; this place is kinda dead," he said. And we just filed out of the place onto the next stage of the evening. I was a little confused why Thomas gave up the machine so easily, but I kept it to myself; I figured he knew it wasn't worth any trouble. The night air had a refreshing chill to it when it met my skin, probably because I had the sweats from that last shot, and the air temp played well off of it.

"You want some of this?" Bob said, as he nudged me with a steel flask. I didn't say anything or ask what it was. I was just happy to have an instant drink to help keep the party going. I put the lips of the flask to my mouth and poured. The instant familiar and bitter oak taste of whiskey registered quickly but didn't slow down the process. I filled my mouth with a healthy shot plus of the stuff and swallowed—followed by a few deep breaths through the nose. I handed the flask back to Bob, who instantly handed it to Frank and then passed to Thomas. When Bob's flask was returned to him, he tilted his head back and poured, probably more than any of us took. He tilted it until it dripped empty into his mouth. "Thanks for leaving me some," he said to the group with a sheepish smile.

We continued to walk and eventually were spit out on the edge of The Dam Square in front of the nobility of the former Dutch Palace. Thomas began to barter with two pedal-bike taxis. "We want you two to race to the Leidsepline," I heard him saying.

"Yes-yes?" the bike driver said, figuring out what Thomas was saying as the locals always do after a five-second pause.

"Yeah, there—how much?" Thomas was in heavy barter mode, or maybe I should say promotion mode, as I knew what he was thinking and the costs of the service were not the immediate issue.

"Fifteen euro," the driver said with an Eastern Block accent. His short, dirt-brown hair could put him as a foot soldier in a Polish army.

"Fifteen for both bikes?" Thomas said in a way that showed surprise at the low fare.

"No, each rider."

"So sixty euro total for the four of us?" Thomas said again, but with more frustration, as this time the price was too high.

"No, you pay he'm fifteen, you pay mee fifteen."

"Sooo thirty, huh?" Thomas studied the situation. "Okay, here is what we will do," Thomas started to lecture the drivers with full concentration on the production. "The winning driver will get twenty euro; the loser gets ten." Then he turned to the group, "And the losing passengers have to pay the entire fare." He delivered that part of the message with the tone you would expect a gambler to use, especially when the total is about fifty American bucks, which would take a serious chunk out of somebody's nightly drinking money.

Frank and I immediately took the bet, more so for the need to win, not the option of losing. I approached the Polish driver—he comes from a tough region; he had to have some heart. "Can you beat this guy?" I said in a low tone.

"Yeah," he said, affirming my question with more of a confident nod so as to give his truth without his partner hearing him. I had already bred some confidence into our horse—a strong shot of adrenaline—and he knew, though not directly, that his male pride was now based on his words.

"GOOOO!" Thomas yelled, forcing Frank and me to jump into the cart. They had the advantage of announcing the start of the race from a seated position, but we had a three-foot advantage, and that was all it took for our driver to take an angle and then the lead. The start was intense; it felt just like the beginning of any athletic competition I had participated in—a strange focus on the task, the mind and body forced to perform in a Darwinist fashion or perish.

"Listen, you know why we're not going to lose, Frank?" I said, loud enough for the driver to hear as to keep him in the huddle without asking for his direct attention. "It's a little cold out tonight, but certainly not enough to warrant earmuffs." Frank looked at me and nodded, like a fullback receiving a play. "Our driver isn't wearing any earmuffs—and do you know why, Frank? Because our driver isn't a pussy."

"YEAH'AH!" Frank yelled and turned to flip off the cart on our tail.

"That's it, man, pound those legs!" I said, as I gave him a reaffirming pat on the shoulder that served as a jockey's whip to the ass. He continued, giving me a nod with his head bobbing, as a cyclist may do to deliver extra power before a climb. Our bike had four wheels; the other had three. That gave them the advantage of speed, but not handling. Our driver obviously knew the closest route to the square, and the fact that our competitor stayed behind us proved this. Most of the race so far had covered small roadways or alleys where passing wasn't an option.

"Slow down right there," Frank said to the driver. "Wait—what?" I said, in a sort of shock. *Why was Frank telling him to slow down? He didn't know where the fuck we were going! Why in the hell would he say that?* I turned to look back; CHRIST, they were right on our tail, able to make a move at the next intersection. Just as I turned around into the cart to question Frank, I heard the sound of chain steel dragging over

175

hollow pipe, followed by a crash and then this loud cackle of laughter from Frank. He had reached out as we were moving and pulled a bike over that fell into their path. I quickly swung back around to get a good look over my other shoulder as to what was happening. I saw Bob, his shadowed silhouette in front of his bike, clearing the path. What struck me as odd was the fact that Bob was looking at us as he picked up the bike, as opposed to just concentrating on getting the bike up quickly—or quicker, I should say. Frank had made his crude and cliché Hollywood chase move that proved to be brilliant in nature, the proverbial slip-and-fall on a banana peel. He and I were now doubled up in laughter, so much so it was starting to hurt; I even heard the driver hum laughter to himself as he pedaled on. "NIICCCE–NIICCCE, FUCKERS," I could hear Thomas yelling, as their goddamn bike had already gained on us. We were winning on pure desire by our driver; the three-wheeler was built just too quick. One open intersection and they would have the opportunity to pass. At that instant we came across a stalled delivery van at the next side street we turned onto; the driver was waving a flashlight to guide bike and car traffic in an organized manner so we had to slow. Their driver had a choice: stay behind us and bank on an opening or circumvent the clog and take an alternate route and use the maneuver to save enough time to make it worth the move. Their driver turned left, cutting off the traffic that inched along. We couldn't follow if we wanted to. They were already off; we slowly flowed along, watching them pedal past us on the opposite side of the road and canal. Just then the white Mercedes in front of us pulled forward and around the stall, opening our right turn up.

"PUSH THIS FUCKER!" I ordered as Frank bailed out the other side to give our driver a power start. They had rounded the corner and were approaching a wider part of the street; a pass here would give us no chance. Our driver's legs turned over like overworked pistons getting the job done. It allowed us to pull it off; we again were able to take an angle on them and foil their hole-shot maneuvering. Our driver did it as the other driver locked his brakes from the move. "Kulta lul," he yelled at our driver, who again was in a head-bobbing stride and humming laughter to himself.

"PLEASE FEEL FREE TO STEP IN FRONT OF THE BIKE CHASING US!" I would say as we passed people. "THEY ARE FILTHY AMERICANS WHO ARE CHASING AND INSULTING OUR CANADIAN WAY OF LIFE!" It's not like I expected anyone to listen or act on the request, but you never know; and, as I said, we needed to win this thing and I was willing to try any angle.

"OUT!" Frank yelled as we hopped out again and pushed the bike up the arching road that crossed over the canal. We jumped back in on the down slope. Thomas and Bob were now copying our effective move, but it wasn't working to their advantage. I knew when Thomas grabbed Bob immediately after making the wager, he was thinking about the lower body weight. Thomas weighs about what I do, around 250; Frank is stout and solid, around 225. Bob is wiry and 150 pounds before taking his morning shit, so it seemed like a smart move. But Bob could not keep up with Thomas' long powerful strides; and though he got out and gave it all he had, his grip on the bike was used more for keeping the bike cart from getting away from him as opposed to giving any help. For Frank and me, it was like pushing a spring football sled.

We shot out of an alleyway right onto Liedespline Strat. This was the widest road we would travel, as it carried two-way traffic; but at this hour, it was all foot traffic, aside from the public transit metros that occasionally paced the drive. Our driver was able to make a sharp cut left, establishing the inside lane for the last half-block to go; the pursuants came out behind us but had to make a wider turn, which was a fatal flaw, as this forced them to cut behind and around a large group of hostel nomads with bags in tow. We had twenty yards on them; our horse pumped, throwing his entire weight into his efforts. "That's it, beat those fuckers who bet against you!" I was in his ear, making him want to win, giving him the reasons. "My friend picked him over you and then placed a bet. You can't lose this; you and I couldn't live with the fact!" His body's entire torso was thrown into each revolution of the pedals. It very much was like being in a horse race; our horse's nose was flared, the finish line in view. The pedestrians looked like the track crowd. They were on their feet—waving their wager, white paper dreams in the air. The underdog was about to pull it off and pay us well; you could hear both drivers breathing with everything their lungs could give by design, and then it was suddenly over—we had won by a length!

Our horse was exhausted, breathing to capacity and smiling. Thomas made good on the bet. He paid both drivers, tipping his well enough to keep the wages fair. I shook our driver's hand and gave him seven euro for his performance. He had a pride in his eyes—and why shouldn't he? He'd earned it; he's drinking milk in the winner's circle tonight.

Chapter Twelve

I woke up the next morning to the smell of frying pan butter and a throbbing headache, two sensations operating at both ends of a spectrum. I heard the sound of a steel utensil tapping cleanly on the side of a glass bowl, and it became clear; Frank was starting our Thanksgiving Day meal early. At least I thought it was early. I checked my phone for the time and was surprised I had slept until 10 a.m, the latest I had slept the entire trip. I was sore, the soreness that is typically beyond being hungover. My muscles hurt; my neck was stiff. Jesus, what had I drunk to deserve this? But through the soreness, I had a slight excitement about it being Thanksgiving, the first I had felt on the trip, even though I had forgotten it was coming. However, the pleasant thought of cooking butter and feast day wasn't detracting me from my headache—it's what I deserved anyhow.

I rifled through my shower bag for some aspirin. I poured four of them in my mouth and started chewing them up. It was a trick my older brother taught me when he went away to college. "Chew up the aspirin; it goes into your system faster," he said. And being he was going away pre-med, I figured it was sound advice. The first several times I did it, I remember the taste being so bitter, it was almost intolerable. However, I had grown to like the taste. Just as in life I had grown to like the taste of wine and coffee.

"Good morning, sunshine," Frank said with his big smile; he was able to look me in the eyes while rapidly whisking a tilted bowl of eggs in his hand. The simple act showed his polished skill in his craft.

"Good morning, bro," I said. At that moment I instantly realized I didn't remember going to bed. Fuck, what did I remember?

"How ya feeling?" Frank asked, as he was looking down while rapidly chopping up chives. Between watching that and figuring out what my answer would be to his question, I didn't have the chance to figure out when I had blacked out the night before.

"My fucking head is killing me," I told him as I rubbed where the bridge of my nose met my forehead.

"There's some Advil in my shower bag if you need it," he said. "Thomas said you had quite the adventure last night."

"Yeah—we all did, right?" I asked.

"For a while," Frank said, "until you guys came home and got on the bikes."

"I'm good; I just took something a couple of minutes ago," I told him about his offer for the Advil. I looked around and noticed Thomas and Bob were gone. "Where are the fellas?" I asked, while I tried to figure out when we got on the bikes.

"I needed a few things: potatoes, tinfoil, butter," Frank said. "So they ran to the market for you?" I asked.

"Yeah," Frank froze and stared at me, "for the second time!" he said and then started laughing hard. "I needed a couple of other things earlier too: nutmeg, cream, rosemary," he explained. "There's so much little shit that I forgot is easily accessible in my apartment back home. In this kitchen I found some salt and pepper and I put those to work too," he explained as he took the game hens from the refrigerator. He unwrapped each and placed them back on top of their white and pink stained butcher papers that he had flattened out. "But yeah—I'm still trying to keep things simple," he said as he had moved on to rinsing a couple of gourd-looking things. "Butternut squash," he said as he saw me eyeing them.

Just then I heard the thud of Thomas' shoulder hitting the front door open. "G'day, mate!" he enthusiastically yelled out. "Happy Thanksgiving!" he followed with, as he set down Frank's rucksack and started pulling groceries from it.

"Good morning, Major," Bob said as he maneuvered past Thomas to go take a seat on the couch.

"You find everything?" Frank asked.

"Yup and then some," Thomas said. He reached into a pocket on the bag and pulled out a plastic container, the kind you would buy a small bunch of sealed blueberries in at a grocery store.

Frank eyed the package as he set up the new run of ingredients. "Blue cheese?" he guessed the content.

"Nope—truffles," Thomas said.

"Nooo fucking way," Frank said with a lot of excitement. "Where did you get those?" he asked.

"Bob found them in a Smart Shop," Thomas said.

"Wait, what? You got them in a Smart Shop? Let me see those," Frank said, taking a break from his prep work to eye the contents. He squinted to read the label on the front. "Psilerotium, psilocin— these are psychedelic drugs!"

"Yeah, no shit," Thomas said. "What did you think they were?"

"Truffles, like you fucking said—for me to cook with."

"Go ahead and cook with them," Thomas said, clearly not grasping that he and Frank were talking about two different items—or maybe he knew and was just playing with Frank. Or maybe he actually wanted Frank to mix them in with something. It didn't matter; Frank was back to work peeling potatoes.

"You need any help with that stuff?" Thomas asked. "Absolutely not. This kitchen is only built for one cook at a time," Frank said. Thomas looked at me and shrugged his shoulders and made his way to the couch.

"How you feeling, Evel Knievel?" Thomas asked.

"What does that mean?" I asked. He just stared at me for a moment.

"Your failed bike stunt?" he said, which was the second bike reference in the few minutes since I'd climbed out of bed. "You don't remember?" he asked with shock.

"No," I said, wondering what it was all about.

"What's the last thing you remember last night?" Thomas asked.

"The bike race," I said.

"You don't remember the Irish pub we went into after? You kept staring at the bartender." At that moment I remembered what he was talking about. We had gone in right after the bike race.

"Yeah, that's right, I do remember going in there; and, as I recall, she was cute," I said.

"Oh, now you're full of memories," Thomas said.

"You get nutmeg?" Frank interrupted.

"Check that side pouch," Thomas answered. "So yeah, I remember going in there," I said. "Do you remember leaving?" Thomas asked. "Well… no," I said.

"There you have it," Thomas said. "We didn't really want to leave, but after the second shot, you told the bartender that you liked to brag about your small penis."

"Bullshit," I said.

"*Bulltrue*, dude," Thomas said. I looked over at Bob, and he was quietly laughing to himself, shaking his head affirmatively at the story. "Yeah, you told her 'it's the new trend; all the girls are talking about small penises in Paris and New York.'" I just sat there and listened; I could recognize my own drunken humor when I heard it.

"Fuck, dude, I hope I didn't make her uncomfortable," I said, feeling a bit bad about it.

"Actually I think she liked you," Thomas said. "Really?" I asked.

"Yeah, you were being pretty funny about it; we all thought so," Thomas explained. "But the one person who didn't like it was her boyfriend who owns the place."

"Oops," I said. "Did he come after me? Wait, wait—a big, but soft balding Dutchman about our age?" I asked.

"Yup, that's him," Thomas affirmed.

"Big pink bastard," I said. Part of the memory was coming back. I just remembered pissing a guy off at the bar; it wasn't the first time in my life.

"Yeah, pink until he got tired of you picking up on his girl; then he went to red and had us tossed out by the dishwasher," Thomas explained.

"The dishwasher? Was he a big guy or something?" I asked. "No, the poor bastard was small; he looked Turkish or Hungarian. He probably appreciated his job enough to have the balls to do what the boss asked," Thomas said. "He was cool about it, simply asked that we pay our bill and leave—so we did. The bar owner stayed at the end of the bar and watched it all."

"I'm glad I didn't protest," I said.

"Us too," Bob said jokingly, just as Frank dropped a large metal spoon on the kitchen floor. "FUCK!" he said as he picked it up and started washing it.

"How was the bartender acting through all this?" I asked. "Unfazed—she clearly has the guy wrapped around her finger," Thomas said. "You told her you'd be back for her number." "What did she say to that?" I asked.

"It's better I not tell you; you'd go back in there," he said.

"Why—I'd be mad?" I asked.

"No, you'd get it," Thomas said with a side smile. "We came home after that?" I asked.

"Yeah, for about three minutes before you insisted we take the bikes to go get some Mediterranean food."

"Mediterranean food?" I asked.

"Yeah, you had it set in your mind. No one else was hungry, but I figured I should go with you to keep you from going back to the bar or getting arrested," he said.

"Well, I guess you were successful at that?" I said.

"Hah, but you almost died."

"Oh yeah—the bike thing—fuck, I can't remember any of it." "We were going down a street where the tram was running," he explained. "You were being funny—or trying to be funny—like you were gonna play chicken with it."

"Jesus—and you let me?" I asked.

"What the fuck was I gonna do with you? You were ahead of me," he said. "The thing was only going like five miles per hour."

"Oh," I said, waiting to hear the part of the story that was dangerous.

"You were riding towards it standing on your pedals; and as you went to swerve around it, the sunken rail grabbed your rear tire and clipped the front of the tram," he explained. I just sat there and didn't say anything, realizing that at the slow pace it was going, it was still enough to grab my bike and pull it and me under its crushing steel wheels.

"Wha'd I do?" I asked.

"You were kind of athletic about it," he said. "It hit the bike and you fell sideways but actually saved yourself by landing and hopping out of the way on your foot that hit first. That surprised me," he said.

"What did the tram operator do?" I asked.

"That's the funny part; he didn't even stop. He looked at us on his way past and just shook his head. You must not be the first drunk he's had to clear off the track," Thomas said. I sat for a second, feeling dumb about the ordeal.

"How's the bike?" was the next thing that came to my mind. "Fuck, I can't believe you don't remember this shit," Thomas said with the expression he wished I did. "The bike was fucked, almost folded. So I threw it in the canal," he said, as if that were the normal thing to do in the situation.

"Wait a second—you threw it in the canal? What the fuck?" I asked.

"Well, as I explained last night, the bike was done. If you had turned it in in that condition, you would be buying them a new bike," he said.

"How am I not doing the same thing after it gets tossed in the canal? And what if they could have fixed it?" I asked.

"Dude, they weren't fixing it. The frame was cracked; the rear end ruined—just listen to me—again," he said. "I pulled the key out of the wheel lock; you're just gonna tell the guy you had it locked up and someone took it," Thomas said with confidence in the plan. "That's why those bikes come with insurance, and the only thing they ask is that you produce a key to prove it was locked."

"You threw it in the canal. Why do I have to go talk to the guy?" I asked, but then stopped myself. "I get it, bro; it's a solid plan, given what you had to work with," I told Thomas. It was true; he had come up with an option to cover me when we were both plastered.

"Funny thing is, dude," Thomas started again, "right after I did it, you started laughing hysterically and calling the plan 'genius,'" he said.

"After a few minutes when you finally stopped laughing so hard, you tried to convince me to throw mine in too and even reached for it ready to do it yourself," he said. "Then you wanted to go to the bike agent right then in the middle of the night," Thomas said. "You just kept saying you wanted to go talk to his white boxer, that he would understand. That's when I convinced you it was time for bed."

"Did we even eat?" I asked. "Nope," he replied.

"So I guess I got to go see about a bike today," I said. Thomas shook his head *yes*. At first I was curious if they would be open on Thanksgiving—and then I came to my senses. "Alright, I may as well get ready and get this out of the way," I said. "What's the plan for the day?"

"You mean, when are we eating?" Frank said with a smile. "Yeah," I said.

"I can have it ready around late afternoon—let's say we plan on eating around 4 or 5 p.m.—sound good?" Frank asked. Everyone agreed that would work, so I showered and got dressed with a knot in my stomach about dealing with the bike rental agency.

I walked along the canal a few blocks until I arrived at the shop. The small bell above the door rang as I stepped in. I could hear the clicking of nails on the wooden floor as the white boxer was the first to greet me. I knelt down and let him sniff my hand and then went to scratch under his ear in the place my boxer enjoyed. It must be a K9 sweet spot, because he immediately turned his head into the pressure of my fingers and made the same feign grunting sounds my dog Blu made when I gave him the same love.

"Oi," the shop keeper said as he entered. I almost felt sick. Not only because I was lying—well, I was lying—but I just didn't like it, either because I wasn't good at it or because I was good at it. Neither was a good trait to have.

"Yes, sir, my bike was stolen last night," I said, wanting to speak as little as possible.

"I see," he said. "Where was the bike last seen?" he asked. I almost felt relieved at the question, as I wouldn't be lying if I really didn't remember where I saw it.

"Outside the Leidseplein," I said—I knew this to be true. "Did you notify the police?" he asked.

"No," I said.

"Why not?" he asked, as my anxiety returned in gushes now that all of a sudden the police were being brought into it.

"Well, it was late—very late—and we didn't come across any," I explained.

"Do you have the wheel lock key?" he asked. I felt a little relief at this question, because I finally had an answer he was looking for. "Yes, yes, right here," I said as I pulled the key from my pocket and handed it to him.

"Goot, that's what I need," he said. "Zat is vat we have insurance for," which also gave me some relief, as now my irresponsibility would be passed on to an insurance company and not the shop owner.

"I'll just need you to fill out a couple of forms and sign," he said. And that was that. As I filled out the false report, I tried to rationalize to myself that the bike was stolen—by Thomas. I didn't ask him to toss the thing out; he took it from me and did it. The spirit of theft lives in there somewhere, I was sure. I came to the line asking if I swore my information to be true. I rationalized to myself that I couldn't remember what was true about the incident, then signed my name and pushed the paper over to the shopkeeper. He eyed it and said, "Goot," again. Then he looked up at me and asked, "Do you require another bike?"

I pedaled my new bike away, but not to the houseboat. It was a crisp late morning day. The thought of the Thanksgiving dinner with friends brought back the childhood feelings of wonder and happiness on a holiday. I just wanted to ride for a while and enjoy things. I joined a steady stream of bike traffic as it traveled through the Jordan. It amazed me how the bike flow went so smoothly, even through intersections that did not have a stop sign or a traffic light, and was as uninterrupted as blood flow through the healthy human body.

After a few blocks, I was in front of Central Station, the hub of the city. From there I could go in different directions. I opted to patrol through the Red Light District. I didn't want anyone to see me in the

Leidseplein area who may have remembered me or worse yet, witnessed me. So I pedaled alongside the small harbor that stood on this end of the District. I crossed over a bridge and found myself back where it all had started the night before.

The District is different in the day, especially during a weekday. It actually holds an innocent charm to it, and the area appears as most neighborhoods in Amsterdam proper. The sun creeps into the streets, slipping in between the buildings that line the lanes. Shopkeepers and pub house employees sweep and mop out their stores. A woman pedals by with a French loaf partially wrapped and stuck into her bike basket. The one thing that shatters it all is when you get to the red windows. You see, the vice never sleeps... always there to cater to those who may work the graveyard shifts or the sex junkies who need to get a fix on their way to work.

I pedaled slowly along, looking at the girls... not in a wanting way. I always make sure to only give them eye contact, not a brushing up and down with the eyes. Only about a quarter of the working parlors were operating at this hour. Then I saw her, possibly the most beautiful I had seen working. She was sweet- looking, a genuine innocence to her appearance, if it were possible at all to be innocent in her profession. I smiled at her as I passed; she smiled back and gave a cute wave. I kept pedaling though. In nature, creatures like the praying mantis can always pursue a mate, a mate that must know what the end result will be but still buys into the moment.

I pedaled by Rock Planet; it was closed, and its steel shutter roll-down door tomb sealed it. The place was cold now and off limits or sleeping, much in the same manner that vampires do at these hours. The place where we lost our slot machine slept in the same way. Suddenly, probably because of the loneliness of the scene, I decided to head back to the houseboat. The smell of decay from the fallen leaves stood out this morning. It was beautiful. Dried, then dampened flora can have a scent as beautiful as a flower and as rugged as leather. It's a true cologne of autumn.

I locked my bike next to the others and shouldered my way through the front door. I was immediately confronted by new scents; spice, butter and bread were prominent, along with the culinary songs of pans being placed in an oven, while the one just pulled out is placed on top of the stove. Frank had pulled out a tray of sweet potatoes and baking potatoes, and he had just placed some Brussels sprouts on a shelf below a tray of bread slices.

"What are the bread slices for?" I asked.

"Croutons—stuffing," Frank responded.

"How'd it go?" Thomas asked. He and Bob were sitting on the floor playing a game of Chinese checkers.

"Easy actually," I responded.

"No shit?" Thomas asked.

"Yeah—got another bike."

"No shit?" Thomas asked in an even higher tone.

"Yeah, no shit," I said. "You act surprised."

"I am," he said. "It's not like I thought it was a foolproof plan; it was a drunk, desperate plan when there was no other plan."

"Besides just paying for the bike," I said.

"Well, yeah—that's no plan," Thomas said as Bob made a double jump on him.

"Yeah, I just told him it was stolen; he asked a couple of questions and then had me sign something," I said.

"What kind of questions?" Thomas asked, while he made a marble jump on Bob.

"Like if we had told any cops." This made Thomas stop what he was doing and regain eye contact with me.

"Wha'd you say?" he asked.

"That it was late and we didn't come across any."

"Wow, that was easy, I guess," Thomas said.

"Yeah, and he got the paperwork mixed up and handed me yours, so I signed your name," I said.

"BULLLSHIT!" he said, with a mixture of 60/40 non-belief in what I just said.

"You're right," I said with a smile. He just went back to concentrating on the board game. "We still eating at 5:00, Frank?" I asked.

"Actually, things are going pretty well. I just need to finish with these hens and then prepare the starches—we could probably go at 3:00 if you're down," he said.

"I'm down," I said. "You guys good with that?"

"With what?" Bob asked as he looked up from the game to ask the question. He had been concentrating hard on a seemingly brainless game. I knew why, though. Thomas is extremely competitive and smart; put those traits together, and you have a winner in most cases, for better or worse.

"We're gonna eat around 3:00," Frank said, as he moved the game hens into oven position. He had them positioned in a way I hadn't seen a bird cooked in. They were set side by side vertically. "You use those cans to set them on?" I asked, as he had the tail end of the hens resting on two beer cans cut in half.

"Yeah," he said as he closed the oven door. "They are used not so much to set the hens on, but more so to catch the juices that run off into them," he explained. "Plus, some of those juices evaporate back into the meat," he said. It was fascinating, having his craft and personality along on the trip on this day of all days, our last full day in Amsterdam.

The day was mild in weather, which was to say sunny and even warm enough to open the double French doors on the boat, which gave an open view of the canal and neighboring boats. It was very picturesque, one you know that may not ever come about again.

"Bam!" Thomas said loudly as his words woke me from my daydream. He had just beat Bob, who continued to look at the board, probably because he didn't know what else to do.

"Want me to roll us a joint?" Thomas asked as he got to his feet. "Uhh... you have to ask that question?" I said.

"Good point," he said as he got to his feet and walked to his luggage bag.

"How you doing, Bob?" I felt compelled to ask. Bob is not shy, but he is quiet. In a boisterous group like this, a man like Bob can get lost and forgotten, even when he is five feet away.

"Oh, life is good," he said smiling. "I suppose if losing at Chinese checkers is the worst part of my day, I don't really have any problems."

"Nice point," I said, and it was.

"Anyone need the bathroom right now?" Bob asked.

Frank was peeling sweet potatoes and stopped and looked up at him when he heard Bob ask the question. "What the fuck? Did we bring our mom on the trip?" he said… and then hysterically laughed. "I'm asking, asshole, because I want to take a shower," Bob explained.

"Okay, Mom," Frank said as he turned to grab a salt shaker behind him. Bob just looked at me and shook his head as he simultaneously gave Frank the ol' waving-thumb-point gesture.

"It's all yours, man," I said.

"Thanks," he said. Bob got up and went across the boat. Outside the bathroom he got into his luggage and grabbed fresh clothes. He then removed his shirt and revealed a large dragon tattoo that ran from his chest and serpentined down his side and ended up in his lower back region. It was all blue ink and borderline prison in design and quality. But as striking as it was in its prominence, it wasn't what totally stood out on his body. He had two swollen scars on his lower back towards his side.

I waited for him to go into the bathroom, then asked Frank, "What are those scars on Bob's back from?" Frank was in the middle of mashing some potatoes. He put the utensil on the counter and licked a small piece of potato off his thumb.

"From being stabbed," Frank said as he turned to the sink to wash his hands.

"Seriously?" I asked.

"Here ya go." Thomas stepped in from the other room with his freshly-rolled spliff. He handed it to me. I wanted to continue with the story, especially before Bob came out from his shower. But Thomas was being generous on the day of thanks so I didn't want to be rude to his offer.

"Hey," I said in a quieter tone. "Frank was telling me a story about Bob getting stabbed," I said to Thomas.

"Oh yeah?" Thomas said to Frank. "What happened?"

"He walked out of a bar in his town and a guy he knew was getting jumped by two other guys," Frank said. As he spoke, I had bitten the ends off the joint and was ready to light it.

"The guy must have been a good friend of his for him to get involved," Thomas asked and then looked at me as I drew in some smoke.

"No... not really," Frank said as he dumped some Brussels sprouts into a boiling pot. "He knew the guy; that was enough for him," Frank said. "Had it been a one-on-one fight, Bob probably wouldn't have gotten involved," Frank said as he bent over to open the oven and check the game hens. "Nice," he said to himself after viewing them. A moment later Bob exited the bathroom. He was wearing shorts and a Grateful Dead T-shirt, his curly hair still wet enough to stretch the curls out a bit more than usual.

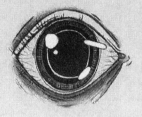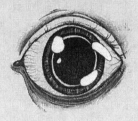

Chapter Thirteen

It was 5:00. An hour had passed since we had consumed our grand meal. We had brought Thanksgiving with us, made it a movable feast of sorts. But now, just like a lion pride after a successful hunt, we were lying around in positions that brought some sort of relief to our stretched-out guts. Frank had delivered, and our stomachs ached with the feeling of overeating, typically a sensation of royalty within a food chain.

Thomas explained that the Smart Shop worker had told him to expect the psilocybe tampanensis to take up to an hour to grab us. "But, of course, taking it on a full stomach is going to slow it down even more," Thomas said to the group.

"Fuck it, let's take it now," Frank said. "It will just take a little longer to kick in." Thomas just shrugged his shoulders and raised his eyebrows, searching the group for any protest. There wasn't any, so he poured the contents out on the counter, and soon after had them separated into four separate but generally even amounts. I couldn't help but notice his pile was barely noticeably larger. But hell, he's Thomas and he bought them and most notably, he separated them.

We each scooped the pile off the counter into a cupped hand. I made Thomas jump like a junkyard dog when he thought he heard a chain-link fence jangle. I just looked at him and winked when I made it appear I was going to scoop the pile in front of him away. He just stared back like a junkyard dog would do to anyone who rattles its chain.

The trip was going to be similar to the mushroom ride. Sometimes you slide slowly into the trip, feeling the effects come on gradually: the sweat, the runny nose, the gag reflex, all the body's efforts to rid whatever the fuck it just ate in the only ways it knows how. Sometimes the ride hits you like an unexpected sea wave just dumped on you, all your senses suddenly on full assault. For a first-timer this can be tough and what lands them in an ambulance from a bad trip. In either case, once you make it through the initial currents and transformation, the ride smooths out. Again, the process seems to mimic the transformation from mortal to vampire, as you slowly feel a dark wave creep over your body—and you welcome it.

Bob came in from out front. "Hey, guys, the boat owner is coming by to collect the rent; and if she thinks we are taking drugs, she might kick us out." This was alarming news because with this ride, if they kick in mid-sentence, it's going to show and be uncontrollable. *No, ma'am, we are not taking drugs on your boat. Wait—did you ask me if we have any drugs or not for us to have drugs? Do you want some drugs?* And that is how it would go down. "Well then, I'm just going to act asleep," I said, as Thomas already had his eyes shut as he sprawled on the couch, still attempting to allow his stomach some surface area. Frank had his MP3 player on and was busy cleaning up the kitchen. "Uh—Major, do you think you could talk to her? I'm worried I'll feel effects and she will know."

"How the fuck am I any better than you? If this shit kicks in on me, it's over."

"Just do it for me, please; you're better at it than me." The statement showed his worry. And after hearing the story about his stabbing, it seemed like a small thing to do for a friend. About forty-five minutes later, the triple click of the door knocker sounded. I got up from my seat to meet my challenge.

"Hello," the boat owner said as she crisply stuck out her hand in a well-rehearsed American-style greeting. "I'm Reina, nice to meet you." She wore a beautiful red woolen coat, perfect for the season, and a black or dark violet beret.

"Hello, please come in to your houseboat." I was hoping the gesture sounded like the joke it was—or did it?

"Thank you," she said in a charming Dutch fashion.

"This is Thomas, Frank, and I think you've dealt with Bob so far?" I asked during the introductions.

"Yesh, I met Bob online when he booked the boat," Reina said with a smile. She crossed the floor and shook everyone's hands, smiling and looking them in the eye.

"I suppose you've come for the rent?" I asked, again trying to add a little humor to my tone.

"Yesh-yesh, if it is okay wit you," she said, applying the same amount of humor in her words.

Bob had collected our money the day before; he went to his bag and pulled it from inside a sock that was stuffed into a shoe. He walked the cash over to her and counted it out in front of her, laying it on the table.

"Thank you," she said. "Have you enjoyed the boat thus far?" she asked.

"Oh yeah," I said. "Immensely," Frank said.

"Frank made use of your kitchen today," I told her. "Made us our Thanksgiving dinner."

"Oh yesh, that's right, it's your American holiday," she said with a smile. Frank had gotten up and moved back into the kitchen. Soon after he presented Reina with a small plate, almost tapas-style for her to sample what he had made. It had a couple of Brussels sprouts that Frank had flash-fried after he boiled them to which he had added minced roasted garlic and small chopped squares of bacon. They were the hit of the meal—or I should say, one of the hits. He put a small piece of game hen next to a caramelized yam. The butternut squash didn't make it through the meal. What Frank shared with Reina was from what little was left that did survive the feast.

Reina ate from each sample, her face giving subtle hints of enjoyment with each bite. "Yeah, guys, I only used about a third of that bacon. I'm going to make BLTs tomorrow for lunch."

"Better make them early; we fly out at 3 p.m.," Thomas said.

"Wait—no shit? I thought you left the day after tomorrow," Frank said.

"I wish," Thomas grinned. "Awfully short stay," Reina said.

"Only a short stay on the boat," I said. "We've been here several days. We were in a hostel, but then Bob invited us onto the boat."

"Ah," Reina said; she then handed frank her empty plate. "That was delicious," she said as she thanked Frank.

"No problem," Frank said as he rinsed the plate and put it in the dishwasher.

"Okay den," she said, "I'm going to be on my way and get out of yours," she told us in her cute way. I walked her to and out the door.

"Thank you for letting us crowd your boat," I told her, happy that I was still feeling okay, as far as I could tell.

"You guys enjoy your stay; it was my pleasure," she said and stuck her hand out again to shake mine. After she walked a few feet away, she disappeared into the misty evening. A cloud cover had come in, and it appeared like rain was likely. I was hoping not though; I was looking forward to our farewell bike tour.

I walked back into the boat. Bob was staring at his hand, so I knew he was feeling something. Thomas handed me a beer; he and the other two already had them. I noticed my head beginning to condensate and the low-level ache in my kidney. I took a few more sips of beer. "Looks like it might rain tonight," I said to Thomas.

"That could be good," he said. "It will get rid of this fog." I took another drink of beer because I felt dehydrated. I sat down—I sat down—I looked at the carpet, and it started to look like a mix of fresh oil-based paints.

"Oh yeah—she arrived," I said, looking at Thomas. "Yeah—I'm there too," Thomas said. I looked at Frank; he had this big smile like the Cheshire cat—he gave me a thumbs-up. I looked out the open French doors. "Rain's here," I said. You could see the drops lightly pelting the water.

"Good timing." He got up and put some music on. It was a song by Cold War Kids; I couldn't tell you the title. I knew the drug was coming over me because it's actually an irritating process. Like I said earlier, when the vampire turns a new victim, the person goes through an internal struggle; as the human "self" dies, there is a struggle. Here, it's a struggle of the mind—though there are things going on physically: sweating, dry heaves, yawning and gut ache. Still, with these things it's a mental process, almost as if the mind asks, *What the fuck is wrong with you, putting that in your mouth and swallowing—you knew what the fuck you were doing—you're no better intellectually than an ape.* And I'd have to admit to myself—to my mind, yeah, I'm just a fucked-up monkey.

"Can you ride a bike?" The question brought me back to reality—or a reality or no reality at all—that's the fucking problem with these things. It's why motherfuckers jump off buildings thinking they can fly. My advice to them: start that journey from the ground. If you can fly, you don't need to do it from a perch.

"Yeah," was what came out, and those words seemed to muse us immediately out of the shelter and into the rain. It fell as softly as an early spring snowfall and turned the environment into a fairytale. We mounted our steeds and were off. The silliness in our thoughts was very real.

We pedaled without talking for a couple of blocks. The bike lightly vibrated as it rolled over the paved brick street. We were paralleling the canal; the cranking pedals made a distinct croaking noise, all out of sync; then on occasion, they came together to sound in unison. The rain wasn't falling enough to be annoying. We wore jeans and sweaters or sweatshirts. The truffles had the body lightly sweating, and it was a blessing to catch a raindrop on the forehead or cheek. They hit the face with the force of a kiss and would run down the cheek like a tear.

We came to the bike-busy intersection of the Jordan on the outskirts of the Red Light. "Let's duck in that place over there and grab a beer," Thomas said. It was a good idea. I wanted to chase my high with the depressant agents in the beer. Keep some sort of level. You know you're on a ride when you need alcohol to help make you feel sober.

The décor of the place involved lots of red walls and white and pink trim, almost like an Old West whorehouse parlor. We ordered a round, placing ourselves at the corner of the bar so we could talk and face each other.

"What's the plan?" I asked.

"What about a ride through Vondel Park?" Thomas suggested. The Park was over by the casino. It was old and had a beautiful front concrete-and-rod-iron-gate entrance. It sounded like the perfect idea.

"Sounds good to me," Frank said. Bob almost too quietly said, "Sure," and then took a drink of his beer. We took a few minutes to finish the beer. Frank sat and stared at his beer.

"What are you looking at?" I asked.

"The bubbles," he said. "They're a trip." So we all sat and stared into the beers. Frank was right. My glass became a Rorschach test of sorts. The bubbles would bring different images to mind. The bubble lights my mom used to put on the Christmas tree were filled with an oil that would heat up and bubble when the lights were turned on. Then the bubbles looked like floating diamonds in liquid; then the beer seemed to turn into amber, the fossilized tree resin material. And then… then it just looked like a glass of beer, but somehow it was more beautiful than a glass of beer.

"Let's go… down the hatch," Thomas said. "I want to hit the park when I'm peaking." And he was right. Our heads were in the right place to see stuff not found in the bar. We went and unlocked the bikes. I put my earbuds in. I knew there wouldn't be a lot of talking on this ride. At least during the pedaling parts. I hit random play and Madonna's "Ray of Light" came on.

The ride was beautiful. The clouds had broken up in the sky like icebergs floating in packs. An almost-full moon showed. It gave enough light to turn the clouds deep blue with silver glowing outlines against an onyx black sky. The front of the houses stayed relatively dark but not hidden, almost like large tombstones. The brick streets shimmered from the rain; moonlight reflected off them. I was so into the moment, and the music was going; then a very real thought came to me, a thought that turned silly when sober from the hallucinogens. But at that moment, as she was piped into my ears and head, I wanted to write Madonna a letter. Tell her to come to Amsterdam, rent a bike and ride on a moonlit night right after a rain. It was something she needed to do. At a minimum, it was something she needed to know. And then the song changed, and so did my train of thoughts. All thoughts before that point had already turned into exhaust.

We were gliding through neighborhoods and soon through the Leidseplein and past the American Hotel. A couple of minutes later, we pulled to a stop at the entrance of the park. An attractive girl walked by us. We each glanced up to look at her. And then Bob, of all people, spoke up.

"Hellloo," he said, trying his damnedest to be charming. But he didn't sound charming; he sounded creepy. She just kept walking;

whether she heard it or not was irrelevant. A wind escaped Frank's lips in the form of a laugh.

"What the fuck was that?" Frank said, now laughing out loud.

"What?" Bob asked, already losing whatever confidence he had gained to try to pick up on a girl.

"You fucking sounded like a serial killer," Frank said, which made all of us laugh. Well, not all of us; Bob wasn't laughing.

"I was just saying 'hi,'" he said.

"More like saying that you were h-i-g-h," Frank said, making us laugh again though, in all truth, I didn't know if that were funny or not at the time; but again Bob had his mind made up about it and still wasn't laughing.

"You guys just want to cruise through?" I asked.

"Let's go," Thomas said. I left my earbuds out this time, wanting to listen to the sounds of the area…whatever that meant. As it was, we ended up pairing off as we pedaled. "How you feeling?" Thomas asked.

"On top of the world for the most part," I said.

"Yeah—me too," he said. "I've tried several drugs, had different highs and lows, but my favorite high is from the psilocybin. The ride lasts a few hours; and, if it's good, it's great. If it's bad, it's a drag—but usually bearable. The worst part about those trips is if you have anything remotely dramatic going on in your life or ghosts of traumas past, they can revisit you in ways that make you rethink things in a deeper and sometimes more twisted way than ever before. It's uncomfortable."

We pedaled through the park. It was dark, with the exception of light posts every so often, like birthday candles stuck haphazardly throughout the area. They didn't give enough light to chase the dark in the park away. But they gave reference to various areas, as well as pointed the way to the foot paths. The trees were, for the most part, silhouetted black shapes, many appearing as the hands of buried corpses, breaking through the soil and reaching for the sky. The grass was dormant. The path curved in windy manners. We pedaled past a large pond; there were a pair of swans who were enjoying an evening swim. They glided in unison, almost appearing mechanical in their synchronized kinetics. Their white bodies gave hope on dark waters. The entire scene was like stepping into a Tim Burton work. It was beautiful; it was truly—literally—surreal. That's what I liked about this high. There are very few places in the world where you get to actually participate in the surreal for any length of time... aside from the mind of a child.

"Let's go over to that tree by that clearing," Thomas said. So we rode over to a large cleared area which had been planted with grass. The bikes were all laid at the base of what had to be a two- hundred-year-old ash tree. Each person just wandered off in his own direction. Thomas and Frank were looking at the sky; Bob stared off across the clearing into the thick growth of forest trees. Who knows what he could see living in there, the possibilities only limited by the imagination and lens of the seeker. I walked to the base of the giant tree and placed my hand on it.

I looked up. It was clear the old-timer was on his way out. It didn't fork much, as was apparent by the large scar where a major branch breakaway had taken a third of the tree away. What was left had lost most of its leaves, though the corpses of some still clung to their branches; but other areas of the tree had completely bare branches that were missing their bark skin, showing that no leaves had grown on them in many seasons. It was dying.

I raised my hand over my head and rested it in the deep and heavy grooves of the ash bark. I stared through the bare area of the tree to see the clouds blowing by at speeds I had never seen clouds move. They almost appeared as clouds in a Hollywood movie set, during a time-lapse scene making them travel very fast for dramatic reasons. The entire scene was covered in the slow strobe-light effect that came from passing clouds which hid the moon and then released its light in heavenly bursts.

The tall tree was slowly twisting in the wind; the height of the branches created enough leverage that I could feel the bark grooves lightly squeezing and releasing my fingertips. It was the tree hugging me back. Everything wants a friend by their side at the time of dying. In this tree's century-old wisdom, it had gained the knowledge of its own mortality. It was beautiful.

"Guys, wanna keep moving?" Thomas asked. I had no idea how long we had been stopped. When you're on these things, it's impossible to keep track of time. And what you find is, it slows time down, which is a neat trick. The only other time I've found a way to slow time down, making an hour feel like three, is sitting through a church service.

"Let's ride through the District," I suggested. Not only because I thought it would be a fun visit while we were still tripping, but in the hopes of seeing the girl in the window from earlier.

"Let's go," Thomas said, and we started out again. We were retracing our bike path back towards the Red Light District. We stopped along the way at the Bulldog in Leidseplein Square. "Grab me a beer; I'll go get the smoke," Thomas said.

"I got these," Bob said.

"Helllooo," Frank said to him and started laughing.

"Fuck you, I'll get everyone's but yours," Bob said to him in retaliation. Moments later he was back but not before Thomas, who had sat down and was already rolling a joint. Bob held three beers in his hands, with them poised in a bowling-pin triangle. He sat one down in front of Thomas and one in front of me; then he sat down holding the third.

"Are you shittin' me?" Frank asked with a little irritation when Bob, in fact, returned without a beer for him.

"Helllooo," he said in a mocking manner. "I couldn't carry them all, you big baby," Bob said as he handed Frank the third beer and then got up and retrieved the fourth that sat on the bar waiting for him. I stared into my glass again, getting lost in the bubbles. The high still ran through my blood-fed brain.

"Cut that shit out and drink," Thomas said. "We're gonna pass this around," he said of the joint, "and then get these beers down and head out." We did exactly that and were out soon after.

We had only pedaled a couple of blocks when Thomas stopped and was looking into a store of some sort. We all caught up and immediately saw the allure that held his attention. We sat and stared like insects into the shop that glowed a warm yellow. It was filled with pastries and candies and hot and cold sugary drinks. There were Stroopwafles, which were like two cookie-sized thin waffles with caramel in between; frosted brownies; éclairs filled with cream or custard; cream puffs filled with clouds; cookies with chunks of chocolate for chips and lemon bars frosted with powdered sugar. It was every stoner's dream, an adult version of Willy Wonka's candy room where everything you saw was edible.

Moments later we had our second feast of the day in front of us. Thomas took the liberty of ordering for the table... or perhaps over-ordering for the table. We gathered around a tall, circular standing table; you could hardly make out the wood top from all the pastries on it.

"Hey, don't touch anything," I said, holding both hands out. "Just stare at it for a second."

"My god, you and your staring," Thomas said. I knew what he meant; I like to stare at things I enjoy and turn away from things I don't: beer bubbles, wicked trees against fantasy sky. Thomas catches me staring at women: beautiful women, average women, ugly women. I stare at them all, not for sexual gratification reasons—not usually, at least—but because I love to observe the human zoo around me. I like to study behaviors. And right now I wanted to watch the behaviors of my pastries.

"Just fucking do it," I told Thomas. Frank and Bob were already on it. I focused on the very center of the table and did my best to relax my vision everywhere else. Sure enough, they started to move. Not like change positions on the table, but more like they were melting colors; a few seconds deeper and it became kaleidoscopic in nature.

"I see it," Frank said. Thomas didn't say anything, though I knew by his expression, his 1000-yard stare, that he saw it—he saw something.

"Okay, let's eat!" I said, looking up. You could see the distance disappear from their faces instantly, like they had come directly out of a hypnotic trance. And it was on. No talking, just chewing... and grunts and moaning noises, made with filled mouths and fresh bites. It didn't take me long—or the group, for that matter—to realize we needed something to wash this all down.

I peeled off first to beat the crowd. I ordered a hot Chocomel. It's a drink like Yoo-hoo, but very popular in Europe. The others ordered the same, without leaving the table. "Make mine cold," Frank said.

We devoured the table top like a pride to the zebra. It never stood a chance. And then we moved on. We unlocked our bikes, and I took off the chain that bound them together. I stood and turned to face the group.

"Where's Thomas?" I asked. The other two just kind of looked around confused as well. Then he appeared, stepping through some pedestrians, holding something in his hand that he took a bite from.

"Gravy stick," he said with his mouth full.

"Are you shitting me? How can you still be hungry?" I asked.

"I'm not," he said and took another bite, "but I don't know when I'll ever be back here again."

"Watch the bikes," I said. "Who else wants one?" I came back with three.

It felt good to be back on the bikes. Our guts were full beyond capacity. Almost anything else was uncomfortable to do, but pedaling seemed to loosen everything up and create more room. We took a turn and were paralleling another canal. We were spaced several feet apart from the other bikes, probably because each rider was back in his own world and wanted to give himself plenty of time to brake or to think about braking before doing so… a process best kept in the back of the mind while on this stuff.

As I approached the end of the street, I noticed where the lane met the street in a drive ramp instead of a curb. A black Mercedes that looked like it was possibly being driven by a professional driver of some kind, maybe a car for hire, was parked half up it to let other cars go around him while he talked on his phone. Anyhow, I stopped short of his passenger-side door and rang my bell. I suppose I could have found a way around him, but why should I? I mean, who is the asshole here anyways? The asshole who doesn't just find a way around the car? Or the asshole who is parked illegally, casually, in the way of the bike path. I rang my bell again, and he just glanced at me while he kept talking. The other three pulled up, and we hit him with a barrage of bells—I mean a real pelting of the noise, like a flock of banshees were upon him, along with about a half-ton of men behind them. He fumbled with his phone to hang it up; and with a funny discombobulated look on his face, he put his already-running car in gear and pulled away, the car jerking in motion as he had put it in the wrong gear. It was silent for about three seconds and then a wave of laughter at the whole thing: gut-stirring, euphoric laughter, possibly the best drug of the trip.

We entered the edge and end of the District, the area where Rock Planet stood. You could see the sign was lit up and alive.

"We gotta do it, right?" Thomas said. Meaning a return trip. At first I would have hesitated. I had a good booze-buzz already and didn't need to add to it or to have it rob me of the spell the stones had me under. But I thought about what he had said moments before, with his mouth filled with gravy stick. *When are we going to be in this place again?* With these circumstances and company? "Yeah, we gotta," I said. We dismounted and locked the bikes. We walked through the doors; I heard something as we did, a drawing-in sound, almost as if we were sucked in, gently, guided by fate's hand—my god, these philosopher stones were good, and thank Christmas Jesus, no urge to fly.

A few small groups dotted the place. I slammed my hand on the mostly-empty bar, "ROCK-PLANET!" I yelled; Thomas followed my lead—it was perfect. Frank and Bob did the same, though I don't think they knew the history of the move. But they were now a part of it; it was already worth going in.

"Four Jagermeisters!" Frank yelled out. Ugh, I felt my throat tighten, but I didn't say anything; I didn't want to be the buzz-kill. And I knew Thomas was feeling the same as me, and he too knew not to turn a free drink down, not in Western Europe at least. So we shot them. Mine went down smoother than I would have thought, but it still wasn't a pleasurable experience.

"ROCK PLANET!" I yelled as I finished mine, a split second before the other three; they said the same thing in turn, but not with as much gusto. I had a feeling their drink didn't go down as smoothly as mine.

Thomas went to take a piss, and I took notice of the rock-n-roll memorabilia the place had on display. I hadn't really paid attention to it the last time we were in there. Lots of stuff that could have been purchased: fake gold record displays and a few random guitars hung on the walls. Something funny—or cute or a little sad—caught my eye. It was an autographed print, made out to The Hard Rock Café. It was by one of the replacement guitar players from the 70s/80s rock band KISS. The musician wasn't known well enough to adorn the Hard Rock's walls, so someone there donated it to the little cousin Rock Planet.

"Let's roll," Thomas said upon his return; and at that, we were out the door. I didn't look back after we left, most likely because the drugs and alcohol were making me feel more nostalgic than needed. But I just wanted to remember the place, as it was, not as we left it. We were back on the bikes, heading to the other end of the District. More stuff there to look at: the old cathedral, the Red-Light ladies, the gawkers, walkers and junkies. We were along the main canal that ran through the District. It shimmered black and was still for the most part, reflecting the houses and flats built above the businesses of the District. A bevy of swans floated by; their legs must have been working, because they were moving—or gliding, I should say—fairly rapidly. Their above-water bodies showed no effort at all though, a true act of grace on Earth. They traveled through the same place where I had seen them swimming earlier. In the spot that reflected red neon, the reflection looked as if it were part of the water's makeup… red glowing ripples being sent out in waves, like a radar page or the pulsating vibrations the heart gives off. I stopped my bike, and I just stared at the water.

"I'll meet you at the end of the block," Thomas said to me as he kept going. "Gonna roll a joint," he said as he pedaled away. The other two followed him. He knew what I was doing and the value in what I was staring at. Even if no other person on the planet would have seen it like I was seeing it—that thought alone made the moment that much more valuable. The water, now choppy from contending ripples, turned to red glitter. The swans had moved on, down the canal and away from me. Drifting away like waking from a sad dream that you didn't want to be awakened from. I headed to the end of the block to meet up with the guys.

"What's up?" I said as I arrived.

"Hey," Bob said. He had been watching Thomas roll what was surely the biggest joint of the trip.

206

"You get what you needed?" Thomas asked. He had grown accustomed to my travel habits and seemingly irrelevant needs, though I knew he understood they weren't irrelevant.

"Yeah, I did," I said. "Looks like you're working on something else I need," I said, eyeing his work. He wet the paper's gum adhesive, sealed it shut and twisted the ends. He bit both ends off and handed it to me—which was cool and unlike Thomas, who oftentimes takes the first drag from his work. I drew in hard, so hard I handed it back to him after a single rip; I knew it was a big one, and I had the lungs developed by college water polo to pull and hold a lot of smoke... cough cough COUGH!

"Can't get off unless you cough," Bob said, saying the old stoner cliché. Frank looked at me with eyes that let me know Bob was about to hear about it.

"What the fuck are you talking about, Bob? Hellooo!" Frank said, fucking with Bob. Bob didn't think it was too funny, but the rest of us did. Frank was just bustin' Bob's balls. Frank did that a lot, but that's because guys know Frank is the type who will be guarding your back in an instant when it's most important. And Frank knew that about Bob. But he still enjoyed jabbing him. We enjoyed it too. And Bob was a sport, or as good of a sport as he could be.

The joint came back to me. "I'm gonna hit this and then just ride some circles, right around here and over there," I said, pointing to the furthest I planned on pedaling.

"Cool, I'm gonna sit here for a while," Thomas said; he had found a public bench by the canal wall. The other two also said they would chill in that spot, so I pedaled away. I knew where I wanted to go. I wanted to go back and see my girl, the one I had passed earlier in the day. I doubted she would be there, but I didn't let that thought stop me from checking.

I pedaled past the first rows of lit windows; I didn't even focus on anyone who wasn't her. Another three girls blurred by. I was getting close to her window; I was getting close to the church.

She was there and her face changed, like she was seeing an old friend. It was genuine, not professional in nature. I know the difference... I think.

"Hi," I said when she cracked her door open wide enough to stand in. She was about five-foot-eight, sandy-blonde straight hair with highlights. She was wearing a shiny black leather bikini. It was as out of place with the weather as it was an impressive piece of clothing. She was so beautiful in it; and if you were a straight male, you would need to have your head checked if you were concerned about the outfit being out of season.

"I was hoping you would come back," she said with a heavy accent, one I couldn't even guess.

"You remember me?" I said, feeling warm inside, but still not exactly sure she did or if most prey circle around and it's a good line to make them feel noticed?

"Yes. You rode a bike by earlier—and you smiled at me," she said.

"Don't most guys smile at you?" I asked.

"Not all—and many have a smile that is not happy," she told me. It was deep. "You want to come in?" she asked.

"I do, but I'm not," I said. The moment was almost soiled by the question. But then I quickly reminded myself who she was and what she was there to do.

"Do I need to let you go back to work?" I asked. It felt weird to say, but out of respect to her, it needed to be asked.

"No, I can talk as long as no one else comes," she said. "You are a big guy; they will probably not stop," she said and then giggled in a very cute way.

"Where are you from?" I asked, while looking into her clear brown almond eyes.

"Georgia," she said. "Things are really tough there." I'm not exactly sure why she offered that second bit of information. Her voice was earnest when she said it though. Maybe it was her best and quickest way to explain why she did what she did. I didn't want to pry.

"You are very pretty," I said.

"I am too a student," she told me, showing an actual modesty in reaction to my compliment.

"Yeah? What do you study?" I asked with interest. "International business," she said. "I wish to get into real estate or real-estate marketing," she said in a studious voice. A wave of respect for her came over me. She was a tough girl. A strong, jewel-encrusted outer shell, holding something beautiful inside as well. Beautiful and tragic, ingredients of life's beautiful dark side.

"You are beautiful and, more importantly, intelligent," I told her. "Beauty will fade; it will betray you—your intelligence won't," I said. She smiled and glanced down and then back up at me. "Can you go to breakfast with me tomorrow?" I heard come out of my mouth, though I knew the answer before she gave it.

"I can't," she said and slightly slumped. "I only do this a limited time and then go back home and take classes. I have very little time aside from this." It seemed believable. But who knows where the truth actually lay. "I tell you what, though," she said. "I'm glad you didn't come in."

"Yeah? Why's that?" I asked.

"Because it is nice to see a man who I would like to meet— aside from this place," she said.

"What's your name?" I asked. "Liliana—Lili," she said.

"I'm glad I didn't come in either, Lili; it was a pleasure to meet you," I said. I laid twenty euro on a small shelf next to her. She looked a little confused.

"That's me buying a bright student her next meal," I said. She smiled, and I kissed her on the cheek; she leaned her face into it. I stepped away and mounted my bike. I put my earbuds in and pressed *random* play. "Bitter Sweet Symphony" came on. I started to pedal away; Thomas was approaching me on his bike. He was speaking to me as he passed. I couldn't hear him; I just casually circled back at him, at the same time he did the same. His lips were still moving, and I was still being an asshole and not saying anything back. The song I had heard countless times over the years seemed more beautiful than ever.

"Follow me," I said to Thomas, hoping he would. We did an oval on our bikes in front of about six windows. I felt like I was flowing well with the stringed instruments of the song…trying to look eloquent. The second circle, I stood on a pedal and stretched a leg straight out behind me, making a simple bike trick look like it took effort. Thomas did the same thing. The second circle I put a knee on my seat and stuck my leg out to the side. Four of the six girls smiled as we did our tricks. Lili was clapping her hands and then holding them close to her body, close to her heart. Thomas then put his feet on his seat and squatted on it, performing the best feat of all. But I couldn't have that; I couldn't have him outdo me in front of my girl. So I stopped my bike and the progression of the oval pedaling. I did a trick I learned in high school. I sat on my own handlebars, facing the seat, and I pedaled in the backwards position, waving good-bye to Lili as I did. She waved back, and I felt my heart leave my body and stay with her.

When I was out of the girls' sights, I stopped my bike and stood and waited for Thomas to catch up. "What was that all about?" he asked. I had my earbuds out.

"I was showing off for my girlfriend," I said. "Oh, you can hear me now?" he asked.

"Of course," I said. Thomas just gave a single huff laugh at me and shook his head.

"What do you guys want to do now?" Thomas asked. "Personally," I said, "I wouldn't mind taking it home for the night." I expected some resistance from the group, especially Thomas, who rarely lets me off the hook from having a good time or continuing a good time.

"Sounds good to me," Frank said. "I'm broke anyway," he followed with and then did his laugh, which always made the group laugh. Bob did a laugh that made his shoulders shrug.

"Yeah?" Thomas said. "Okay, let's go back. I have some hash I bought yesterday; we can relax and get into that." So we pedaled back to the houseboat. Most of the scenery on the way back had grown familiar over the past several days. I felt I was saying goodbye to friends as I passed; the canals, the small shops we patronized, certain canal bridges, the large ash trees in the Jordan all took on a special meaning this night. The town had become a friend unto herself. And as with everything that is good, but limited in time, the time left became more precious.

We were getting close to the boat. The canal bridges were outlined in white lights. Another longer bridge hosted three arches, each adorned as well. A light mist rose from the water, sea spirits which softened the scene into the surreal once again.

We pulled up to the boat and locked our bikes for the night. Once inside, Thomas turned on the heat and then opened the double French doors. Both were good moves. I attached my music to the stereo and put on Lenny Kravitz' "In My Life Today," a fucking beautiful song.

Thomas was digging in his bag for the hash and pipe. Frank and Bob were sitting on the couch. Only the oven overhead light was on, and it provided all the light the room needed. I lit a couple of candles which were on the small dining table.

"Come out here," Thomas instructed us as he walked out on the small deck of the boat. Once there, I regretted not spending more time on it. It was just inches above the canal water and ran the distance of the boat, allowing unprecedented views of life on the canal.

Thomas was situating a small chunk of hash into a wire pipe, which isn't really a pipe in the conventional way. It is more of a finger-held wire ladle of sorts. It holds the hash, and the flame is added from underneath. Once the stuff catches flame, you extinguish it, leaving only a heavy stream of smoke lifting from the smoldering drug, kind of how one would light incense.

"Here," he said as he handed it to me. The smoke stayed in a concentrated formation; I put it just under my lips and sucked in a long drag, then pulled my face away as I held my breath, which I could only do for a few seconds before a cough robbed me of the bounty. A plume of blue smoke let out against the dark clouds. Seconds later everyone in the group was coughing.

Hash for the most part is marijuana concentrate. The high is almost an organic high that the pill pushers are usually chasing with their drug of choice. You just become really relaxed and a little dumb to your cares, whereas with weed oftentimes after you smoke, you can go out and be active if you choose to. Hash doesn't debilitate you like pills. You may slow down, but your speech shouldn't get too slurred. You will want to sink into a couch and just veg while on hash. But when you do that after taking pills, oftentimes you can't get back up to make a sandwich or grab a beer.

We had some small talk on the deck for a few minutes. Though the stones had mostly worn off, the dark water kept an air of enchantment within it. "Looks like the rain might return tonight," Thomas said as he looked up into the sky. We all looked up too but didn't say anything.

"What time you flying out tomorrow?" Frank asked.

"We fly out of Schiphol at noon and into Heathrow, then out of Heathrow for Los Angeles at 3:40," I answered.

"At least it's not a long layover," Frank said.

"Yeah," I said, too worn-out to say anything else about it. "You look done, dude," Frank said to me. "You can have the bed tonight; I'll crash on the couch."

"Awesome, dude, thank you," I said.

"What about me?" Thomas asked, half-joking.

"Take it up with Major," Frank said. "It's his bed now." "I'll split it with you, bro," I told Thomas.

"I may sleep on the living-room floor. You snore too loud," he said smiling, though he was being serious.

"One favor though," Frank asked.

"Yeah—what's up?" I said.

"Can I use your laptop? I want to go online and catch up on some college football," he said.

"Hey, I think I'll lay some bets on weekend games too," Thomas said.

"Cool," I said and went inside to grab the computer; a bed for the use of it was more than a fair trade. I walked it into the room and set it soundly on the table that held the still-burning candles and plugged it in. The screen appeared, and I turned it over to the boys. Then I went to the bedroom to lie down. The bed was right next to a large square window. I drew the blinds open and cracked the window open a few inches. I then lay back in the bed with my head propped on some pillows, looking out the window at the sky and then down at the water. The pair of swans swam by at a hurried pace; I wondered where they were going. About thirty seconds later, the rain started to fall. Heavy rain. It gave itself applause as it collided with the canal water. The sky lit up in the distance. Seconds later, the sound of thunder rolled. I continued to stare out the window, as if I were in love and everything I loved was on the other side of that windowpane. Sometime soon after, I drifted off to sleep.

It felt like I had been asleep for a day. It felt like I had just shut my eyes. I slept so soundly that both perspectives were true. I don't think I woke once through the night. My cell clock said it was 8:45. I could hear Frank in the kitchen, and I could smell bacon, which is the best scent a man can wake up to. Sometimes musky perfume is good too.

I walked into the front room. Bob was out on the couch. Thomas did, in fact, make a nest on the floor. He had his blanket pulled over his head, trying to stave off the inevitable light of the day.

"How'd you sleep?" Frank asked as he sliced a tomato.

"Best sleep of the trip, dude," I told him.

"Good to hear," he said as he grabbed a plate and put the slices on them.

"What are you making?" I asked.

"Something I wanted to make you guys for lunch," he said, "but I know you have to split early, so I'll make them now—BLTs. I didn't get into that bacon as much as I thought I would for the Thanksgiving meal, so I figured I'd do something with it now."

The ingredients looked amazing. "Check this out," Frank said as he held a slice of bacon towards me. "Take it." It was nothing like the bacon back home, at least not the typical store-bought stuff. It was thick cut, and though it had a marble of fat within it, it remained leaner than what we typically have. It was the majority of the meat, like you found back home. I took a bite and instantly knew it was the best bacon I had ever had.

"That's good shit, Frank," I said.

"Right?" he responded with a cook's joy in his eyes. I finished my slice and turned to Thomas.

"Dude, we probably should get ready," I told him. "Hmm?" came from under his cover.

"Our flight leaves at noon, its 9 a.m. now, and we should be at the airport at least an hour-and-a-half early. Airport officials were asking for international flights to get there closer to three hours, but that was to make things easier on them. Something's seriously wrong with them if they can't process us through in half that time." Thomas stirred to life and sat up. He leaned back on one arm like a kickstand and rubbed his eyes with the other hand.

"Alright, gonna shower," he said as he rose to his feet.

"Frank made us some bacon sandwiches," I said as he shuffled by. He looked at the plate of sandwiches, which Frank had neatly cut in half, through a squinted eye. Thomas nodded and grunted in affirmation and kept going into the bathroom.

"He'll eat when he gets out," I told Frank. "He wants to wash first," though I know Frank already knew that.

"He's like a raccoon," Frank said, "washing before eating." Then he did his laugh. And like everything else good on this trip, I knew I was going to miss that too. I ate a couple of sandwich halves, probably complimenting Frank three more times. Though good produce, especially a warm-weather fruit like the tomato, can be hard to find in Europe this time of year, Frank did; and their sweetness, mixed with the smoke of the bacon and the tart of the mayonnaise, made each bite ambrosial in nature.

Moments later the bathroom door opened, and a plume of steam belched out. "That's better," Thomas said as he emerged. His wet hair was brushed back but still messy, as if he did it with his hand. As he walked by, he picked up a half-sandwich and kept walking. He took a bite and almost froze. "Mmmh," he got out of his full mouth. He chewed, swallowed and turned around. "This is fuuking good, Frank," he said and then took another bite and continued to his bag to get dressed.

We got packed and had forty-five minutes to get to the airport to stay on schedule. We exchanged contact info with Frank and Bob. "I'm going to be going to Hawaii to work at a sushi place in the next month or so; Bob's going to come out with me and get some work in construction," he said. "My phone number and email address will stay the same, so keep in touch; maybe we can hook up on the islands in the near future."

"You never know, man," Thomas said before shaking Frank's hand and then leaning to give him a bro-hug. He did the same to Bob, and so did I. And we said our goodbyes. The thick, solid boat door closed behind us; the knocker tapped when it shut—it felt like even the boat was saying goodbye to us.

We made our way to Central Station and onto our train's platform. "I'm glad we fly directly into Heathrow," Thomas said.

"Yeah, me too," I said.

"Why didn't we fly out from there the first time?" Thomas asked.

"Because we couldn't get a flight, just a return," I answered.

"Hmm," Thomas responded in an understanding tone; then he became distracted at all the activity of the station going on around us. A couple of minutes passed, and our train arrived at our feet. We boarded and sat on a pair of seats that faced each other. We each took adjacent seats; the move gave us the most legroom on the train. We stayed quiet on the ride, both just staring out the window. It was a gray day out, just a shade light of being rain clouds. I almost put my earbuds in, but decided to just keep my ears open to the sounds at hand: the conductor's occasional voice announcing an approaching station, the consistent clacking of the steel wheels on the rail. I looked out the window, watched the scenery pass from the city life of Amsterdam: the larger, more modern section of town, to an industrial area, with shipping cranes off in the near distance. Then we hit the green countryside with natural pastures and canals dissecting the area and the famed windmills, some waving, some sitting still. We passed the canal system, made to create land. Much of Holland is below sea level, hence the name "The Netherlands" or "low lands." As the train rolled on, we would approach-stop-pass another small village. After about twenty-five minutes, the conductor said a familiar understandable word, "Schiphol."

We disembarked at the airport. Most European places have very efficient public transportation. Holland is no different. The train pulls into a station built right under the airport. You disembark, take a few steps to the escalator and arrive a level up in the heart of the airport ticketing section.

We went to the easy Jet ticket window and checked our bags. We had exactly an hour and forty minutes; and though it was a Friday, the airport wasn't swamped like it would be back home the day after Thanksgiving, the first moment it's allowable for sons-in- law to leave the wife's family home.

"I'm hungry," I told Thomas.

"I am too, but I might eat at the next stop; I need to buy some gifts," he said. So we agreed to just meet at the gate and went our separate ways. I walked by the food court; there were several places to eat, but one stood out and I didn't know why: Burger King. I'm not even that big of a fan of the place. I'm more of a McDonald's type, sadly enough. But for some reason, I had an overwhelming craving for a Whopper, so I stepped up to the counter and ordered a double. "Would you like the meal?" the kid behind the register asked in good-enough English to warrant getting a job at an airport restaurant. I glanced at the price difference and accepted. The price was typical of airport pricing; and being in a socialist country, paying in euros, it came out bordering sit-down-dining prices. But when you have a craving, you slay it like a junkie when you get the chance.

My number was called, and I was on my way to grab my order when I noticed the posted sign: mayonnaise and ketchup packs thirty-five cents, about fifty cents a pack American. Fucking Europe. A beautiful place where healthcare is free to citizens, but not fast-food condiments.

I finished quickly, probably because there was a low-level angst about airport travel you keep until you reach your gate. Security took about thirty minutes, and I arrived to the gate; Thomas wasn't there yet. I chose to stay standing; I knew we had a long day of sitting ahead of us.

A voice announced they would be boarding our flight and still no Thomas, though there was over a half-hour until they would shut the doors on us. Without thinking, I boarded when our section was called to do so. After I sat down, I realized that if Thomas didn't make it on, I'd be sealed in and it would turn into a nightmare with us in two different countries, trying to meet up and get home. Though I was already on and making the next flight on time, it would be more Thomas' quest to get home. And then it dawned on me; he was driving us home from Los Angeles, and my angst announced itself again.

216

Most of the plane had boarded and settled and we were under ten minutes from closing the door when he popped in, ducking through the door and then walking the aisle in my direction. Thomas gave a head nod when he saw me. He put his bag of purchases in the overhead and dropped heavily into the seat next to me. "Hey," he said and then fumbled for his seatbelt. He never brought up his timing, as it just didn't appear to be a concern. I turned to look out the window, and moments later the jet lurched in reverse and then thrust lightly forward to taxi; soon after, we flew above the weather. "This is bullshit," Thomas said as we waited at the luggage carousel for his bag that wasn't appearing. I had my luggage, but we were to the part where the same few unclaimed bags had made several laps around and none of them were his. The good news of a short layover became the concerning news now.

"Let's go to their customer service," Thomas said as he turned and walked away, frustrated. We walked to the end of the luggage carousels and spoke to a representative. She took Thomas's ticket information and studied the screen in front of her.

"It doesn't appear to have been checked onto the plane, sir," the representative said.

"Yeah, I kinda got that," Thomas said; he was a little short, but understandably so. "So what does that mean?" he asked. "Do you know where it is?"

"It's not showing up as being checked," she said. "Stand by, please," and she picked up a phone and spoke to someone somewhere about the situation. Then she hung up the phone. "I'm sorry, sir, we are not locating it," she reported. "But if you will just fill out this form, we will contact you when it's found."

"*If* it's found?" Thomas said, already beginning to fill out the form.

"Yes, sir, *if* it's found," she said.

"Let's go," Thomas said after filling out the lost-bag form. We were cutting it close again, and Heathrow was buzzing with more activity than Schiphol. I had to recheck my bag with our original carrier, and we had to go through security again. After a long but fast-moving line, we ultimately made it through and back into our seats on a much-larger air bus. Thomas had the window seat this leg; he sat quietly and looked out the window. The thrust soon pulled us into our seats, and we were off. We were headed home.

"Fffuuuck," Thomas said, almost as if it were forced out of a frustrated mouth. "The fucking car keys were in my bag." I stared at him for a second and then looked straight ahead, processing what was just said. I put my earbuds back in. I reclined my seat and played Duran Duran's "New Moon on Monday," a song of hope, a song to enjoy in anticipation of the next adventure we would face upon touchdown in Los Angeles eleven hours ahead of us.

The End

My Friend Ben...

The bold gold chime from the
Clock Big Ben,
As soothing as a churches hymn,

Standing proud for a
hundred-and-fifty years,
While seeing his country both
cry and cheer,

But there is something about his
hello,
Something reminding you there's
a time to go,

He says to enjoy life while it
lasts,
Because all too soon the future
will be the past.

Major Rogers resides in Visalia, California, but considers the world his back yard. He lives with a pack of French Bulldogs, and usually a house guest or four. He enjoys writing in a pseudo-fiction style, so his antics don't offend his mom or the church. He hopes in his writings to motivate taxi drivers, bartenders, rock stars, and college students to discover the joy of reading adventure, and he hopes you'll come along for the ride too.

Made in the USA
San Bernardino, CA
26 March 2019